Uncivilised

Subhadra Das is a writer, historian, broadcaster and comedian who looks at the relationship between science and society. She specialises in the history and philosophy of science, particularly the history of scientific racism and eugenics, and for nine years was Curator of the Science Collections at University College London. She has written and presented podcasts and stand-up comedy shows, curated museum exhibitions and has appeared on radio and TV.

Uncivilised

Ten Lies That Made the West

SUBHADRA DAS

CORONET

First published in Great Britain in 2024 by Coronet
An imprint of Hodder & Stoughton Limited
An Hachette UK company

This paperback edition published in 2025

The authorised representative in the EEA is Hachette Ireland, 8 Castlecourt
Centre, Dublin 15, D15 XTP3, Ireland (email: info@hbgi.ie)

3

A CIP catalogue record for this title is available from the British Library

Paperback ISBN 9781399704397
ebook ISBN 9781399704373

Typeset in Bembo by Hewer Text UK Ltd, Edinburgh
Printed and bound in Great Britain by Clays Ltd, Elcograf S.p.A.

Hodder & Stoughton policy is to use papers that are natural, renewable
and recyclable products and made from wood grown in sustainable
forests. The logging and manufacturing processes are expected to
conform to the environmental regulations of the country of origin.

Hodder & Stoughton Limited
Carmelite House
50 Victoria Embankment
London EC4Y 0DZ

www.hodder.co.uk

For my parents

'A great portion of the world suffers from your civilisation.'

Rabindranath Tagore, New York, 1930.

Contents

Introduction

The story goes that when a journalist asked Mahatma Gandhi what he thought about Western civilisation, the sage took a beat before replying, 'I think it would be a good idea.' Do a little digging, and you will find that, like all the best stories, this one probably isn't true. The quip was first attributed to Gandhi in 1967, nearly two full decades after his death, and it seems to be the reworking of an old joke that had been doing the rounds as a comic filler, in publications like *Life* magazine, since the 1920s. What's interesting here is not so much whether Gandhi said it, but that it should so consistently be attributed to him. The original joke went:

> *'What's your opinion of civilisation?'*
> *'I think it's a good idea, someone ought to start it.'*

Let's face it, that was hardly going to set the world alight. Yet put the same words into the mouth of one of the most influential civil rights leaders of the twentieth century, and suddenly they pack a much stronger punch. Make that leader Gandhi and a critique of centuries of history, power and hypocrisy is encompassed in a single sentence.

To start with, Mohandas Karamchand Gandhi was as Western-ised – and by extension as *civilised* – as colonised Indian subjects came. As a young man he wore sharp suits, learned to play the violin and studied law in London. He was the poster child for the colonial civilising mission – the product of an education and governmental system that, on the face of it, allowed him to flourish as a British subject. That ideal, though, did not last long. When he finished his education and went to live and practise law in South Africa, the gloss began to chip away, reality showing through. Neither Gandhi's fancy London education nor sublime tailoring provided any protection against the racial discrimination he faced almost from the moment he set foot in his new home. The dramatic origin story of the Mahatma – the leader with the great soul – describes when he was violently removed from a first-class train carriage because a white man had complained, refusing to travel with an Indian – even if that Indian had paid for his own ticket. This, according to legend, was the moment when Gandhi made it his mission to ensure his colonisers lived up to their own 'civilised' ideals.

Gandhi's story is, of course, more complicated than the legend would have us believe. As a lawyer in South Africa, he advocated for the rights of his fellow South Asians over and above Black South Africans, essentially reifying existing racist legal codes. Later in his life, he insisted on sleeping naked in the same bed as some of the young women of his household, supposedly, by his own account, as a means of strengthening himself through abstinence. It remains the case, however, that when he moved back to British-ruled India, Gandhi showed up the hypocrisy of an empire that claimed to believe in justice, equality, liberty, democracy and self-rule, but clearly only as far as its white citizens were concerned. He highlighted its brutality when he persuaded his followers to engage in non-violent protest, and many of them had their heads broken for their pains. He advocated for equal rights for women and for Dalits (commonly and derogatorily known as 'untouchables', the oppressed people at the bottom of the Hindu caste system). In short, he dedicated his life to revealing the truth about everything he'd been taught was possible in a civilised society and stood up for true equality and freedom. So, whatever your opinion of Gandhi may be, his story contains an important idea: Western civilisation is not all it's cracked up to be.

We all have our own ideas about what it means to be civilised. For me, it's when I turn up in a new place and find free and accessible public toilets. When you travel the world, you can never entirely be guaranteed a warm welcome. So, when it turns out that people who have never seen me before, who, up until this moment, didn't even know I existed, nonetheless thought ahead and considered my needs and the needs of other strangers, I find myself reassured about humanity.

There are, of course, more well-established notions of civilisation. To be civilised incorporates ideas of progress and advancement. The city, with all its complex infrastructure and urbanity is, we are told, more advanced and civilised than the countryside or the wilderness. A civilised person – as opposed to a savage or a barbarian – is rational, educated, well-behaved, law-abiding. For much of its history, crucially, it has been an analogue notion. This is to say that for all that is civilised, on the other side of the coin are things and people who are *uncivi-lised*. For the ancient Greeks the distinction was simple: anyone who didn't speak Greek was a barbarian. For the ancient Romans, anyone described as 'civis' was a city-dweller, distinct from people who lived and worked in the countryside. I mention these examples because both the ancient Greeks and Romans are considered the cultural ancestors of how we now understand 'civilisation'. As we are going to see, starting from the Enlightenment, through to the twentieth century and into our present, the word took on a new, more particular meaning. It's this meaning that I'm interested in, and the story of how the word 'civilisation' eventually settled companionably alongside the word 'Western'.

What exactly do we mean by Western civilisation? This is not an easy question to answer because, despite some appearances, there is no explicit written manifesto for Western civilisation. For all those who argue that the West is in danger of collapsing or falling victim to external forces (and people have done so pretty much since the beginning), their definitions of what is threatened are as particular and numerous as their theories.

Within all of these, though, we can pick out a set of recurring themes. Definitions of Western civilisation include things to value – art, education and time, for example, alongside individual liberties and freedoms. There are also certain governing principles. We are led to believe that a scientific approach is the best, indeed, the only way to understand the world around us. Democracy, the system of government where the power lies with the people, is seen as a better and fairer approach than the stranglehold of dictatorial or fascist regimes, all within the advanced, civilised context of the nation-state. This is accompanied by a strong belief in justice as governed by the rule of law. Justice, we are told, is blind. The knowledge you gain from your education has the potential to make you powerful, as do the words on the written page.

So far, so splendid, no? Rational thought, human progress, liberality and equality under the law. What's not to love? These premises – and promises – are at the heart of our society, the vows that bind and hold us in place and the laws that govern us. But consider for a moment: how do we know these things to be true? Who taught them to us? Are they for real? And how do we know we can trust them? What would it mean if the ideas at the heart of Western civilisation are actually lies?

To understand why I'm asking these questions, it is important to understand what holds Western civilisation together, beyond these ideals. The clue lies in the word 'Western', and the fact that this particular distinction has never purely been a question of geography. Throughout the heartlands of Western civilisation, from the small kingdoms of Europe, through the open plains of North America, across the stretch of Australia, and in enclaves all over the world, the one thing they all have in common is obvious: the West is where the white people are.

When Western civilisation came to take on the meanings, customs and values we associate with it today – democracy, justice, rationality, to name but a few – it came in tandem with growing European imperial ambition and power. It was the colonisers who determined where and what was civilised, and they defined it in their own image. As such, settler colonies outside of Europe – in North and South America, Australia, New Zealand and South Africa – all over the globe, in fact, West of everywhere and nowhere, are now considered to make up the Western civilised world. By self-definition, these places were not simply more powerful, but more advanced – socially, culturally and intellectually – than the rest.

The self-proclaimed ascendancy of the West relegated the rest of the world to an intellectual backwater, held in place by the big lie of civilisation: that these were backward people with backward ideas, who had made no true contribution to humanity and its advancement. Of course, this really isn't the case. Non-western ideals and the people deemed non-Western and, therefore, *un*civilised, have been here all along, despite our ignoring them. In fact, it is often those very people, like Gandhi, who have fought for supposedly Western civilised values to be upheld and held Western powers to account when they failed to live up to their own ideals. It is these people I am interested in. The ones who were told 'justice is blind', 'knowledge is power' or 'the pen is mightier than the sword', who believed in those ideas and believed they should apply to everyone. I want to understand the seductive power of these promises, and the truth about who they are for.

At this point you may be wondering if this is a thread worth pulling on. Why argue with the things that are supposed to be an inherent good in and of themselves? In such precarious times, surely they are better left unquestioned? Part of the answer is that it's a historian's job not to take historical arguments at face value. In the case of a strong brand like Western civilisation, it's important to see if the product actually delivers what it promises. These truths are not self-evident. In fact, some of them are not true. As apocryphal Gandhi so wittily pointed out, much of what is supposed to be Western civilisation is not what it says on the tin. Its lies divide us, disenfranchise us and bring us down in ways we should, at the very least, be mindful of.

Throughout this book, we are going to interrogate what it means to be part of the civilised West, how these ideas came about in the first place and, crucially, if they actually are what they claim to be. These aren't historical lies in the mould of when the Russians failed to tell the rest of the world about the Chernobyl disaster. It's more the case that Western civilisation is, in many ways (at least ten, as we're going to see), a triumph of branding over reality. If we look at the history of the 'West', we can see that Western civilisation was not simply a product, but a process. The 'civilising mission' was also a vision and an excuse for colonising nations, such as England, Spain, Portugal and others to go out and make the rest of the world not simply their own, but also in their own image.

In a way this book is also a survivor's guide for those embarking on a critical journey to scrutinise Western civilisation. It's not simply about exposing the lies behind these ideas, but about coming around to understanding how we fooled ourselves into thinking they were true in the first place. It's a key to what some of the terms we so blithely use really mean and what some of the implicit arguments are. Often these are not spelled out, but they run through our conceptions of the West, first as definitely distinct from and then definitively superior to the rest. If we even briefly skim the surface of our recent history, we see it isn't necessarily so. What is actually involved here is power play. It was never about what – or who – was civilised or not but always about *who got to say so*.

Western civilisation has always talked a big game. In fact, it claimed – and still claims – to be the only game in town. This book is about how the line between the civilised West and the *un*civilised 'Other' depends on how we choose to draw it, about how we see the world and how we see each other. It's also about the people who were written out of this very particular way of looking at the world, and what it might look like if we wrote them back in. While the jury remains out on whether the concept of Western civilisation is a good thing, at the very least, the ideas that underpin it deserve a much closer look.

Chapter One

NULLIUS IN VERBA

Tucked away in the storerooms of University College London's state-of-the-art teaching museum is a metal box. It's flat like a cigarette case, only much longer – just over a foot long – and it doesn't contain any cigarettes. If you flip open the two clasps along one long edge, you will see laid out before you thirty samples of synthetic human hair, all of different colours and textures. Most of them mimic straight hair, running the gamut of blonde and brunette. The palest flaxen shades are in the middle, changing by degrees to darker shades of brown on either side. The last three samples on the right show different shades of red hair. Black hair is represented by the last four samples on the left. Like most of the others in the box, the innermost of these shows straight hair. The three outermost demonstrate black hair with varying degrees of curl. Altogether, the thing gives an impression of an antique hairdresser's sample kit. It's mildly creepy in the way of so many historical curiosities, but otherwise seems fairly innocuous. Take a look at the faint engraving on the top left-hand side of the lid however, and you will find a clue that there is something more sinister going on here.

In old-fashioned cursive writing the object itself tells us what it is: '*Haarfarbentafel*', which, roughly translated from German means 'hair colour gauge'. The inscription also spells out a name: Prof Dr Eugen Fischer. A German anthropologist, in 1927 Fischer was appointed Director of the Kaiser Wilhelm Institute of Anthropology, Human Heredity and Eugenics. His anthropological research informed his beliefs that miscegenation – so-called race mixing – should be discouraged in the interests of maintaining Aryan racial purity. Fischer's scientific research would go on to inform the Nuremberg Laws, the antisemitic and racist legal codes that underpinned the Nazi state during the 1930s and into the Second World War. These laws would go on to target and legitimise the persecution and murder of disabled people and racialised groups of people, including Jewish, Black and Roma people, in acts so terrible we had to come up with new terms to describe them: genocide and crimes against humanity.

Fischer's hair colour gauge was the first object I got to know when I was one of the newly appointed curators of the UCL Science Collections in 2012. You may think, as I certainly used to, that all museum curators know everything there is to know about their collections, but the reality is that we all have to start from somewhere, and for me, this was it. My job was to make the historical science collections at the university available for teaching, research and public engagement. One of the first tasks on my to-do list was to help a couple of my academic colleagues who were teaching on the Museum Studies course. They wanted to assign a research project to their students that involved taking a deep dive into the archives in relation to museum objects about which relatively little was known. The metal box of hair samples fitted the bill and the students went on to meet the brief and more. Thanks to their research, we now had lots of new, and frankly horrifying, information about the object, like who made it, when and how they used it and to what purpose.

We could say with some certainty that the device was designed by a eugenicist scientist to study the children of local women and European soldiers in the colony of German South West Africa (now Namibia). He did this against the backdrop of the Herero and Namaqua genocide (1904–8) – now acknowledged as the first genocide of the twentieth century. Fischer's research was seen as proof that 'racial characteristics' – like hair and eye colour – were passed from parents to their children. In other words, it was seen to prove that 'race' had a basis in biology. Similar devices were made and used in racial studies in other parts of the world later in the twentieth century, including Nazi Germany, just a few decades later.

As a former UCL student who was now a member of staff, and knowing its reputation as being at the cutting edge of scientific research, I had always been under the impression that we were the good guys. All of this research, however, threw up a new question, one that would go on to both frame and haunt my career as the curator of a historical science collection at one of London's, if not the world's, leading universities. If the hair gauge was, in fact, an object designed by a race scientist who went on to become a Nazi, what on earth was it doing *here*? The answer lies in the history of science. More particularly, it lies in what science means to us in our civilised society. To find the answer, as with most things, we have to go all the way back to the beginning.

*

If Western civilisation were a city, science would be its citadel. Built on higher ground, at the heart of the settlement, science is the bastion of a rational, civilised society, a solid fortress that is supposed to be built on observation, reason and truth for the benefit of all concerned.

Civilised people, as we have come to know them, are not prey to myths and superstition. They do not succumb to fear, irrationality or the other base emotions of 'savages'. They do not have unquestioning faith in what they cannot see for themselves, be it God or monsters. Instead, civilised people are able to look at the world objectively, without prejudice or bias and, through the application of reason, lay their hands upon the truth. To be scientific, then, is to be as civilised as it gets. The methods of science require scientists to be as rational as they possibly can – to pause and look at the bigger picture. They need to step out of the hubbub and the messiness of their everyday lives and look at what is really going on. It's this separation of scientists from the very things they are studying which is held to be the greatest strength of the scientific method. Science, we are led to believe, does not trouble itself with philosophy, reputation, power or any other such social and cultural fripperies: it deals with reality.

One of the most celebrated figures in the history of science is Francis Bacon, a seventeenth-century English lawyer, politically disgraced Lord Chancellor (he took bribes and got caught) and the man generally credited with drawing up one of the earliest iterations of the scientific method as we think of it today. The Baconian method of science relied on the physical examination and detailed observation of the natural world to gather data as the direct path to the truth. This was as opposed to the existing theology or moral philosophy of his day, which bothered itself with trying to work out what was right and wrong. Instead, Bacon placed his sole focus on what could demonstrably be proved. For Bacon and other early scientists like him, the scientific method was a tool that allowed them to be more practical – and in some ways more democratic. Rather than defer to the word of God in the Bible, for example, or the word of Aristotle from classical sources, anyone could – and should – go forth and find things out for themselves.

This is the scientific method in its earliest form as we

recognise it. Bacon and his peers also had the benefit of developing a whole new slew of scientific instruments for measuring the world around them – the telescope, the microscope, the barometer, clocks and watches, sextants and surveying equipment – all of which are still used today. According to Bacon, these instruments, along with careful observation and experiment, would lead reliably and directly to the truth. When, after years of lobbying by Bacon, Charles II granted a charter to the Royal Society, this freedom of thought and focus on hard facts to the exclusion of everything else was integral to its mission. So integral, in fact, that the Royal Society's motto remains engraved above a door in its London headquarters to this very day: Nullius in verba – take no one's word for it. Do not rely on testimony when you can depend on facts. It was this faith in the experimental philosophy that laid the foundations for modern Western science.

In the centuries that followed, Bacon was held up as a beacon for Enlightenment thought in the seventeenth and eighteenth centuries. European Enlightenment thinkers rejected the existing religious and classical philosophies in favour of what they believed to be a more effective and useful approach to understanding and living in the world. As the name Enlightenment suggests, thinkers during this period were keen to expose the old ways of doing things to the bright light of reason. It was an idea that crossed art and academia, that saw Voltaire skewer the French nobility in satire, Jean-Jacques Rousseau advocate for educational reform and Denis Diderot attempt to compile the entirety of human knowledge into his *Encyclopédie*.

For Enlightenment thinkers, no subject was beyond the bounds of human understanding, and to pursue that understanding was key to what it meant to be alive, to be human and to contribute to the work of the world. In the now immortal words of René Descartes: 'I think, therefore I am.' Finally, after centuries of stumbling around in the darkness of religion, myth and superstition, humankind had taken a firm hold of the torch of reason, which would now light the way on our collective journey to the truth. The pure light of reason, though, managed to cast some long, troubling shadows. Our collective journey turned out not to be so unambiguously unified. European scientific endeavours would go on to show, or so it seemed, that some people were more capable of rational thinking than others.

*

I used to think I was no good at science because when I was at school, I found chemistry and physics so unspeakably boring. In truth, it's because I wasn't very good at maths. While I could get a handle on the concepts of chemistry – about how the different parts of an atom work, for example, or how different scientists like Niels Bohr and Ernest Rutherford had worked this out – when asked to calculate molality (or was it *molarity*?), I immediately felt my brain start to glaze over.

When it came to computing the implications of a hypothesis, say, or really, just computing anything, I found myself yearning to go back to reading, for example, the graphic novel about the Holocaust I had started the night before. Why speculate about things you can't even see, I figured, when there is so much documented about the history of the world that you can? As such, the social sciences were healthily represented on my schedule. I was first in the queue to sign up for the anthropology and psychology options in high school and I studied archaeology at university. Rather than try to make the world – and the people in it – add up like a chemical equation, it made better sense to me to try to understand them as they were, instead.

This distinction in my academic preferences, it turned out, related to the difference between what are called the hard sciences and the soft sciences. The hard sciences include chemistry, astronomy, physics and mathematics. They are not 'hard' simply because they are difficult, but rather in the sense that they deal with solid things that can be measured or observed in ways that are consistent and predictable. In a hard science, it's possible to ask a question and, through the application of reason and the scientific method, come up with something of an answer.

Conversely, the 'soft' sciences include archaeology, anthropology, sociology and psychology. They deal with soft, squishy things, like people. Ask a question in the soft sciences, and the odds are you'll end up with an unsatisfactory answer, along with a lot of other questions. The soft sciences are no less rigorous or useful than the hard sciences, but there appears to be a consensus that their conclusions are more ill-defined and harder to demonstrate. We can safely say, for example, that electrons orbit the nucleus of an atom. It's much less easy to definitively say how different societies work, or why individuals or groups of people behave the way they do. Despite this – or possibly because of it – I had a feeling that the social sciences weren't really sciences at all. It, therefore, seemed ironic that when I landed my dream job of being a museum curator, I was put in charge of science collections.

Being a science curator turned out to be a good news–bad news scenario for me. The good news was that the job was all about the history and philosophy of science rather than the science itself. So, I could use my research and archiving skills to tell the wider story of the history of science at UCL, where I was now settling into my museum career. The bad news was the actual content of that history. This was especially true of the Galton Collection.

Named for Sir Francis Galton, on the face of it, this was yet another historical science collection, like any of the others I had been assigned to work with. Just as with electrical engineering, physiology, medical physics, chemistry and the like, the Galton Collection was made up of historical objects related to the study of genetics at the university. In reality, it was much – very much – more than that. And, after only a few weeks in the job, everything I thought I knew about science had been blown spectacularly out of the water.

After ten years of working and teaching with the collection, I can safely say that Francis Galton is the most important and influential Victorian scientist most people have never heard of. Before I started working for UCL Museums, I had never heard of him, and I wasn't alone. Over the years, it's become clear that many undergraduates, summer school students, members of the public, even many of the faculty don't know about him either. Despite being a key figure in the history of a whole bunch of sciences – meteorology, crime science, statistics, sociology and genetics – Galton's name only rarely appears in school history textbooks or in science documentaries. This is probably because Galton was a race scientist. He spent much of his life studying human behaviour and heredity and, in 1883, he coined the term 'eugenics' – the study and practice of selectively breeding human beings – and, by doing so, established a whole new field of science.

Galton was a racist and a colonialist, and those ideas informed his approach to his science. It took a good five years of being a science curator for me to feel brave enough to even say that. First off, as attempts to separate the scientist from their science go, it fails outright. For another thing, we aren't very good at talking about race. We're not good at looking at its impact, considering how it works or resolving the legacy of the damage it left in its wake. We're also not good at understanding where the idea of 'race' comes from, and particularly how science and the magic of rational thinking was used to establish 'race' as an idea in the first place.

*

You may be familiar with the phrase 'race is a social construct'. This is an important concept because it acknowledges that 'race' is made up of social and cultural ideas, and that there is no objective truth in either the idea of biologically fixed, inherited characteristics or the idea of racial hierarchy. The oldest and most prevalent theory of racial hierarchy is called white supremacy. This is the mistaken idea that people racialised as 'white' are supposedly racially superior to everyone else. 'Race is a social construct' is an important tool in the box of arguments against white supremacy. It works to remind us that it is impossible for one group of people to be superior to others on the basis of an arbitrary idea. There is, however, a problem with the phrase. Taken by itself, it loses half the story. Some people solve this problem by adding a follow-up clause: 'Race is a social construct, *but racism has a very real effect on people's lives.*' This seems to be working relatively well, but to my mind it doesn't do enough. In fact, on the face of it, it's kind of paradoxical – how can something that isn't real have real effects?

For me, when it comes to race, the real question we should all be asking is: if it is a social construct, how did we come around to constructing it in the first place? The answer? We did it with science. It turns out that, before it was eventually disavowed and disproved, race was an important scientific idea. In fact, race, as we now understand it, was in part conceived of as an observable, measurable, hard fact.

The word 'race' was first used in the late sixteenth century in the same way we use the words 'type' or 'sort' today. It specifically distinguished between different varieties of living things that were supposed to have something in common. Where you drew the line as to what constituted a race depended on the thing you were talking about. So, it once made as much sense for an innovative gardener to talk about an exciting new race of carrots they had succeeded in growing, as it did for the English poet Edmund Spenser, writing in 1590, to describe 'the race of woman kind' in his epic poem *The Faerie Queene.*

The beginnings of the way we understand 'race' today, as seeming functional units of humanity, can be traced back to the eighteenth century. Before this time Westerners, and indeed everyone else, had noted physical differences between groups of people living in different places, but they did not assign a value to those differences. The name Ethiopia, for example, comes from the Greek for 'burnt face', as the ancient Greeks had noticed that people from this part of the world had skin darkened by the sun. There was no judgement associated with the term, merely an acknowledgement of physical difference. If the Greeks considered themselves to be civilised and the Ethiopians to be barbarians, this delineation was not based on the way they looked – it was based on their culture and behaviour along with the insurmountable problem that they were not Greek. The use of 'race' in the context of Enlightenment science in the eighteenth century changed all that. It arose within taxonomy, the study of the classification of life on Earth, a branch of biology that originally fell under the umbrella term of 'natural history'.

In 1735, for example, the Swedish biologist Carl Linnaeus – who is generally known as 'The Father of Taxonomy' – published his seminal work *Systema Naturae* in which he classified humans under the term 'Anthropomorpha' (people shaped) and divided us into four groups: Europeans, Americans, Asians and Africans. Linnaeus' classification wasn't solely based on appearances, it incorporated human culture and behaviour too. In later editions, for example, he described Europeans as 'acute, inventive ... Governed by laws'. Africans, by contrast, he called 'crafty, indolent, negligent ... Governed by caprice'. What you are looking at here is white supremacy, propped up by the work of a man held up to be one of the leading minds of European thought.

Linnaeus, sadly, was not alone. In 1776, a few decades later and the year that saw the foundation of the great new civilised nation of the United States of America, Johann Friedrich Blumenbach's *On the Natural Varieties of Mankind* was published, listing five categories of humans: Mongolians, Ethiopians, Americans, Malays and, in its first ever outing, Caucasians. These, according to Blumenbach, were the single ancestor of all humanity, being 'the most handsome and becoming', on account of having 'the most beautiful form of skull'. Blumenbach's theories, along with the work of many of his fellow European scientists, concerned themselves with the big question of humanity. This was no longer 'who are we and what is our purpose in life?' (that was now a problem relegated to philosophers), but 'what is a human and how did they come to be here?' This single question was the common goal that bridged what we see today as the division of the hard and soft sciences. Whether you were a biologist, a zoologist, a geologist, an anthropologist or an archaeologist, this was your single guiding mission.

For much of the eighteenth century, and into the nineteenth, the answer to this question and the related research was framed in racial terms. Out of this arose two opposing theories. The first, monogenism (from the Greek, combining the words 'single' and 'birth') held that all human beings constituted a single species. By contrast, advocates of polygenism (meaning 'many' plus 'birth') maintained that the observable different races of people had separate biological origins. In other words, it held that white people, and other arbitrarily defined racialised groups of people, were so different from each other as to constitute different species. To us in the twenty-first century, polygenism sounds like racist nonsense for a very good reason – that is exactly what it is. In their day, though, for much of the time these two theories were circulating, a good deal of the scientific research supported polygenism. It was through the painstaking data gathering and research of a British scientist named Charles Darwin that everything changed.

Along with Isaac Newton and Albert Einstein, Darwin is considered one of the greatest thinkers in the history of science. His theory of evolution by natural selection provided an over-arching framework for how we understand how life on Earth came about and how it changes over time. Darwin expounded his theory in a book titled *On the Origin of Species*. The book's title clearly refers to the debate between monogenists and poly-genists, and, through his research, Darwin came down in support of the former. Darwin's theory rang the death knell for polygen-ism because it showed that species can change over time, and that new species can arise out of old ones. The logical implica-tion of this idea was that all life, including human life, descended from a common ancestor. Evolution also suggested that there was no design in nature. How a species developed, thrived or went extinct was down to nothing more than chance. You can't have a system of racial hierarchy if all life derives from a common ancestor and is the result of nothing more than sheer luck.

While Darwin's theory was generally accepted by his fellow scientists, the yoke of scientific racism proved harder to throw off. This was down to a number of things, for one the fact that even though monogenists like Darwin believed that all humans were the same species, they nonetheless held on to the delineations of race as distinctions within that single species. Another reason came down to language. Darwin eventually adopted the economist Herbert Spencer's phrase 'survival of the fittest' as another way of describing natural selection. By that, he meant that those individuals best adapted to a particular environment had the greatest chance of surviving and producing offspring, thus carrying on the species. If the environment changed, it was likely that different individuals might find themselves a better fit to the changed habitat. Unfortunately, given the context of race science and racial theory, the phrase can also be understood more generically as those individuals who are the most fit, in absolute terms, are the ones most likely to survive. For biologists in the nineteenth century, the frame of race science persisted. The people who were the most fit, in their eyes, were the people they thought of as white.

The story of Charles Darwin, his work and his revolutionary theory is the stuff of science legend. That of Francis Galton – who happened to be Darwin's first cousin – is generally less well known, but his work is nonetheless just as influential. Galton's ideas were as innovative as they were disastrous. Darwin had begun *Origin* with descriptions of how domesticated animals were bred. This was a way of showing how specific traits like the curliness of wool or the quality of milk could be managed over time through selective breeding. Galton was happy to go one step further. If, as Darwin had demonstrated, humans were a species just like any other, why not try to breed them better? This idea laid the groundwork for Galton's eugenics. He believed that if scientists could provide the government with enough biological and statistical data about the population, they could encourage and reward 'fit' individuals to have children. This, Galton believed, would ensure the future health, purity and success of the 'British race'.

The flip side of Galton's idea was that 'unfit' people should be stopped from having children, or stopped from existing altogether. Eugenics was both an extension and a rebranding of earlier concepts of race science. Astonishingly, it framed much of what was considered progressive thinking in the first half of the twentieth century. In particular, it fuelled sterilisation programmes, carried out against disabled people and people with learning disabilities in countries all over the world, particularly in the United States. This infamously culminated in the Nazis' targeting of people who were deemed physically and mentally 'defective', first with the 1933 law introducing the forced sterilisation of 'hereditarily diseased offspring' – people with conditions such as epilepsy, alcoholism and schizophrenia – and then in 1939, Aktion T4, which legitimised the murder of children under the age of three with physical and learning disabilities. Sadly, this was one part of a larger eugenics programme, targeting people deemed racially, morally and culturally inferior, particularly the murder of six million Jews in the Holocaust.

This is an appalling and disturbing part of history, but, as the newly appointed curator of the Galton Collection, I was really shocked by how that history – a history that I thought I already knew from school and graphic novels – was only one part of a much bigger, equally disturbing story. I learned that the Nazis had not pulled their ideas out of the air. Instead, that they were based in a well-established scientific discourse, originating in and churned out of Western universities and research laboratories starting in the eighteenth century. What's more, it was work that had been done disturbingly close to home. The Museum Studies student research revealed that Eugen Fischer's hair colour gauge, having been used by its designer during a genocide in Namibia, was also used by Karl Pearson, UCL's – and the world's – first Professor of Eugenics, to carry out studies on the children of Jewish immigrants to Britain.

The Galton Collection comprises the stretch of human scientific endeavour. It is a monument in miniature to the marvels of rational power and empiricism. The collection contains objects, devices and prototypes used by Galton to advance the science of biology as we know it. There are the cress seeds he gathered and analysed by size in the course of experiments that established the mathematical principles of correlation and regression to the mean. There is the quincunx – a machine of Galton's own devising that illustrates regression as a statistical principle, a mathematical window into the future science of genetics decades before anyone knew what genes were and how they worked. Instruments of race science – head measurers, eye colour and hair colour charts – sit alongside these marvels. Altogether, they are testimony to one of the most serious misconceptions of Western science: the idea humanity is somehow objectively quantifiable. That the wide, immeasurable expanse of all our consciousness, emotions and shared experiences can somehow be reduced and represented by a series of numbers in a chart.

Are we to expect scientists to be infallible, to never make mistakes? Of course not. Any decent scientist knows that being proved wrong is all part of the process. But when it's clear that we have been making the same mistakes over and over again, when it's clear that there is a direction of travel here that steeps inequality upon inequality, that is worth shining a spotlight on – and dissecting. What the Galton Collection helps us understand is that it's not how such catastrophic mistakes in the search for truth were made, but why. *Why* did these so-called men of science pursue such a baseless line of enquiry, and then accept a range of evidence with no foundation? Quite simply, it is because they chose to. This was the order they believed in, and things they believed had been proved true. This was the whole history of science, race and eugenics, tucked away in a university archive and held tight under the lid of a slim metal box. When we open up that lid, we can look more closely at that history and how we came to the idea we now call Western civilisation.

*

If you were to visit Tate Britain in London – like the civilised person that you are – you can see a painting that is a handy window with a view looking out over Western civilisation. It's a landscape by the acclaimed English artist J.M.W. Turner, titled *The Golden Bough*. The painting shows a scene from Virgil's *Aeneid,* the epic founding myth of the Roman Empire and, by dint of the *translatio studii* – the transfer of learning from the ancient classical to the modern European civilised world – it came to be seen as part of the founding myth of the British Empire too. The scene in *The Golden Bough* shows the Cumaean Sibyl, a mystic and prophetess, standing on the shores of Lake Avernus, holding aloft a branch from a golden tree. The hero, Aeneas, has brought it as a gift for Proserpine, Queen of the Underworld, so that she will allow him to talk to his dead father and fulfil the prophecy that will lead to the founding of Rome.

In Virgil's epic poem, the golden bough is a symbol of light and life, a talisman to ward off death and ensure safe passage through the Underworld. There are various theories as to what kind of tree the branch actually came from. Translations of Virgil's text name it as a holm oak, a Mediterranean evergreen, but the British sociologist J.G. Frazer thought it might have been mistletoe.

Mistletoe has a long and rich symbolic history in the West: in Norse mythology a mistletoe spear was used to kill the god Baldur and, in some Christian traditions, the wooden cross on which Christ was crucified was thought to have been made of mistletoe. As Aeneas, Baldur and Jesus Christ are all supposed to have returned from the dead to live and reign again, it's easy enough to see why the idea appealed to Frazer. He wrote about this, and his broader theory of religion, culture and civilisation, in a multi-volume work with the same title as Turner's painting, the first of which was published in 1890, with further volumes and iterations published over the early decades of the twentieth century. Frazer's *Golden Bough* built on many decades of enquiry into human history that we now think of as falling under the banner of the social sciences.

The Golden Bough was a politically controversial work. Frazer did not shy away from the fact that one of the central tenets of Christianity, like the founding myths of many other civilisations, including that of Aeneas and the founding of Rome, involved the sacrifice, death and resurrection of a king. He made it sound as though Christianity, which had been both the high-water mark and the driving force of Europe for more than a millennium, was simply a religion just like any other. For Frazer, that was very much the point. He theorised that the ways in which societies transition from 'savage' to 'primitive' to 'civilised', was through a progression in belief systems. The first stage featured magic and superstition, then came formal religions and, eventually, science and rational thought.

Frazer's work crystallised existing ideas about cultural development, progress and civilisation. Earlier versions of these ideas, of course, were bound up with scientific notions of race. As was the case with taxonomy and the classification of life on Earth, the seeming hard-science observations of physical appearance continued to be bound up with other more abstract qualities like intelligence and behaviour. When it came to civilisation, there were other objective, measurable, hard science observations to be made. James Cowles Prichard, a leading nineteenth-century British ethnologist, believed that the fair skin and the supposedly greater intelligence of Europeans were the direct result of the civilising process that darker-skinned people had yet to experience. Henri de Saint-Simon was less optimistic about whether civilisation could be transformative. He justified France's reinstitution of slavery by saying there was no way Black Africans could obtain the intellectual heights of white Europeans. The anthropologist Frederic Farrar agreed. In his 1866 lecture entitled 'Aptitude of Races', Farrar divided the people of the world into three groups: savage, semi-civilised and civilised. He defined those he saw as savages as being 'without a past and without a future', 'irredeemable', unfixable and, like living fossils, frozen in time.

Through the work of Farrar and other race scientists, civilisation itself became a fixed biological characteristic, to be observed and measured just like skin colour, skull shape and hair texture. In other words, it became a racial characteristic. As you can see, much of this discourse was still conjecture, but, through the sheer weight of what was now well-established scientific practice, it was taken and read as fact. While individual scientists quibbled over the details, one idea became firmly entrenched. Civilisation, as a racial characteristic, was now a fixed and, seemingly, objective scientific truth. While its ideas may have been imagined, the power of science to shape our world was very real indeed. As Robert Knox, a Scottish anatomist and anthropologist who had expounded his own racial theories put it, 'Race is everything: literature, science, art, in a word, civilization, depend upon it.'

What does all this mean for us? Well, for starters, it helps us have a clearer picture of how we got to where we are. It accounts for the social injustices we see all over our so-called civilised society, the embedded social inequalities that continue to replicate as if by their own accord. It also accounts to some degree for how it is so difficult to talk about and disprove these harmful ideas. Even when Darwin had demonstrated that human evolution was down to chance, the die was already cast. Science was the frame for understanding the world, and within its confines our humanity became a subject that was up for debate. There remains room for people who feel entitled to continue asking these questions. Asking the questions is clever, rational and civilised. Particularly when those people whose humanity you are questioning no longer have a right of return to your argument. The potent combination of science, race and civilisation meant that when non-Westerners might simply have been perceived to be doing backward or wrong things, now it was the case that they themselves were wrong, down to their very bones.

As such, the answer to the question of humanity could now only be proved in one specific way, through the methods of science itself. When people from outside the West, particularly people not racialised as white, tell you that they, too, are human beings, you cannot take their word for it. The onus is not on you to believe them, but on them to prove to you that this is true.

Race becomes a very broad church in this sense, because it encompasses the myriad complex ways in which our identities can be marginalised, be it through disability, gender, sexuality, class or body size. There is a right way to be, and anything that doesn't conform is false by definition. With the odds stacked like this, good luck proving anything different. There is no arguing with race, and, by extension, very little point in arguing with racists, at least as far as the science alone is concerned. They would have us believe that race is a reality, and science is their alibi. It allows them to be distant, safely elsewhere. We don't have to take *their word* for it, the *science* shows us the truth. Nullius in verba. No arguing with that. But take a closer look at the wider historical context, and it becomes clear that the foundations of science – and race science in particular – were serving a deeper purpose. To be white and civilised, it turned out, was also to be powerful.

*

Science, of course, does not happen in a vacuum. Beyond trying to determine an objective truth about the world we live in, Francis Bacon, and his fellow scientifically minded thinkers at the Royal Society, had political ambitions from the start. One of the most famous aphorisms attributed to Bacon is 'knowledge is power', and he saw his scientific method and philosophy as a new way of thinking for a new world. For Europeans in the seventeenth century, this was literally the 'New World', as the Scientific Revolution and the Enlightenment were happening at the same time as the European discovery of the Americas, an enormous pole to pole landmass that none of their existing sources (neither the Bible nor the ancient Greeks) could have known of or predicted. To learn more about the Americas was not simply about discovery for discovery's sake, there was enormous potential wealth and power to be found there.

Over the following centuries, one of the foundations Western scientists went on to so diligently observe and build their racial theories on was a world built on the profits of chattel slavery. It was made possible by the unpaid labour of the enslaved African people that Europeans had brought to their colonies in the Americas and the Caribbean. As such, race classification was born from a turbulent period in European colonial history when there was every colonialist and capitalist imperative to keep slavery going.

The very early boom of the plantation colonies was built on the work of indentured servants of both European and African descent. These workers shared reasonably equal standing to begin with. Many of the African workers went on to earn their freedom, going on to vote, intermarry with Europeans and own property. But, as labour from England diminished and restlessness among their workers grew, the colony leaders started to look for a way to ensure an easily controlled and distinct workforce. The scientific categorisation of race in the eighteenth and nineteenth centuries shored up earlier laws – particularly the 1661 Slave Code in Barbados, later in Virginia – that enforced the different legal treatment of white and Black servants, and supported the complete enslavement and disenfranchisement of the latter. By proving the African people to be lesser, as scientifically not equal, as racially inferior, it was justifiable to keep them enslaved and dehumanised as property.

Scientific hierarchies that consistently placed white people at the top and Black people at the bottom, then, were based on a political reality, not a biological one. It is a painful irony that as the abolitionist movement grew, fuelled by Enlightenment ideals of liberty, equality and freedom in the late eighteenth century, so did this restrictive science of race, used to justify the status quo. From the first creation of their scientific fields, anthropologists and archaeologists studied the lives of people and the workings of societies past and present in ways that upheld notions of European expansion and imperialism. They suggested that non-white people were physically ill-suited for leadership, and so it made sense for white people to be in charge. Scientific descriptions of 'race' were deployed to justify continuing the subjugation of Black people, postulating that white people were more intelligent and physically fit for overseeing work than Black people, whose supposed lack of intelligence and excess of physical strength made them ideal for working on cotton and sugar plantations in the colonies.

The work of Western race scientists in the eighteenth and nineteenth centuries supported those who had become rich and powerful on the profits of slavery to become even more rich and even more powerful. It justified their imperial and economic ambitions, and that work continued long after the abolition of slavery. The Slave Trade Act ended the trading of humans and slavery in the British Isles in 1807 (though not across the Empire until 1833, and not in the British Raj until 1843). At that moment Britain was at the beginning of what came to be known as the Imperial Century, a period when roughly four hundred million people were added to the Empire. As the economic and social fabric of colonies were shredded under the boots of imperial armies, Western scientists continued to argue that colonised people were clearly naturally inferior, rather than made that way through colonial violence, oppression and, indeed, through science itself.

Western science is a strong brand. So strong, in fact, that it doesn't usually bother to call itself 'Western'. We in the West perceive science as a clear path to the objective truth and an unmitigated force for good. The wider view of the history of science – the things we got right and the things we got wrong – tells a different story. It stands to reason no one can have a monopoly on science, that is to say, anyone can look at the world in systematic and questioning ways. For much of its history, though, science in the West has claimed just that while doing exactly the opposite. The Western scientific gaze on the world was not as simple as observation, it was tied inextricably to purpose. Our very sense of civilisation was bound up from the beginning with what we wanted to set it against. By the late 1800s, Westerners had been playing and winning at 'civilisation' for more than a century. In this context, science was a double whammy. First, Westerners called themselves civilised because their society was based on rational thought and science. Then, it turned out, their science revealed that non-Westerners were uncivilised, on account of being incapable of rational, scientific thought.

As we will see in the following chapters, the belief in this seemingly inexorable journey on the road to rationality – like Frazer's three step programme from savage to civilised – is a recurring theme in Western thought. It is, perhaps, our foundation myth. It is the central belief that underpins all the other beliefs we have about ourselves. It's why we take our science as fact, our laws as fair and just, and our democracy as sacrosanct. Belief in the rational truth of its own ideas is perhaps the essence of Western civilisation. It is also the first of many lies on which the idea of the West is built. Race science – the hard and soft science facts that uphold white supremacy – is not rational. It never has been. Nonetheless, Western scientists took the word of their fellows at home and abroad over the word of the people they were supposed to be studying. They took their own word for it that the West was best, and theirs was the one, only, civilised way of doing things. To take no one's word for it may be the scientific thing to do. Given the history of where our science has got us, it may also, perhaps be true that if we listened to other people, we might uncover things that shake us to the very core of all that we've been led to believe.

The work of anthropologists, archaeologists and historians framed a number of assumptions about rational thought and science in relation to civilisation that are still with us today. European ideas about Western civilisation ran in parallel with their ideas about how race separated the West from 'the rest'. Their ideas about rationality as a sign of progress effectively relegated the rest of the world to being an intellectual backwater, less advanced and stuck behind the West in its ways of thinking and being. If we are interested in the truth of the matter, though, it's worth knowing that this is by no means the whole story.

The reality is that there are other people and other stories here too. To ignore their contribution is to participate in one of the lies of Western civilisation and to endorse a historical narrative that upholds one people over another. This book is about how and why our stories have been told a certain way. It is about the truth as we have been taught it, alongside the truth – and the people – we have been taught to ignore. For anyone who cares to look, they have been here all along. The reality, as I learned about Francis Galton during my time working at UCL's museums, is that the absence of their stories is a story in itself.

Chapter Two

KNOWLEDGE IS POWER

I almost always misspell the 'canon' in 'Western canon' first time around. Used in this context, the Ancient Greek word for 'measuring rod', has come to mean a standard against which to measure all kinds of things, in this case an established list of texts that an educated person should be familiar with. Instead, I can't help writing it as 'cannon', a weapon used to blow others to smithereens. I wish this were only an expression but will sadly direct you to what officials of the British Raj did to Indian soldiers found guilty of desertion in the aftermath of the 1857 Uprising against colonial rule. It may be that my subconscious finds this metaphor more apt. It certainly speaks to the power of education, of our words and language – and the ways they shape how we see the world and people around us.

The dangerous power of education is the subject of a 1969 film called *The Prime of Miss Jean Brodie*. Based on the novel by Scottish writer Muriel Spark, the film follows the career and exploits of an eccentric woman with intellectual pretensions played by the mesmerising Maggie Smith (who won the Academy Award for Best Actress for her portrayal). Miss Brodie plays out the prime of her life as a teacher at the Marcia Blaine School for Girls in 1930s' Edinburgh. Among her many areas of expertise are Renaissance art, opera, romantic love – and manipulation. Smith makes Jay Presson Allen's screenplay sparkle with her spot-on delivery of witticisms and quotable quotes. My particular favourite comes early in the film when Miss Brodie learns that some of the girls in her class have joined the Girl Guides. 'For those who like that sort of thing,' she drawls, 'that is the sort of thing they like.'

While the plot combines the growing threat of fascism in the 1930s with everyday office politics, along with underage sex and ideas around duty, truth, loyalty and betrayal, *The Prime of Miss Jean Brodie* is also something of a treatise on education. When confronted by the headmistress, Miss Mackay (played in the film by the equally brilliant Celia Johnson), Miss Brodie explains how her mission as an educator is informed by using etymology, particularly the Latin origins of certain words.

'To me,' she says, 'education is a leading out. The word education comes from the root "ex", meaning "out", and "duco . . ." "I lead". To me, education is simply a leading out of what is already there.'

'I had hoped,' counters Miss Mackay, 'there might also be a certain amount of putting in.'

Miss Brodie is having none of this. 'That would not be education,' she insists, 'but intrusion. From the root prefix "in", meaning "in", and the stem "trudo", "I thrust". Ergo, to thrust a lot of information into a pupil's head!'

Here Jean Brodie is concisely summarising a popular and highly romantic Western philosophy of education – Jean-Jacques Rousseau's part-essay, part-novel *Emile, or On Education*, written in the mid-eighteenth century. According to Rousseau, the most important lesson a child can learn is how to be a child. He advocated a child-centred approach to parenting and teaching, saying a child should be allowed to wander free in nature, be left to learn at their own pace and should learn only those things that are really worth knowing. Religious study and books, he suggested, were best avoided, and the role of the tutor was to guard against external influences, particularly those of organised religion. Rousseau was not writing in a secular age, and the response to *Emile* was somewhat heated. The ideas it contained were considered so dangerous, the book was publicly burned in Paris and Geneva following its publication.

Teaching in theory and teaching in practice, however, turn out to be different things. The inherent irony of Jean Brodie, teaching impressionable little girls while she was in her prime, was that her methods were pretty intrusive in and of themselves. In her admiration of the Italian dictator Mussolini and his vision for a New Rome – a new civilisation – she is, for want of a better term, a prime example of how it is difficult to give credence to the ideas of fascists without becoming one yourself. It also turns out that, if we look at the bigger picture of the idea of education in the West, Miss Mackay really was on to a winner. Education is, indeed, very much a process of putting both knowledge and ideas *in* to students' minds. It is, as such, very much part of the civilising process. Education is not a neutral process, though, nor has it ever been exclusively to the good of all concerned. Francis Bacon was right, your knowledge may be your power, but, as we are going to see, it also depends on how powerful your teachers are to start with.

*

Despite Rousseau's best efforts, education in the West has, for the most part, been prescriptive. Our future potential as a citizen – whether we get to go to university, whether we have access to the job market that a university degree enables, how much money we make and, in turn, where we are able to educate our own children – is judged by how we perform in exams whose questions have, by consensus, 'correct' answers. Education in the West is not so much about its so-called *intent* – to create free-thinking people – but about its *result*. It's about what we think happens, or is supposed to happen, when we formally teach people things.

A good example of this comes from July 2021, when then UK Education Secretary Gavin Williamson announced a new programme to teach Latin in a selection of state secondary schools. For some, this was good news. The public historian and classicist Mary Beard said she was delighted. 'Studying classics opens up history to us, from early dramas, that two thousand years on are still part of the theatrical repertoire, to some foundational philosophy, from democracy to empire, from powerful rulers to the enslaved.'

Historians like Francis Young took to Twitter to say that Latin is not only a direct line to the classical world of ancient Rome, but also a window to the medieval and early modern world up to the 1700s, where Latin was the language of religion, government and written records. Knowing how to speak Latin isn't solely about chowing down on the works of Marcus Aurelius or digging into the minutiae of Julius Caesar's political career, his sex life or, more usually, both. In fact, it opens up more than a millennium of historical goings-on throughout Europe – that is, the whole of the Latin-speaking, civilised world at that time.

Interestingly though, improving educational standards was not Williamson's main goal. It was social change. 'We know Latin has a reputation as an elitist subject which is only reserved for the privileged few,' he said on the programme's announcement. 'But the subject can bring so many benefits to young people, so I want to put an end to that divide.'

The first part of Williamson's statement is spot on: the need for greater parity in UK education is patently clear. A 2020 British Council survey showed only one in fifty state schools teaches Latin at Key Stage 3 (ages eleven to fourteen), compared to nearly half of independent schools. The second part of the statement, though, doesn't tell the full story. It fundamentally misunderstands a key point about the history of education in Britain, which is this: it is not studying Latin that makes you privileged, it's that privileged people are the ones who get to have their children educated in Latin. Still, giving Williamson the benefit of the doubt for a moment, let's say he's right, and learning Latin really can break down social barriers. That being the case, what exactly do we mean when we talk about Latin and the classics more broadly?

Beard's definition is a relatively concise one: the classics are those works from ancient Greece and Rome – poetry, history, biography, plays, philosophy – considered worthy of study. This is in part because their ideas have survived for so long, and also because of some inherent value, usually left undefined. While the works themselves are thousands of years old, the ways in which they are taught date to the modern era. Socially speaking, it was an elite pursuit from the start. In fact, our word for 'class' and 'the classics' share the same Latin root. At the risk of falling into a vortex, we need to use a bit of Latin etymology in order to really understand what is going on here.

Both 'the classics' and 'class' come from the root *clamare*, meaning 'to call out'. Originally, a 'classic' was a war trumpet, used to summon a group of people together. The economic connotation of 'class' comes from when Servius Tullius, the sixth of the legendary early kings of Rome, clamoured for a census in order to better plan his military campaigns. Tullius' census divided people into different groups, or classes, based on their wealth and possessions. In eighteenth-century Europe two thousand years later, the Industrial Revolution resulted in a new distribution of wealth across society and the idea of 'middle' and 'working' classes came into everyday use. The term 'the classics' also comes from the Roman census, where the top six classes of men with the most money and property were called the *classici*, that is, 'top men'. The second-century Roman miscellanist Aulus Gellius extended the term to the leading writers, calling them *scriptores classici* – 'top writers'. When you consider that Gellius and his contemporaries distinguished the *scriptores classici* from the *scriptores proletarii* – the everyday run of writers – you can see that a classical education, with the wealthy upper classes reading the works of the top writers, was about separating the elite from working people from the very beginning.

The classics have variously passed in and out of fashion in Europe since the classical period itself, with revivals under the first Holy Roman Emperor Charlemagne in the eighth and nine centuries, under three of his successors – all called Otto – in the tenth century, and then again in the twelfth. It's this last revival that was most influential on the Italian Renaissance, the intellectual and cultural movement usually dated to the fifteenth century, although its roots went back further. Not only did the twelfth century see a renewed interest and more vigorous study of classical works, it was also the time when the first European universities were established, and these ideas first added to organised curricula (or, courses of study).

It was following the Glorious Revolution of 1688, when James II and VII of England, Ireland and Scotland was deposed from the throne by William of Orange and James's daughter, Mary II – seen as the historic moment when power shifted from the monarch to parliament, that a classical education became the defining feature of a new type of social figure: the English Gentleman. These were men taught in an increasingly formal school system (as opposed to wealthy young men being taught at home by a private tutor), well-versed in Latin and Greek languages and literature as a kind of conspicuous consumption. Here, the classics came to signify intellectual and moral superiority, as well as class distinction. They were the great unifying factor that delineated the educated gentleman's son from his working-class equivalent because, as the philosopher John Grote put it, they spoke 'the language of intellectual communion among civilised men'. In other words, your father could be a tradesman or a peer, but with a copy of Dryden's translation of Virgil's *Aeneid* under your arm, you could find kinship and unity with others of your ilk by signalling that you were both pursuing a common goal: to look posh.

We know that in England 'the classics' as the study of ancient authors by rich young men was well entrenched by 1684, because a self-described group of 'several young men privately educated in Hatton Garden' published their own translation of a work by Eutropius, the fourth-century official who wrote a history of the founding of Rome. This was the time when London was emerging like an imperially-minded phoenix from the ashes of the Great Fire in 1666, and there was a clear notion, as Francis Bacon – disgraced Lord Chancellor and founder of the scientific method – had expressed it, that knowledge was power. Lewis Maidwell, teacher at the Hatton Garden school, wrote in his introduction to the book that if only the English would take the education of their sons more seriously 'the sleepy genius of our Nation would rouse itself'. Education wasn't simply about broadening minds, it would play a key role in broadening the horizons and cementing the power of the British Empire too.

Virgil's *Aeneid* in particular performed another function here. Along with signalling social and intellectual aspirations, it also embodied an ambition for empire. The epic work by the first century BCE Roman poet follows Trojan hero Aeneas who, having left his home in the aftermath of the Trojan War, goes on to found the city of Rome. He does this on the orders of the god Jupiter, who promises that from Rome will come *'imperium sine fine'*, 'an empire without end'. Although unfinished, the *Aeneid* became an instant classic in the ancient Roman world because its story linked a historical and mythical Rome directly to Virgil's contemporary Rome under the rule of the emperor Augustus. It went straight into the classroom and has been there ever since, its presence ebbing and flowing as the classics have always done. Alfred, Lord Tennyson was such a big fan that he began a nineteenth-century revival of Virgil almost single-handedly. So were his fellow poet T. S. Eliot and Enoch Powell, the UK MP whose infamous 'rivers of blood' anti-immigration speech was named for the lines he quoted from the epic, spoken to Aeneas by the oracle of Apollo at Delphi. Powell was following a long-established tradition of administrators throughout the Empire quoting lines from Virgil to each other. Why wouldn't they, when those words were so consistently useful to the project of Empire? '*Tu regere imperio populos, Romane, memento*', Virgil wrote, which, in Dryden's translation, reads: 'But, Rome, 'tis thine alone, with awful sway / To rule mankind, and make the world obey'.

In the classics, Britain found a magic mirror, one that reflected the past in the glory that was Greece and the grandeur that was Rome, and also showed imperial visions of the future, based on that history. As early as the 1840s, leading Victorian thinker

Thomas Carlyle had announced that Britain was the new Rome, and the British were the New Romans (Jean Brodie's hero Mussolini, who was also keen on Latin, would say exactly the same thing about Italy a mere ninety years later). The classical era provided useful models for Empire too. For aspiring British imperialists over the turn of the nineteenth century, it was handy to co-opt the idea of a society supported by slavery, and also one that played up to the idea of enslavers as physically and racially superior, as the British perceived the ancient Greek states of Athens and Sparta. When it came to running a huge, global empire from a tiny set of islands less than one-hundredth of its total size, the British turned to the ancient Roman model of systematically hierarchical society and strongly centralised, violent imperial control. It's this co-opting of the classics in the interests of Western imperialism that continues to inform white supremacists today. Whether it is a mistaken racialised view of the classical world as exclusively white (which it wasn't), or the idea that as the physical and cultural – that is to say the racial – inheritors of the classical world, the white West was civilising its colonised peoples, this is the same idea that has been at play in the West for the last two centuries. Perhaps unsurprisingly, it was an idea Westerners thought was worth spreading.

*

Britain's imperial visions were crystallised in the middle of the nineteenth century in the form of the Indian Civil Service entrance examination, designed by classical educators with both classics students and imperial ambitions in mind. As Benjamin Jowett, Master of Balliol College, Oxford, put it: 'I should like to rule the world through my pupils.' Jowett saw to it that the classics were central to the ICS exam, and deemed there was no problem with the requirement for Latin and Ancient Greek being given double the weight of Sanskrit and Arabic. So, in effect, being able to quote Virgil and the other Greats was more use to you than any kind of knowledge about the place you were actually supposed to be administering (although one Indian, a high-caste Brahmin, did pass the exam to much acclaim in 1867). Prime Minister William Gladstone approved of the exams, believing that intellectual competition would play to the natural superiority of the *hoi aristoi* (as opposed to the hoi polloi, i.e. everyone else).

The ICS exam was the brainchild of another educational administrator, Thomas Babington Macaulay, whose *Lays of Ancient Rome* ('lay' in the sense of a ballad or narrative poem, this was not some early Victorian bonkbuster) was one of the most popular publications of the nineteenth century. As a schoolboy, Winston Churchill memorised the book, a supposed sign of his great intelligence and education. Today, Macaulay is more notorious for his 'Minute on Indian Education', which included the infamous words, 'I have conversed both here and at home with men distinguished by their proficiency in the Eastern tongues ... I have never found one among them who could deny that a single shelf of a good European library was worth the whole native literature of India and Arabia.'

As was the case with so many scientists, Macaulay took the word of his Western fellows over and above everyone else. Rather than learn the languages, history and customs of South Asian people, Macaulay put forward an assimilation model of British civilisation as the means of creating a better integrated empire, built by and through education. What was required, according to Macaulay, was: 'An intermediary class who may be interpreters between us and the millions whom we govern; a class of persons,

Indian in blood and colour, but English in taste and opinions, in morals and in intellect.'

Every time I read that sentence it makes my blood run cold. Although I had never heard of Macaulay until I started to learn more about the history of the British Empire, he is very much the ghost at the banquet of my education. (In fact, this quotation from *Macbeth* is in special deference to him and his belief that, by his day, the work of English writers like Shakespeare had started to surpass that of the ancient Greeks). As the child of Indian parents raised in an international community in the Middle East, with English as my first language despite Bangla being my mother tongue, I am arguably one of Macaulay's metaphorical grandchildren. My parents had moved to Abu Dhabi in the late 1970s, having lived in the UK for just over a decade. They both worked for the NHS (Mum as a gynaecologist, obstetrician and surgeon and Dad as a pharmacist) and despite being happy to take a professional leap into the unknown, when it came to the education of their only child, they insisted on betting on a sure thing and enrolled me at the one British primary school in the city. This was the one school that claimed to take a more Jean Brodie approach to education. Rather than the rote learning my parents had both suffered through at school, their daughter would have the benefit of a more enlightened system, designed to nurture and bring out the best in me. They were also clearly aware of Macaulay's claim, echoing through the generations, that a British education was the best in the world. So, unlike the other kids of our various South Asian family friends, who went to Indian or International Curriculum schools, I went first to a British primary school and then later to the American Community School.

Talk about the best laid plans.

Both were really tiny Western enclaves, and going to school every day was in many ways a much longer journey than the drive across town. During primary school, I remember going to services at the neighbouring Anglican church for Easter, Harvest Festival and Mothering Sunday, and singing Christmas carols by candlelight around the swimming pool. I also remember enthusiastically waving a tiny Union Jack when Princess Anne came to visit. There were school sports days replete with sack and egg-and-spoon races, and, as many of the teachers were Scottish, we did Scottish country dancing and held a mini Highland games. As for middle and high school, it was like stepping into every American TV show or high school movie you've ever seen, the only difference being a much stricter dress code. We ran laps in gym class, there were pep rallies, elaborate high school musicals, a school newspaper (on which I was a columnist and editor) and mums from the Booster Club sold hot dogs at lunchtime every Wednesday.

All of these things put together made for a cultural experience that made me feel like I'd grown up in the West, even if it was the West in the Middle East. This was doubly true when it came to the curriculum. Despite growing up in a place where summer temperatures could hit above 50° Celsius in the shade, I learned about freezing Dickensian Christmases and Sir Walter Raleigh laying down his cloak so Elizabeth I could walk over a puddle. History classes included all the standards, from the Vikings to the Tudors, and, through what can only be described as a greedy use of the Puffin Book Club, I read all kinds of books from Roald Dahl, Allan Ahlberg and Jules Older through to Arthur Conan Doyle and Agatha Christie, all of which painted in exquisite detail what life was like in an England where I felt as though I already lived. English class – strangely at both schools

– filled in the gaps with Charlotte Brontë and Joseph Conrad, and a solid diet of poetry. I was lucky that I liked poetry, and that it was easy enough to memorise the works of all the usual suspects: Wordsworth, Keats, Shelley, Byron and Coleridge, along with the Americans – Ralph Waldo Emerson, Henry David Thoreau, and Walt Whitman. They were almost all men, almost exclusively white and all strangely thrilled by being outdoors, which, I supposed, made sense because where they were it wasn't so hot. You can't tell it by looking at me, but, educationally speaking, I'm as white as they come.

In ways that I am now solidly ashamed of, I conformed to the model minority stereotype of South Asian children in Western schools in that I was very good at it, and this kept my parents happy. True, I ditched playing the piano one grade before the top qualification, but that was so that I could focus on taking Advanced Placement college level classes in my last two years of high school. I was valedictorian of my high school class (ending my speech with a quote from Tennyson's 'Ulysses') and this was all part of the project of getting a place at a good, that is to say, English university, attendance at which was non-negotiable. And there, the trend continued.

I remember in my first year as an archaeology undergraduate, I managed to fill some dead air in a seminar by waffling on about Percy Bysshe Shelley's poem 'Ozymandias'. This was not entirely off topic, being a poem about power, memory and time. It must have made an impression on the tutor, because I remember him asking me afterwards where I'd gone to school. When I told him I had an American high school diploma and, save for the last three months had lived my entire life in Abu Dhabi, he seemed surprised. 'Well,' he said, 'you are certainly much better read than the rest of them.'

For all this success though, there were odd moments of dissonance. When I showed my dad a project I was working on about the British in India, he went quiet for a bit before saying, 'You know, they don't teach you everything.' Well, duh, I remember thinking. There's a lot out there, obviously they can't teach all of it, they have to be selective. I don't know what prompted my dad to say what he did. I don't know what it took for him to say, for what I think was the first and only time, something critical about the system of Western education he had so enthusiastically thrown me into until then. It could have been any number of things: I may have been studying Advanced Placement English Language and Literature, but I was illiterate in Bangla; I could recite the whole of 'The Lady of Shalott' and 'The Road Not Taken' from memory but barely knew anything by Rabindranath Tagore, Nobel laureate and the pride of not just West Bengal but the whole of India. If pushed, I probably would have argued that the Empire wasn't all bad, after all it had given us the English language, democracy and railways.

I was a little nerd who loved history and the music of poetry, who had done what her teachers had asked her to and, through doing so, had become indoctrinated in a certain way of being and speaking that would stand me in good stead in an academic setting. I know first-hand that it helps to know your poetry. Not for its own sake, but for what it is able to signify. In the West, being immersed in the works of Tagore from birth will get you nowhere. Troll out a bit of Shelley, on the other hand, and it shows that you are able to fit in. I may look Brown on the outside, but I'm white on the inside. All told, more than a century and a half after Macaulay came up with the idea, I am, simultaneously, the dregs but also the epitome of his vision of British education as a civilising force.

For Macaulay and his imperial-minded contemporaries, as Rome had civilised Britain, so Britain could civilise the rest of the world. The Greeks proved useful here too, particularly Aristotle, his *Nicomachean Ethics* framing the idea of a paternalistic elite as the engine driving civilisation forward. This is what Rudyard Kipling was talking about in his hugely popular poem, 'The White Man's Burden', exhorting the nation to 'Send forth the best ye breed / Go, bind your sons in exile / To serve your captives' need.' British imperialists even modelled themselves on ancient Greek and Roman historical figures like Alexander the Great, Julius Caesar, and Caesar Augustus (funnily enough, all the ones we learned about at school). Alexander, in particular, who had been taught by Aristotle and whose empire had also extended to South Asia, was seen as a civiliser of savages, and yet another imperial role model. Technological advances like the steamship, railways and the electric telegraph allowed for the British to spread their influence much further and more quickly than the Romans had done, and these agents of change were eventually spoken about as an end in themselves, in the absence of the politics and economic aspects involved.

In their book *A People's History of Classics*, Edith Hall and Henry Stead explode the idea that the upper classes managed to hold on to a monopoly on the classics. They tell the stories of working people who used the classics to break through class divides. In recounting the history of trade unions and individual people like bodybuilder and showman Eugen Sandow, Hall and Stead share stories of aspiration and resistance, showing how working class people 'used the classics to prove their intellectual calibre, to express their plight and signal their consciousness of the class system.'

Despite the fact that the upper class monopoly on the classics was confounded from the start, it's sadly the case that the image of a civilised and well-educated person as someone able to quote at will from the writings of Virgil, Homer or Pericles is still very much with us today. It speaks to the enduring power of our language and educational system in all its forms to elevate as well as to oppress.

*

We're used to the idea that a formal education, above and beyond the classics, can be prescriptive in ways that are socially unhelpful. We don't need to go back too far to a time when Home Economics was exclusively taught to women students, or when those same women students needed letters of introduction and special interviews to establish their good character before being able to attend university. Insulting and infuriating as this was, it pales in comparison to considerably more traumatic and sinister aspects of education in the Empire. Within Britain itself, Welsh children were bullied and beaten out of speaking the Welsh language. In British settler colonies like Canada, Australia and the United States, Indigenous children were forcibly removed from their parents and put into residential 'schools'. Here they were punished and stigmatised for speaking their own languages and sometimes starved, tortured and outright killed, all in the service of an underlying theory that through assimilation they would eventually be 'bred out' of the population, die out and disappear.

Under the banner of 'Empire', the West could use whatever force and means it liked to establish and maintain its supremacy. In the aftermath of Empire, the Western canon in particular and Western knowledge more broadly, combined to make a powerful political tool. When the nations of Europe were retreating from their former colonies in the twentieth century, ostensibly leaving them free and independent, cultural theorists like Ngũgĩ wa Thiong'o and Edward Said pointed out that models of Western education that upheld Westerners as the pinnacle of civilisation remained behind. They showed how Latin, Ancient Greek and English were not simply neutral lingua franca – a set of useful common languages – but a complex and sophisticated means of controlling thoughts and ideas. Culture is as much a form of imperialism as winning a battle and planting a flag. As such, it is not simply lands that get colonised, its people's minds too.

Towards the end of the 1960s and the beginning of the 1970s, a series of publications exposed a travesty baked in to the British educational system. One of these was a leaked report entitled 'Haringey Comprehensive Schools' (1969), which widely became known as the Doulton Report, named after its author. This document sparked dismay and outrage among the local North London Black community, when it stated that academic standards would be compromised in schools with large numbers of West Indian pupils, because those children were generally recognised as having much lower IQs than white English students. In what was clearly a move to mitigate this perceived problem of Black children in their schools, a follow-up 'Report to the Education Committee on Comprehensive Education' recommended that Haringey Council banded the schools in the borough according to the academic ability of their students.

Even though he had been dead for fifty-eight years by that point, I think it's safe to say that Francis Galton would have approved of this course of action. In Galton's vision for a state run on eugenic principles, the quantification of intelligence played a key role. The most intelligent, he argued, should be supported and encouraged to reproduce, while the least intelligent should be prevented from doing so. In the 1920s, psychologists such as Charles Spearman and Cyril Burt made Galton's vision a reality by designing and developing standardised intelligence tests along with an idea for standardising intelligence itself. Burt's research on the heritability of intelligence – what we now think of as the genetics of intelligence – profoundly shaped Britain's system of formal education by introducing the 11+ exam. The 11+ was the test of a lifetime. If you scored highly and were deemed to be of high intelligence, it could land you a place at one of the prestigious grammar schools. The grammar in question was, of course, Latin, and a grammar school education was a much-vaunted path to success at school at beyond.

Standardised intelligence tests determined a child's IQ, or intelligence quotient, and whether they were of average, above average or below average intelligence. Today we think of people in that last category as having learning disabilities or special educational needs. Back in the 1960s, they were deemed 'educationally subnormal' and sometimes sent to special boarding schools set up for 'educationally subnormal' children.

A few years after the Haringey school reports, in May 1971, educationalist Bernard Coard published his seminal book, *How the West Indian Child Is Made Educationally Sub-normal in the British School System*. Based on his own personal experience as a schoolteacher, Coard showed that a disproportionate number of Black children were being put into the boarding schools, having been deemed intellectually inferior to their white counterparts. The reason for this, as the educational psychologist Mollie Hunte explained in support of Coard's argument, was that the tests were culturally biased against Black children. Speaking to

Sue Lawley on the radio show *Desert Island Discs,* the Black dub poet Linton Kwesi Johnson – who in 2002, became only the second living poet to be invited to produce a collection for the Penguin Modern Classics series – described how this worked. 'They would give you little tests to do,' he explained. '. . . like they'd ask you to draw a house, for example, and you come from the Caribbean, and the houses there don't have chimneys. So, you draw a house without a chimney pot, and somehow that would make you "educationally subnormal."'

Professor Gus John, a renowned educationalist and activist in the fight against institutional racism in schools, has also said that an ignorance of issues around language were at play here too. There was no appreciation, John says, that Jamaican Patois – while based on English – used completely different words from standard English – a distinction that none of the people issuing the intelligence tests had accounted for. While the children of Indian immigrants were seen to speak different languages and were supported to learn standard English, the kids from West Indian households were not granted the same privileges. They were ignored, diminished and left behind. While the benefits of a grammar school classical education were actively lifting some students up, at the other end of the scale, the racist assumptions that Black children were not worth the effort of educating was pulling them down.

Their parents were having none of it. Protests led by the West Indian Standing Conference and the North London West Indian Association managed to get the Haringey schools project shelved. Black parents all over the country then turned their efforts to making up for the shortfall of their children's education in mainstream schools. Their efforts informed the Black Supplementary School Movement, which arose in the sixties, where, on Saturdays, Black parents taught their own lessons in whatever spaces they could find – from local community centres to church halls, Portakabins and even their own front rooms.

'Part of the reason these schools were so popular,' according to Kehinde Andrews, who wrote a book on the history of the movement, 'is because they were dealing with the deficits in Maths and English in the mainstream schools.' Alongside this, the Black Saturday Schools encouraged creativity and confidence in their students. A newsletter from the Winnie Mandela Supplementary School, which convened every week in a set of Portakabins in Bayham Street in North London, features an interview with Ms Robinson, the drama teacher. 'The problem is basically one of confidence,' she said.

> I see my job as helping the children develop confidence in their own West Indian roots. I teach them West Indian folk songs and stories and try to give them a pride in their heritage. West Indian culture is thought of in this society as not being quite the same level as British culture. If the children are given some support in this area, it helps them to stand up to it.

The interview with Ms Robinson and other teachers and parents at the Winnie Mandela Supplementary School is illustrated with a black and white photograph of a five-year-old boy, with what can only be described as an adorable grin. This is Kingslee, one of the school's pupils, and he is quoted as saying 'We do better work here.' Today, you and I know Kingslee better as the writer, hip-hop artist and social entrepreneur Akala. He has spoken more recently about what his Saturday School education has meant to him, and what it means with regard to education in this country more broadly.

For me, my passion for learning world history came from Pan-African Saturday School. So, as a young Afro-Caribbean child growing up, if I had swallowed the Eurocentric curriculum that told me that Black people's only role in the human story, was, first of all, as being slaves, then getting set free by William Wilberforce, then the Civil Rights Movement in America, I probably wouldn't have had very much pride in my own identity. Luckily, I didn't swallow that curriculum 'cos I went to a separate Saturday School ... I was a lucky recipient of some of that knowledge, and it meant that I didn't feel inferior to what I was being taught. So I could engage with Shakespeare, or Newton, or Plato because I didn't feel intimidated by that, 'cos I didn't feel that people like me had never contributed anything to human progress.

Akala's comments were part of the conversation following a blistering presentation at the Oxford Union. Part history lesson, part highly informed polemic, he spoke in great detail about African intellectual contributions and achievements, and also how, through the lenses of racism and imperialism, these achievements were made to disappear. The stories we tell our children are important. If we make an effort to imbue all our children with confidence and pride in their history, the rest falls into place.

*

The resistance to Euro-critical and decolonial movements in education reproduce the old Empire in miniature. They uphold the Western canon as a continuing neutral good and dismiss its critics as either ignorant or politically motivated. As we've seen throughout this chapter though, Western education has always been political, both at home and overseas. A look at the history of education in the West shows us that it was less of a theory and more of a tool for delineating differences, particularly differences in class, but also, as we saw with science, differences between so-called races. It is a knowledge monopoly that needs confronting. The educational theorist Paulo Freire made no bones about it: 'There is no such thing as neutral education,' he wrote. 'Education either functions as an instrument to bring about conformity or freedom.' I expect we all know which of the two we would choose for ourselves and our children, but looking at the history of education in the West, we can see that these distinctions are often not as clear cut as they would appear to be. The idea that education was about indoctrination, particularly about the positive role, benefits and importance of Empire is not in question. The question is about what we can change. And one of the easiest changes to make is acknowledging how the white curriculum is constructed, along with the historical and political contexts that shape who we deem to be knowledgeable, educated and civilised.

I can't count a classical education among the list of my many privileges, but I was brought up bilingual, and have always been interested in the origins and exact meanings of words. What *exactly* does this mean? Where *exactly* do our ideas come from? How *exactly* is knowledge constructed? There is power in this knowledge, if it is knowledge we make for ourselves. And be under no misapprehension, education has always been about power.

My father understood the power of education, not to lift me up and to widen my horizons, but to help me establish my place in the world. 'They can take away everything else,' he told me, 'but once you've got it, they can't take away your education.' I can only wish for you all that you could have a parent or a guardian like my dad, who understood both the value of an education and also some of the price we have to pay to get it.

While there is no getting away from the fact that I am one of Macaulay's grandchildren, I am also the granddaughter of Sri Thakurdas Ray, noted Kolkata architect and devoted reader of books from Rabindranath Tagore to Sukumar Ray, Sarat Chandra Chattopadhyay and, I am reliably informed, P. G. Wodehouse. He passed this love of reading on to his daughter – my mother, Dr Sonali Das – which meant that I grew up in a house full of books that fostered a love of reading as an everyday pleasure. Everything about my life and education tells me the binary between 'the West and the rest' is the false one. I am nothing if not living proof that it is not a question of being either all Brown or all white, of being civilised or uncivilised: I am living proof that you can be both. The ability of knowledge to empower us lies at the heart of education. And what entrenches both that knowledge and that power? The ability to impart it.

Chapter Three

THE PEN IS MIGHTIER
THAN THE SWORD

I made a strong play to win the education game. In high school I took a whole load of AP – Advanced Placement – university-level classes in history, English, art and calculus. While these proved invaluable for getting into university, they all required a huge investment of time and effort, particularly a lot of writing. I have always wanted to be a writer. I tell everyone I love writing, but that's not entirely true. The truth is that I love *having written*. The process of writing – the focus, concentration, thinking, in short, the work it requires – I can do almost entirely without. This being the case, I had filled the rest of my schedule with classes that did not create homework: choir, modern dance, theatre, even PE, and all of which, lucky for me, were graded on effort. I made a strategic error, though, when I ticked the box for 'Newspaper', which had a reputation as being a bit of a party class. While I'm not a party person, this was exactly the kind of walk-through class required. Except, of course, here, suddenly, was a whole other heap of writing, that, worse still, demanded a regular physical output. Along with being a staff writer, I was made a columnist because there were pages to fill and no one else wanted to do it. The paper was published monthly, and, for two years, I found myself bouncing, sometimes jubilantly, often not, from one deadline to the next.

By my senior year, I had risen to the rank of editor. This meant making other people write things as well as continuing to write myself. Looking back through the old issues from that year, I see that one solution we had all come up with for this was to not actually do any writing at all. The pages are filled with comics, lists of music and movies, student profiles and quizzes. My favourite of these was a satirical quiz put together by some friends of mine. Among the cheap but also hilarious swipes at then US President Bill Clinton, was a single question on literature:

'Who wrote Goethe's *Faust*?'

If anything, it's punchier today than it was when it was first written in the late 1990s, after the internet was invented, but before Google had become a verb. Every time I read it, it makes me smile and, at the same time, forces me to resist the visceral urge to reach for my phone to check, just in case. The inspiration for this question was the title of a film that had come out a couple of years earlier. Directed by Baz Luhrmann and starring Leonardo DiCaprio and Claire Danes in the lead roles, it was called *William Shakespeare's Romeo + Juliet*. In our newspaper office (read: school computer lab), the snippier among us wondered if we had missed Charles Dickens' or Jane Austen's *Romeo and Juliet*.

The joke's on us though, as there exists a significant body of published research based on the idea that someone other than Shakespeare wrote the plays and poems attributed to him. One of the first people to make this argument was an American woman named Delia Bacon. In 1853, Bacon travelled to England with the express plan to discredit Shakespeare. Bacon was convinced that the works were actually written by her namesake (but not relation), our old friend, Sir Francis Bacon. According to Delia, being a disgraced lord chancellor and coming up with a whole new scientific paradigm hadn't been sufficiently challenging for Francis Bacon: he had also written all of the works attributed to Shakespeare. She spent several months researching the various locations associated with Francis's career in order to prove her point. Her method involved sitting in these places and absorbing the 'atmospheres', a sort of PhD by vibes.

Despite being more than a little eccentric in her output, and not having been born particularly rich, Delia Bacon had a number of well-known and wealthy supporters, including the writers Ralph Waldo Emerson, Thomas Carlyle and Nathaniel Hawthorne. In 1857, she published a book – *The Philosophy of the Plays of Shakespeare Unfolded* – making an overlong and excruciatingly detailed argument in Francis Bacon's favour, all without actually naming him. Delia Bacon's was a sad life. She was very likely delusional and she died two years after the book was published, alone and having been institutionalised, believing herself to be the Holy Ghost. It seems unlikely that Francis Bacon wrote the works of Shakespeare, given that he was busy doing and writing lots of other things. In addition to *Novum Organum*, in which he had outlined his ideas for the scientific method and for which he remains famous, he also wrote a number of essays, including one in which he summarily dismissed the theatre as a good use of anyone's time. Delia's idea did not die with her, though. In her wake, American writers Mark Twain and Henry James took on the mantle of supporting her case.

These anti-Stratfordian arguments (that is, arguments that the works of Shakespeare were not written by the actor of that name who came from Stratford-upon-Avon), like all good conspiracy theories, are based on supposedly hidden and cryptic clues in the text of the works. People unconvinced of Shakespeare's bona fides scrutinise his works and supposedly decipher them in order to get at the truth. Another candidate for having written Shakespeare is Edward de Vere, the seventeenth Earl of Oxford. This began as the theory of a Gateshead schoolteacher called J. Thomas Looney, who managed to get his book *Shakespeare Identified* published in 1920. In it, he claimed that the real William Shakespeare lacked the learning and polish required to write the works attributed to him, and so they were more likely to have been written by someone more posh. Oxford seemed a likely candidate, given his social class and connections, including Elizabeth I. This argument is also applied to Christopher Marlowe – Shakespeare's contemporary, fellow playwright and another candidate for Shakespeare's throne. Oxford's fans don't seem to mind that these men died many years before the last of Shakespeare's works were written. They also don't account for why either Marlowe or Oxford should want to do this work under a name not their own.

In a refreshing turn, there are some women writers in the fray here too, such as Mary Sidney, Countess of Pembroke, whose candidacy is also based on her social network. Mary's brother was the poet Philip Sidney, her uncle was Robert Dudley, the Earl of Leicester, and Mary herself was friends with the poet Edmund Spenser (already known to us as having penned *The Faerie Queene*). Another branch of the theory suggests that Shakespeare's works were actually written by a syndicate of different people, a sort of League of Extraordinary Elizabethans, including Francis Bacon, Mary Sidney, Sir Philip Sidney and Sir Walter Raleigh. Seen in this light, some of these stories practically write themselves.

The assumption that lies at the heart of these theories is that Shakespeare's works cover and demonstrate expertise in so many different subject areas, from law to medicine to politics and state affairs, that they could not possibly have all sprung from the quill of the son of a dowdy, provincial, Warwickshire glove maker. It's true that while there are reams and reams of his writing in the collected folios, given his position in the Western canon there is next to nothing in terms of written records about Shakespeare's actual life. What records there are, though, do testify that he did exist, was an author of plays and sonnets, was well-educated and came from a relatively well-placed family, even if they were not nobility. And no one in Shakespeare's lifetime, or even in the few hundred years that followed, doubted that he wrote his own plays. How then do these conspiracy theories manage to be quite so involved and quite so persistent? How is it more reasonable to think that two men, who died well before the last of Shakespeare's works were written, were, in fact, their actual authors? How are academic careers built, books written and plays produced by people who don't buy the fact that Shakespeare wrote Shakespeare?

Part of the answer is that that is how conspiracy theories work – the more convoluted and arcane, the better. But it's also worth looking at the ways in which academics and intellectuals were thinking about the world in the eighteenth and nineteenth centuries. We've seen how, by the turn of the twentieth century, changing ideas in science were starting to frame ideas about human society, particularly with regard to human biology.

Francis Galton was influential in foregrounding the idea that intelligence in all its forms, including genius, was passed down from one generation to the next. For Galton, and many of his contemporaries, scientific research demonstrated that highly intelligent men tended to have highly intelligent fathers. Doctors were related to doctors, judges to judges and so forth. Sadly for us, Galton framed this phenomenon as what we have come to think of as the genetic heritability of intelligence, rather than the benefits of wealth, privilege, and, as we have also seen, access to education. In this context, it made perfect sense that Shakespeare, who was relatively low-born and dismissed by Delia Bacon as a 'stupid, illiterate, third-rate play actor', could not have been a great writer.

If historians, sociologists and anthropologists have a kink, it's for writing. They are mesmerised by the written word in its myriad and powerful forms. They marvel at the typography, the intricacies of letter forms and the varieties of fonts. They lose themselves in the interplay between ink and papyrus and parchment. They spend whole careers learning to read and decode lost ancient languages, from hieroglyphs to cuneiform. Put this way, it's easy to understand the appeal of writing. It is a magical medium that allows everything from common or garden accounting and tax calculations to epic poems to be read, experienced and understood through space and time, by people born hundreds, even thousands of years apart. If we take a closer look at the history of writing, though, it's possible to see that there is something else going on here.

The written word is a tool for conveying art, ideas and information in much the same way that a loaded gun is a tool for conveying bullets through the air. The person doing the conveying is, by default, powerful. The intriguing affair of who wrote Shakespeare's work has been, in part, made possible by his relative absence in the written record. This has left a void that could be filled with other people's ideas, including ideas that they themselves have been able to have published. This tells us something about the power of writing and the nature of ideas – the ideas that survive, the stories that get told and, importantly, the ones that don't. In reality, texts – both ancient or otherwise – do not only speak for themselves.

*

Much of the early study of writing relates directly to the history of civilisation. As nineteenth and early twentieth century European archaeologists began to uncover ancient civilisations in Egypt and Mesopotamia, they started to build theories about how those ancient civilisations related to their modern selves. Linguists and philologists came up with grand theories, linking players of the biblical past to the ancient Greeks and Romans, whose written genius was eventually passed down to Europe.

There were some inconvenient truths to gloss over here. For one thing, the ancient Greeks weren't big on writing at all. Both the *Iliad* and the *Odyssey*, the Greek epics that remain mainstays of a classical education and are ascribed to the poet Homer, were originally spoken word pieces, passed down from performer to performer over the generations. 'Homer' was more likely a collective of poets and storytellers who, over centuries, recited, reworked, honed and perfected lines that were eventually written down at some point between the eighth and sixth centuries BCE. If anything, the Greek epics have more in common with hip hop than they do with Shakespeare, and all of these works depend on the rhythm of the spoken word to connect and engage with their audiences. Even in what we know from works that were written down, the written word was suspect. Letters are used as plot points for characters to misunderstand each other, usually with disastrous and tragic consequences. In Euripides' play *Hippolytus*, for example, Theseus finds a letter written by his wife Phaedra – who has just died by suicide – falsely accusing Theseus's son Hippolytus of having raped her. When Theseus takes the written word of his dead wife over the protestations of his living son and exiles him, yet another death is added to the score. While doing nothing for the #MeToo movement (portraying women as lying about rape for the sake of advancing your plot is not a good look), Euripides was wise to the fact that the written word was not necessarily the unvarnished truth, and that it pays not to believe everything you read.

Nevertheless, many eighteenth and nineteenth-century scholars focused on those aspects of the history of writing that strengthened the Western pedigree. This has now settled into a rollicking ride from cuneiform – the 'wedge-shaped' writing first developed in Sumer in Mesopotamia, through ancient Egyptian hieroglyphs and finally on to the phonetic alphabet popularised across the Mediterranean, that is, from the Near East to the world of the classical Greeks.

Through the combined efforts of philologists – researchers who specialise in the study of ancient texts – and linguists – those who study languages – a whole range of theories about the development of civilisation sprang up. Some stuck to the Holy Land as the beginnings of civilised living, as demonstrated by clay tablets with prototypic writing for accounting that later blossomed into full length narratives like the *Epic of Gilgamesh*. This was a particular favourite as it told the story of the world being flooded, which was thought to prove the truth of Noah's flood in the Bible. Others thought that the oldest texts were developed by the people of the Indus Valley civilisation, in what is now Pakistan. When he was assigned to sit on the Supreme Court of Bengal in 1783, the acclaimed linguist William Jones was astonished by the similarities he saw between Sanskrit – an ancient South Asian written language – and other linguistic forms he was already familiar with, including Persian and, of course, Greek and Latin. In his *Third Anniversary Discourse on the Hindus*, presented to the Asiatic Society in 1786, Jones concluded that all of these languages descended from a common ancestral language, which he called Proto-Indo-European. This, along with other racial theories, conceptualised the Indus peoples as the Aryan race, feeding into the same school of thought that in turn fed Hitler's vision of modern Germans as being descended from this first civilised and, therefore, superior race of people. While our contemporary ideas about the history of writing are considerably less overtly racist, there remains a nagging colonial hangover in the obsession with trying to work out who came up with writing first.

Primacy, though, was only one of the defining factors of writing for civilisation. Another was complexity, and particularly how some scripts became more and more complex as time went on. The main division here is between pictographic scripts like Chinese and Japanese, and phonetic scripts, where the characters represent sounds rather than things or ideas. Phonetic scripts, like Phoenician (from which we get the word 'phonetic'), Sanskrit, Greek and Latin were considered more advanced than pictographic scripts on account of this difference. This was despite the fact that pictographic scripts require readers to learn hundreds upon thousands of unique characters, whereas even the largest phonetic alphabets are usually made up of only a few dozen characters.

It's now generally thought that one of the reasons it took Europeans so long to decipher ancient Egyptian hieroglyphs was their starting assumption that hieroglyphs were, by definition, less complex than phonetic scripts, and so, to start with, European scholars failed to spot that hieroglyphs were, in fact, representations of the sounds of the language of the ancient Egyptians. European scholars continued to make the same mistake by creating notions of civilisation in their own image. They were 'civilised people', their written language was phonetic, therefore it stood to reason that different, older languages were less complex by default.

This assumption, that civilisation could be traced by how closely written text reflected a modern phonetic language, became entrenched in scholarship. At the start of the nineteenth century, some anthropologists got to thinking that words themselves – particularly written words – were like artefacts, that is to say, ancient objects that could be used to investigate and understand the ways in which the early humans who had made them thought. To do this, they linked language directly to the structure of the human mind. One of the leading thinkers in this area was the Reverend Dr Hugh Blair, the University of Edinburgh's Professor of Rhetoric and Belles-lettres (literally 'beautiful writing', meaning any kind of writing deemed an art form, like poetry or drama). Writing towards the end of the eighteenth century, Blair's work, along with that of others in his field, laid the groundwork for comparing different cultures and civilisations with each other based on their written scripts. These were the early days of the subjects that would become anthropology and archaeology. As the theories developed, they started to build principles linking language, culture and progress.

Blair's thinking was based on a number of set assumptions about the process of thinking itself. He held that ideas were made from physical, sensory experiences, or combinations of other ideas. A set of ideas put together made a thought, and a collection of thoughts together formed a memory. According to Blair, when someone is thinking, ideas flow across their mind's eye in quick succession, as a train of thoughts, or a chain of reasoning. Put altogether, the sum total is rational thinking. Blair believed that words were physical signs of ideas. As such, he believed there was a strong connection between rationality, language and the written word. And so, simply studying how a people's language changed over time should reveal how capable they were of constructing rational thought structures. While this all sounds very abstract and theoretical, Blair's philosophy was actually a handy shortcut that allowed Western scholars to make assumptions about people based on, for example, the grammar or other structures of their language, rather than the actual meaning of the words and thoughts they were expressing.

Blair divided the progress of history into three stages: primitive, ancient and modern, according to what he saw as the progress of language and culture. Primitive people, as Blair defined them, had no written language and relied solely on spoken and gestural languages. The latter ranged from the sign language used by some Indigenous peoples in North America to the broader gestures of the Mediterranean cultures (the stereotype that Italians talk with their hands goes all this way back, it seems). As Blair linked language to morality and cognitive ability, he believed that the second stage – as demonstrated by ancient people like the Chinese, Egyptians, Hebrews, Greeks and Romans – allowed for the development of writing. This was not so much a guiding principle that Blair stated outright, but rather an unquestioned, implicit logic: an argument strengthened by its own assumptions. Blair arrived at his third stage: modern people – specifically, unsurprisingly, modern Europeans – as both spoken and written language developed. He argued that modern Europeans had reached the peak of human development as their language had become ever more complex and ordered on the page.

If this tripartite system of progress is starting to look familiar to you, there's a good reason for that. It's all part of the same thought process that held that human societies progress through stages, from savage, to barbaric, to civilised. Blair wrote that, 'though among barbarous nations, and in the rude, uncivilised ages of the world, the stock of these words might be small, it must have always increased, as mankind advanced in the arts of reason and reflection'.

He was also explicit about the connection between the development of written language and rationality. 'The more any nation is improved by science, and the more perfect their Language becomes,' he wrote, 'we may naturally expect, that it will abound the more with connective particles; expressing relations of things and transitions of thought, which escaped a grosser view.' (I particularly love that Blair used a semicolon to express this idea. When it comes down to it, what could be more civilised than a semicolon?)

For Blair then, written language was not so much a triumph of style over substance, but a theory that determined style *was* substance. For those European academics who studied such things, the idea was established that not only were certain ways of thinking better – more civilised – than others, but also that only certain people were capable of thinking in civilised ways. It's telling that when Captain Cook was sent to find the Great Southern Land, one of his orders included finding out if the people who lived there had a method for communicating at a distance, as Western scientists had with writing. It was a way of finding out to what degree those people were like the Europeans and to what degree they were different. When 'newly discovered' peoples were found to have no formal written language, colonising Europeans assumed, again and again, that they were not as advanced in their ways of thinking, that they existed at a more primitive stage of human development and, as such, their ideas were not worth knowing. That is simply not the case.

*

According to the history books, the downfall of one of the great non-Western civilisations of the world turned on the treatment of a piece of writing. The piece of writing was a breviary – a book issued by the Catholic Church containing instructions for how to carry out religious services, and it had been presented to the last Inka Atawallpa by a Franciscan friar who was part of the entourage of the Spanish conquistador Francisco Pizarro. This particular breviary was accompanied by a recitation of the notorious Requerimiento, a speech Spanish colonisers read out to the people they met on their imperial explorations, calling on them to discard their own gods in favour of Christianity, and to replace their own rulers in favour of the King of Spain. Atawallpa had only recently cemented his position as Inka – the name of the ruler, and also the name of the people they ruled – following a long period of political instability (the transliteration of Inka in their own language, Runa Simi, is spelled with a 'k', unlike the more commonly used Spanish Inca, spelled with a 'c'). As the new emperor of the largest empire on Earth, he had been willing to meet with the visiting foreigners, but he had no time for this nonsense. He ignored the Requerimiento, and, as for the holy book – which to him might as well have been a bit of kitchen roll – he tossed it aside. In doing this, Atawallpa was seen by the Spaniards to have desecrated Holy Writ. This was their excuse for what they did next.

No sooner had the breviary hit the ground, did the Spanish unleash hell. It's difficult to look at this event as anything other than an ambush. The meeting between the Inka and the Spaniards had been a grand political affair, the Inka being escorted by some five or six thousand soldiers to the city of Cajamarca, with all of the pomp and grandeur you would expect from a state visit. The Spanish attack turned it into a scene from *The Godfather*, only in the northern Peruvian highlands instead of an Italian restaurant in New York City. On Pizarro's order, signalled by two shots from the cannons that had been hidden just out of sight, his armoured men on horseback charged the city's square. Carnage ensued. By nightfall, thousands of the Inka lords and soldiers were dead, shot by guns and crossbows, sliced through by Toledo steel or crushed under the feet of the warhorses. Pizarro was able to capture Atawallpa and extract from him the promise of huge quantities of gold and silver. The Spanish force that accomplished this outrage were a tiny group of a mere 168 men.

Over the following centuries, Western historians puzzled over just what it was that had led to such a small group of soldiers (supported by many local groups willing to join forces against Atawallpa) overwhelming an entire empire in one fell swoop. The theories settled on the idea that this was done through sheer force of will and superior technology. The list of the Spanish advantages includes guns, cannons, armour and horses, none of which the Inka had seen before, and all of which left them totally overwhelmed. In the frame of the idea of civilisation, with all the racist connotations involved, the superiority of the Spanish war machine was extended to apply to the Spanish themselves. As such, the outcome of the outrage of Cajamarca was effectively preordained. Of course, the Spanish, with their advanced civilisation and racial superiority, made short work of the uncivilised Inka.

This was far from the whole story. At the time Pizarro rocked up in Cajamarca in 1532, the Inka Empire was the largest in the world. It was certainly bigger than any of the rising empires elsewhere, be they in Russia, China, the Ottoman state and Great Zimbabwe. It was also a relatively new empire, roughly a century and a half old, built by the Inka people through the consolidation of various parts of pre-existing empires, from the ancient Chavín and Moche to the more recent Wari and Tiwanaku, which had collapsed at the end of the first millennium. All of these different empires were fed by a complex economy that worked vertically, with people taking advantage of the different microclimates across the various levels of the vertiginous Andes, where different crops were grown at different altitudes. This was not a high control type of empire – the Inka allowed their different constituent peoples to continue to pretty much rule themselves in a federal system, with an economy based on reciprocity and central provision. The Inka didn't use currency. In itself, this wasn't unusual – it was much the same case in feudal Europe as far as everyday people were concerned – but they also didn't have markets. Rather than depending on a system of goods exchange, all of the resources of the empire, from food to textiles and beyond, were managed by the central government and stored in way stations and warehouses for everyone's access and use. This was clearly a highly effective and productive system despite the challenging environment and intemperate climate of western South America – the Spanish found stores full to overflowing with high quality, surplus goods.

The Inka Empire satisfies many of the requirements to be counted as an advanced civilisation. They had a complex

political system with a centralised government, one that deliberately shifted people to different areas of the empire in order
to quell rebellion and encourage social cohesion. They also
instituted a system similar to European feudalism where people
were obliged to work for the state (that is, for the Inka themselves) for set parts of the year. They prioritised the use of a
single language throughout the empire; the language of the
Inka conquerors called Runa Simi, literally 'the mouth of the
people'.

The Inka had highly advanced technology, although, notably
from the Western viewpoint, they used neither the wheel, iron
nor the arch. They developed special techniques for freeze-
drying potatoes and llama meat, and their architecture was so
monumental and in such hard-to-reach places that it boggled
the minds of the Spaniards. The central plaza of Awkaypata in
the capital Cusco was nearly 32,000 square metres large (about
the size of 124 tennis courts) and lined with white sand that had
been carried up the 3,399 metres from the Pacific shore. This
was the meeting point of the segments that made up 'The Land
of the Four Quarters', what the Inka called their own country.
It was the centre of their empire and, for the Inka Pachakuti
who designed it, the centre of the universe. Cusco and other
Inka cities were built up of enormous palace complexes, residential villas and temples, where the building stones were cut
so accurately to shape that, as Pizarro's cousin Pedro described
it, 'the point of a pin could not have been inserted into one of
the joints'.

The Inka had everything, it seemed, except for a system of
writing.

For many years, this apparent inconsistency was called the
'Inca Paradox', supposedly the puzzling anthropological

phenomenon that the Inka built their civilisation – with all of its complex requirements for architecture, engineering and bureaucracy – without a system of recording any of those things. If this sounds too good to be true, that's because it's not. While the Inka didn't have a written language as the rest of the world understood it, that is, marks on paper, they had their own unique recording system of knotted threads, called khipu. Until relatively recently, when anyone troubled themselves to think about them, the khipu were generally considered to be a basic system for counting or calculating, as had been the case with the earlier versions of cuneiform in Mesopotamia. Research over the last decade, though, has revealed that the Inka khipu are, in fact, a recording system that is as complex as any written language, anywhere in the world that we know of today.

Each Inka khipu bundle consists of a number of threads, usually varying from a few to the low hundreds, but a couple have up to 1,500 cords. The threads are made out of different materials, dyed in different colours and knotted in three different ways at a series of different points along their length. In the 1920s, the American anthropologist Leland Locke studied the khipus in the collection at the American Museum of Natural History and worked out that the placement of the knots along the length of some of the thread represented a decimal system of numbers and could be read like an abacus, with units of tens, hundreds, thousands and tens of thousands. Nearly one hundred years later, in 2016, Manny Medrano and Gary Urton, anthropologists based at Harvard, worked out there was much more going on in the khipu than just accounting. By making highly detailed and painstaking comparisons with a Spanish census form, Medrano and Urton were able to work out that the khipu they were studying was a parallel record of the different individuals recorded in that census, with the pendant cords hitched to the primary cord according to which large family group in the region they belonged to. Even better, Sabine Hyland, from the University of St Andrews, was invited by the inhabitants of San Juan de Collata to come and study the khipus that had been preserved there by the community. Having done so, Hyland has proposed that those khipu may also be a phonetic recording system, with their myriad combinations of materials, colours, direction of ply and direction of knots standing for different sounds and whole words – a combined phonetic and pictographic alphabet, read not in two dimensions, but in three. The khipus from San Juan de Collata post-date the Spanish invasion, so it's possible that their design and use was influenced by the methods of Spanish writing, but even this speaks to the malleability of the khipu as a recording system. Taken altogether, the Inka may not have had writing, but they did have a complex and sophisticated recording system – one that, due to Western assumptions about the superiority of Western ways of doing things, has remained all but invisible to us until now.

These developments in various prestigious academic institutions are doubtless interesting and exciting, but amidst the thrall of all this innovative research, I can't help but feel we're forgetting something. While it's wonderful that researchers are making great leaps in deciphering the khipu, this doesn't account for how we lost sight of them in the first place. There have been generations of scholars, from historians to anthropologists to museum curators who have looked upon the khipu without thinking that there was anything within them to be discovered. It seems that when you make civilisation in your own image, your ability to see things of interest and value in other cultures is severely compromised.

The Spanish conquistadors had known about the khipu, of course. Inca Garcilaso de la Vega – an early third-culture kid who was the son of an Inka mother and a conquistador father – wrote in 1609 that the Inkas 'recorded on knots everything that could be counted, even mentioning battles and fights, all the embassies that had come to visit the Inca, and all the speeches and arguments they had uttered'. The khipu bundles were read by khipukamayuq, or 'knot-keepers', who, it seems, kept such accurate and accessible records that the conquering Spaniards clearly saw them as a threat. Two and a half decades earlier, in 1583, the Spanish had passed an order that all the khipu in Peru should be burned as idolatrous objects. This was a convenient end to records that might have contradicted the Spanish account of goings on in South America. It was the same trick they used in 1562, when Spanish conquistador Diego de Landa ordered the burning of hundreds of Maya cult objects, including twenty-seven books. It wasn't just the Spanish guns and steel that defeated the Inka Empire, it was their stories too. So, the history of the Inka – their story and their ability to tell that story and be heard – does turn on a piece of writing. It's just not the kind of writing we thought it was.

*

Even if you've never been interested in archaeology or anthropology, it's likely you've heard that it was aliens that built the great pyramids in Egypt. Aliens were, it turns out, also responsible for building the pyramids of other ancient civilisations, from the Pyramid of the Sun and the Pyramid of the Moon at Teotihuacán in central Mexico, El Castillo at Chichén Itzá in the Yucatan Peninsula, the Great Pyramid in the Aztec capital of Tenochtitlan and the Inka's great temple at Cusco in Peru. If this seems implausible to you – or maybe you are just not that into aliens – there are many other competing theories about the origins of civilisation that might appeal to you instead. Perhaps the true pyramid builders were the inhabitants of the lost city of Atlantis, who took their specialist knowledge with them when their island nation was lost under the waves? Or there's the Hollow Earth theory, that an advanced race of people live in the tropical hollow centre of the Earth, intervening in the lives of different societies all over the planet by means of an advanced network of tunnels. An astonishing amount of public archaeology today – books, magazines, documentaries – relate these racist theories, and they sadly appear to be as popular as they are disappointing and wrong.

It's easy for lots of us to dismiss all this talk of aliens, Atlantis and Hollow Earth as the uninformed witterings of a paranoid fringe of delusional people. The reality, though, is that they are far from uninformed (the information may be wrong, but there sure is a lot of it), and actually, these ideas, to some degree, are the logical extrapolations of actual archaeological and anthropological theories.

If we are to believe the theories of J. G. Frazer, Thomas Babington Macaulay and Hugh Blair, it stands to reason that uncivilised, non-white, non-Western people were simply not intellectually or technologically capable of building the cities and monuments among which they lived. European scholars once thought that Great Zimbabwe – a fourteenth-century fortified city located between the Zambezi and Limpopo rivers and once home to an estimated 18,000 people – was a replica of the Queen of Sheba's palace in Jerusalem, because they believed African people were incapable of carrying out such complicated feats of architecture and engineering by themselves. When he visited there in 1871, German explorer Karl Mauch insisted that it was more likely that Great Zimbabwe was built by biblical people from 1,500 years earlier and 8,000 kilometres away, rather than by the local people. 'A civilised nation,' he wrote, 'must once have lived there.' And of course, that civilisation could not be a local one. The racism inherent in these views is implicit and it's not an argument put forward about older Western civilisations. No one suggests aliens were responsible for building the Temple of Artemis in modern-day Turkey, the Parthenon in Athens or the Colosseum in Rome. On the flip side of the same racist coin, there are researchers who spent their careers in search of ancient and lost white races, figuring, with all this nascent civilisation going on all over the place, they must be *somewhere*.

Some other things are worth clarifying. While it's certainly the case that ancient Egyptians made artefacts out of extra-terrestrial iron, this is not because they were aliens, but because meteorites fell to Earth and were historically traded between ancient peoples. Atlantis was not a real place, but a fictional one dreamt up as a thought experiment by the Greek philosopher Plato as a cautionary tale against democracy. We should be sceptical of people who find it easier to believe that monumental architecture in the non-Western world is the work of fictional space invaders than of actual people. And when we talk about 'prehistoric peoples', we need to be more mindful that the absence of their written history is not the absence of a history altogether.

In the last three chapters, we've seen the growth and embedding of a system of thinking about non-white people based on the supposed fact that they did not have thoughts or ideas worth paying attention to and that, by extension, they themselves were not worth paying attention to. At the very least, this means we've been missing out on a view of the world that has been there all along. The khipu were there in front of our faces, and we simply passed them by, in favour of other stories about a paradoxical people who were civilised and illiterate at the same time.

The story of the Inka khipu may lead you to question what counts as writing. It may also lead you to question how useful, and indeed how limiting and potentially harmful the frame of Western civilisation can be when it comes to the ways in which we look at non-Western people. Sherlock Holmes famously said that it was 'a capital mistake to theorise before one has data. Insensibly one begins to twist facts to suit theories, instead of theories to suit facts.' Sherlock Holmes was, of course, fictional, yet Western scientists, particularly Western anthropologists, theorised ahead of their data all the time in ways that systematically diminished the power and agency of non-Western peoples.

The logic of these scholars was significantly flawed. They did not account for practical aspects like preservation. For all that we have studied and fetishised the classical world, the odds are that precious little of the writing produced there has actually lasted long enough for us to see it. As medieval historians are at constant pains to remind us, the 'Dark' in 'Dark Ages' refers to a lack of sources, rather than a period of intellectual decline. Over several centuries, starting in 1403, in Ming Dynasty China, more than 11,000 volumes of an encyclopaedia were compiled and lost to nothing other than the ravages of time. When it came to looking beyond the borders of Europe, it was also the case that scholars didn't think much beyond their own hypocrisy. In the United States, enslaved Africans were deliberately kept from learning to read and write in a bid to keep them disempowered. In the Caribbean, British plantation owners supplied enslaved people with a specially redacted version of the Bible, carefully edited to leave out the contents abolitionists were using to argue against slavery itself. Just as we saw with education, when the Western world-view frames what you can read and, by extension, what you can know and understand, it can be used to control you.

Writing and writing technology certainly give us a direct line to swathes of historical information and codify all of literature, encompassing prose, poetry and drama. We make a mistake, though, if we think that writing is the only line to all those things and if we assume that supposedly 'savage' or otherwise 'primitive' people are not as intellectually capable as those of us so comfortably ensconced in the written world.

Much of early or ancient writing makes for pretty tedious reading. The odd epic poem aside, it is mostly made up of account books, documenting trades, taxes, tributes and censuses – the filed administrative paperwork of ancient civilisations, often long gone. But there is a power, a value inherent in the written word, so much so that it has been possible to wield it as a weapon to determine whose stories got told and whose didn't. In our supposedly civilised Western world, it's not that the pen is mightier than the sword, it's that your pen is only really mighty if you happen to be holding a sword in the first place, Toledo steel glinting in the sunlight.

The written word, however sophisticated it may be as linguistic technology, functions by default as a historical record. It speaks to ownership and precedence and, therefore, speaks to power. In the West, writing, as defined by its own standards, was established as the sign of civilisation. By extension, the lack of writing or a written record in any society, be they ancient, historic or non-Western, marked them out as uncivilised. As a result, we have lost out on – or in the Spanish and others' cases purposely destroyed – their stories. All written accounts of the Inka date to after the Spanish conquest. Which is to say, at no point do we really have the Inka's own account of themselves. They were not allowed to tell their own story. And even if they had been, would anyone in the West have listened?

Chapter Four

JUSTICE IS BLIND

When, some time in the second century BCE, the Roman comic poet Caecilius Statius wrote, 'sæpe est etiam sub palliolo sordido sapientia', he was, of course, talking about the famous TV detective Columbo. I know this seems unlikely, some may say impossible, because the writer pre-dates the TV show by roughly two millennia, but hear me out. In translation this Latin phrase means 'wisdom is often hidden under a shabby coat'. So who else could it be referring to? Shabby though his coat may be, I have a lot of time for Columbo. Which is lucky, because there are a lot of repeats. There is something infinitely comforting about the fact that, when pitted against some of the most intelligent and cunning murderers out there, we know Columbo will always crack the case, usually in a highly conscientious and ingenious manner (and not, as my husband uncharitably puts it, by simply annoying the criminal into confessing).

Columbo is not alone in his indomitability. Between him, Hercule Poirot, Miss Marple, Inspectors Montalbano and Morse, I can take my pick of lavish television adaptations to snuggle up with on a weekend afternoon. My ritual in this is very particular. First comes the arrangement of a fortress of cushions and a fluffy blanket, followed by the bringing together of season-appropriate snacks and tea. I then bed myself in like a bear going into hibernation, safe in the knowledge that, come the denouement when the detective has worked everything out and the identity of the criminal is about to be revealed, I will be fast asleep. It took me a little time to work out what it is about the moment in a detective drama when it becomes clear that the case is solved that is so soporific. It is certainly the case that detective dramas are comforting. The writer and literary critic Alison Light has called detective fiction, particularly the stories written in the interwar 'Golden Age', 'the mental equivalent of pottering', a process by which chaos and disorder are sifted through and everything ends up neat and tidy. While Light makes perfect sense, I would go one step further: my sleep is the sleep of the just – the delicious oblivion of someone who can rest safe in the knowledge that, somewhere out there, justice is being done. The righteous have triumphed, the criminal has been brought to book, all is right in the world.

I need hardly tell you that real life is not like it is in detective dramas. For one thing, there is no way that Jessica Fletcher could solve all those murders and still get her books written on time. For another, the notion of justice in the West is not so easily or so convincingly pinned down. This is because there is a fundamental difference between what we consider justice to be and how the law works in reality. If we go back to the ancient Greeks – rounding up the usual suspects in our search for civilisation – we can see the idea of justice as it appears in the form of the goddess Dike – a daughter of Zeus who, along with her mother Themis, was one of two personifications of justice (earthly and heavenly justice, respectfully). Dike was usually depicted as a young woman, wearing a laurel wreath and carrying a set of scales, in which to weigh the balance of justice. Her Roman name was Iustitia and, in this form, along with the scales, she also carries a sword. From the Renaissance onwards, she is occasionally depicted as blindfolded – a metaphorical reference to the fact that justice should be applied equally to everyone, regardless of their wealth, power or social status. In Ancient Greek, The word *dikē* literally meant 'finger', and so the idea was that justice was about pointing out – or indicating – the right thing to do. At its most basic, then, Spike Lee had it right. As the title of his incredibly powerful 1989 film reminds us, justice has a moral dimension. When it comes to ensuring justice in our society, the onus is on us to *Do the Right Thing*. Almost immediately, though, this idea became more complicated, and it's a complication that relates to that blindfold. Justice cannot exist in the abstract, it happens here, in the real world. We cannot meaningfully dispense justice until we acknowledge that injustice needs to be dealt with, in the interests of what is fair and right. So, if justice is about doing the right thing, who gets to say what's right?

Broadly speaking, historically the answer to this question has been whoever is in charge. Just as it was in the previous chapter about writing, and as with the Roman vision of Iustitia, it's whoever is carrying the sword. 'Might equals right' may be a rather blunt instrument, but for much of history, throughout the world, it has been the instrument of the law nonetheless. In the West, there were some exceptions to this, particularly in the classical world. As we are going to see in more detail in the next chapter, legal developments in ancient Athens helped to establish Athenian democracy, and so, to a degree, was instrumental in the equal distribution of power. In the Roman Republic, where there was no professional legal class, commoners were appointed as an iudex in order to sit in judgement cases. For the most part, though, the law, and the justice it was supposed to purvey, was the sole jurisdiction of a privileged few. In part, the story of the development of Western civilisation is the story of how the law supposedly came to be applied to the benefit of not just the elite but to everyone in society. You'll have noticed that I say, 'supposedly'. This is because, when we actually look at how the laws in the West have changed over the centuries, the picture is rather different. Instead of evolving to the benefit of all concerned as a universal facet of Western civilisation, I would argue that the power of the legal system has stayed exactly where it always has been: in the hands of a privileged few. As such, the justice it purveys is distinctly slanted in favour of some people, to the detriment of others.

Our journey into the quagmire of Western justice begins with a single, historical legal document. It so happens that this single document is a symbol of many more Western ideals than justice alone – it is often referred to in the context of the foundations of democracy and individual freedom, which means that it is going to crop up more than once in this book. It is, of course, the Magna Carta, and it's a big sneeze in the Western ideal of justice because, for the last few centuries, it has been held up as the acme of the ideal of liberty and equality for all in the eyes of the law. This is interesting because, when you look at the history of the Magna Carta, the story is not as straightforward as your local pub quiz would have you believe.

*

In 2012, David Cameron, then UK Prime Minister, appeared on the *Late Show with David Letterman* and was subjected to an interview he clearly had not been prepared for. Opening under the banner, 'do you mind if I ask you a lot of dumb American questions?', Letterman launched into an interrogation that brought to mind the Life in the UK citizenship test. In the usual run of things, this test is used to ensure that potential new UK citizens, as part of the process of naturalisation, are familiar with British culture and values. For the most part, Cameron showed himself to be highly knowledgeable about Britain, its population, politics and history, albeit with a few notable gaps. While he could explain the complexities of the Good Friday Agreement, he didn't know who had written the words to 'Rule Britannia'. Most infamously, though, Cameron failed to provide an accurate literal translation of 'Magna Carta'. Again, it was the detail that let this classically educated prime minister down.

'You have found me out,' he said to Letterman, before joking, 'That is bad, I have ended my career on your show tonight.' With the outcome of the Brexit referendum that forced his resignation still four years in the future (for starters), this, of course, was far from the case. Nevertheless, and seemingly to make up for his public disgrace, Cameron went on to champion the need for greater public knowledge of Magna Carta. In June 2014, a year ahead of the document's eight-hundredth anniversary, he wrote an article in which he said: 'The remaining copies of that charter may have faded, but its principles shine as brightly as ever, and they paved the way for the democracy, the equality, the respect and the laws that make Britain, Britain.' It turns out, David Cameron was wrong about this too. We're going to look at what he got wrong about democracy in the following chapter, Power to the People. Here and now, though it's particularly interesting to see how he was wrong about British justice, with the ideals of equality and the law. Because as far as these things are concerned, Magna Carta is really only half the story.

In its original context, Magna Carta was not a document that espoused universal ideas of justice and equality for all. It was an agreement made between an extremely small number of extremely rich and powerful men. Chief among them was King John, the son of the Plantagenet King Henry II and successor to his elder brother, Richard I, more famously known as the Lionheart. Historical sources agree that King John was not nice to know. Apart from being the king who agreed to Magna Carta, he is probably best known as the bad (or, according to the Disney version, the phoney) king of England from the legend of Robin Hood. True, John was no good at being king. In a series of military failures, he managed to lose the provinces of Normandy and Anjou to the French. As the head of the English court, his failings included the murder of his own nephew, theft and lechery (sadly the latter is not usually considered a failing in royalty, but John made mistresses of his noblemen's wives, and this turned out to be a bad move, politically speaking). Given how the story of the Magna Carta has since been told, there is a lot invested in making King John look like a bad guy and we would be wise to look upon this list of disgraces with some scepticism. We should remember that in the fairy tale of the journey from tyranny to civil liberties, King John was necessarily framed as the bad guy who lost out to the march of progress. That being said, the medieval historian John Gillingham once famously said, 'King John was a shit', and a description that concise is difficult to resist.

King John was such a shit that a group of barons who owed him loyalty rose up against him on two separate occasions. In a story that doesn't get told as often as it should, the result of these two rebellions, on both occasions, was Magna Carta. It all started in 1214, when John's transgressions overran him when he lost at the Battle of Bouvines. He returned to England in abject disgrace and with his finances seriously compromised. This was money he had effectively stolen from his barons, a small group of the wealthy social elite who owned land and castles and who, under the system of medieval feudalism, owed him loyalty. It seems that a generation earlier, under King John's father Henry II, the barons were happy to go along with the idea that the king was the sole source of divine justice and right. With John, they saw there was little point in having a despot for a king if he couldn't be counted on to be effective. When John failed to make good on his airy promises of winning back French territories for England, and lost their money doing it, the barons had had enough. They rose in revolt, captured the city of London and forced the king into making a legal agreement that was specifically written to curtail his power.

The history books tell us that Magna Carta was sealed in 1215 at Runnymede, a field near Windsor. Everything in this document, from outlining the freedoms of the English Church and of the City of London, to protecting baronial inheritances and limits on the number and placement of fish weirs that could be built along the Thames, increased the barons' freedoms and access to resources while curbing those of the king. The real revolution of the Magna Carta sealed in 1215, though, came in its final clause. Known as the security clause, it empowered twenty-five barons to force the king to keep to the charter. For the first time, the king was answerable to earthly authorities. This was the beginnings of equality under the law.

As beginnings go, the 1215 Magna Carta wasn't much to write home about. It was effectively cancelled within a few weeks of being sealed as King John, spectacular douchebag that he was, convinced his friend Pope Innocent III to intercede on his behalf. The first incarnation of Magna Carta, then, was barely in effect for a few months. In retaliation, the barons rose up a second time in what is, confusingly, called the First Barons' War.

A quick historical aside: some people would have you believe that since the Norman Conquest in 1066, the British Isles has never fallen to an invading foreign force. This is not true. In 1215, the English Barons brought in the French to help them fight their own king in a venture that was so successful that, for a few months, Prince Louis was in charge of half of England. The only thing that stopped a long, drawn-out civil war was that, for once, John did the decent thing and died. Magna Carta – which had been reissued in 1216 having been stripped of many of its radical clauses – formed part of the peace accord in 1217 when the barons booted out the French and made their peace with the English crown by swearing their loyalty to the new child king, Henry III. Both the 1216 and 1217 versions of Magna Carta were agreed under the auspices of William Marshal, who had been appointed Regent until the new king came of age. Just under a decade later, in 1225, Henry III reissued a revised, and I'm pleased to say, final version of Magna Carta, albeit one with fewer limitations on the king's power. The security clause was already notably absent from the 1216 Magna Carta and, slightly concerning to those of us with an interest in greater justice and equality for all, this is the version that has been passed down in English Law ever since. The king, even if it was a different king, had got his own way in the end. How disappointing that the idea that royalty should be held accountable for their actions in the eyes of the law was a fleeting reality that barely lasted a few weeks eight hundred years ago.

More disappointing still is that whichever version you look at, Magna Carta was, in fact, only ever a deal between a very small number of highly privileged men. Magna Carta was good news for the barons. By contrast, everybody else – the rest of us non-barons – had very little recourse in the law. Why then, is Magna

Carta such a big deal? Why is it that, even today, some people, when they have been issued with a parking fine or a mask mandate, seem to instinctively, albeit mistakenly, reach for an eight-hundred-year-old legal document as a means of guarding their liberties and freedoms? The answer lies in when a seventeenth-century English lawyer called Edward Coke guided Parliament as they took the next steps on the precarious path to greater equality for all people under the law. In 1628, in reaction to King Charles I imposing martial law in order to pay for his army, Coke helped put together a set of documents that once again aimed to limit the power of the king. One of these went on to become the Habeas Corpus Act of 1679, which asserted that no one could be detained without having a formal charge made against them or imprisoned without the benefit of a trial. More immediately, when it seemed unlikely that a legal agreement could be reached between the King and Parliament, Coke suggested Parliament draw up a petition to present to the King. After much parliamentary wrangling, this came to be called the Petition of Right.

Guaranteeing a set of 'rights and liberties', the Petition of Right stated, among other things, that no one could be forced to pay taxes without an Act of Parliament (so not at the King's whim), no one could be arrested or imprisoned without knowing the charge against them and no one could be forced to house members of the Army or Navy unless they agreed to do it. The foundation of Coke's opposition to Charles I came from a pair of clauses buried in the middle of Magna Carta (starting with Clause 39 in the 1215 version, and clause 29 in the 1225 version). In translation from the Latin, they read as: 'No free man is to be arrested, or imprisoned, or disseised, or outlawed, or exiled, or in any other way ruined, nor will we go against him or send against him, except by the lawful judgement of his peers or by the law of the land'; and 'To no one will we sell, to no one will we deny or delay justice.' It was thanks to Coke and his legal efforts that the symbolic (if not the actual legal) power of the Magna Carta tipped into the modern age. Framed as a guarantee of liberty and justice for all, the principles of that small part of Magna Carta runs through the veins of documents from the English Bill of Rights to the US Constitution, the International Declaration of Human Rights and the Geneva Convention. Justice was no longer the sole purview of gods and kings, it could be dispensed and defended down here on Earth.

The literal translation of Magna Carta, as David Cameron would hopefully be able to tell you today, is 'Great Charter'. Having learned this, and about King John, the barons, the fish weirs and the security clause, the question it never occurred to me to ask is: 'great' compared to what? In part, this is down to Edward Coke's seventeenth century metaphorical reframing of Magna Carta as the greatest ever legal document, the standard bearer for justice in a liberal democracy. According to Coke, Magna Carta was great in itself, on account of the high, universal Western values of liberty and justice that it espoused. And, of course, it's Coke's reinterpretation of Magna Carta that we have held up for centuries, particularly since its highly successful rebranding, in the nineteenth century, during the victorious fight for American independence. Historically, though, we are missing something. We are missing the fact that alongside the Great Charter, there was another, smaller charter. It was called the Charter of the Forest and, if we really want to think about justice and equality for all, we would do well to remember it.

The Charter of the Forest was issued alongside the revised Magna Carta by William Marshal under the auspices of the new king, Henry III, in 1217. While the Great Charter applied to the king's greater subjects – the rebellious barons – the Charter of the Forest was more relevant to the wider English population in ways that to modern eyes are quite astonishing. At the time it was issued, it applied to about half of the territory of England, these being Forest Lands over which various kings had claimed ownership since the Norman invasion in 1066. This land was specially reserved for venison and vert, that is, land preserved for the king's hunting. In accordance with the Charter of the Forest, all of the forest land delineated since the time of Henry II (the present king's grandfather) became *disaforested*, that is, taken out of the king's hands so the barons could do what they wanted with it. More crucially, though, this charter also guaranteed the liberty and livelihood of ordinary people by placing limits on what the barons and other English nobility were able to do. This included rights of pannage, such as giving ordinary people the right to graze their cattle on the king's lands from Michaelmas to Martinmas, the right to put their pigs into the woods where they could eat acorns and the right to use turf and wood from the forest land to fuel their fires. In today's terms, the Charter of the Forest is absolutely mind-blowing. It guaranteed access to resources for everyone, not just the rich and powerful. Imagine being able to tap directly into the nation's gas supply or wander over and plug your phone into the National Grid, and still be completely within your rights, and without having to pay for them. Imagine being able to freely wander through the countryside without falling foul of trespass signs, signs forbidding swimming or, worst of all, private golf courses.

Fundamentally, these were common rights given to common people, ensuring they could access food, fuel, tools and medicine. The Charter of the Forest instituted so much more radical change than Magna Carta, in any of its versions, ever did. It also legitimised customary rights in ways that were the beginnings of working-class politics. It was a document that was well known and in daily use long after Magna Carta was mostly irrelevant by the end of the thirteenth century. Forest people knew they had rights, they knew what those rights were and were willing to defend them. When you know about the Charter of the Forest, it makes perfect sense that the Peasant's Revolt of 1381 was sparked in the forest lands of Essex and Kent.

Before you run off to join the barricades, sadly it falls to me to tell you that the Charter of the Forest was revoked in the astonishingly recent year of 1971. For most of us, though, it had slipped from view long before that. Efforts made by the wealthy to enclose and keep their land to themselves go as far back as the twelfth century, and they were on the rise from the fifteenth all the way up to the seventeenth century. Over the course of Britain's imperial age, during the eighteenth and nineteenth centuries, the landlords whose power had been held in check by the Charter of the Forest started to find ways around the statute by arguing that enclosing the land would allow for more effective farming.

One of the great advocates for the enclosure movement was Arthur Young, an agricultural writer from the eighteenth into the nineteenth century who was dismayed at how 'the Goths and Vandals of open fields touch the civilization of enclosures'. For Young and its other fans, enclosure represented the most enlightened and rational way to manage the land. Rather than leave it open for the 'barbaric' common people to cultivate collaboratively, as they had done for centuries and as was their legal right, Young argued for closing off the land using fences and hedges so that the landowners could introduce new crops

– turnips, apparently, were all the rage – and farming technologies, like the four crop rotation system. This was a very useful argument for ambitious, politically minded people, some of them newly rich from their investments in the colonies, for whom land ownership represented much more than the simple means to a livelihood. For them, land ownership was the easiest path to status through establishing themselves as a justice of the peace. This local role, entrusted to ensure justice and keep the peace, was similar to that of the iudex in the Roman Republic in that common people could be appointed to it. As such, it was a gateway to gaining greater authority, greater political power and the potential to make even more money.

While there had been enclosure in various, sporadic forms in the previous centuries, the thing that set the enclosure movement of the eighteenth century apart was that it was overwhelmingly a legal phenomenon. Starting from 1604, there were a slew of enclosure bills and laws culminating in the Inclosure Act of 1845. Looking back, this might smack of conspiracy? The reality, while considerably more mundane, is nonetheless still demoralising. The legal system in Britain had been set up so as to allow parliamentary law to be able to override the common law. This was a means of ensuring that deadlocks in legal disputes could be resolved. In the case of the enclosure movement, though, the people who were petitioning Parliament to allow them to enclose their lands were Parliamentarians themselves, and they made decisions that served their limited collective interest. Here again, we see the same story that we have seen before, with the lives of the many impoverished overlooked in favour of the privileged few.

Over three hundred years, coming into the twentieth century, some 2,800,000 hectares of land have been subject to enclosure

– that's one-fifth of the total area of England. The enclosure movement is, really, the natural outcome of capitalism, the high-water mark for a civilised economy that was also in the ascendancy during the eighteenth century and the rise of Britain's imperial age. When your economy depends on the profits from the production and trade of commodities, it makes no sense to allow common access to natural resources, because that is where your profit comes from. Today we may gripe when selfish landlords fence off their properties and don't allow ramblers their legal right of way, but the real things we have lost through enclosure are so much more than that. In the West, in the twenty-first century, land continues to be a highly exclusive commodity. When we remember the Charter of the Forest, it really brings to the forefront what we believe justice to mean: what we hold dear, what we seem to be willing to live with and what we are willing to fight for. It turns out that when your justice depends on the laws, the justice you get is only ever as good as your lawmakers.

*

The land that history books refer to as America was originally carried up from the bottom of the ocean by a water beetle, who was Beaver's grandchild. It was kept in place above the water by four cords tied to the sky. When the land was still soft, Buzzard flew over it and where his wings touched the earth valleys were made, causing the mountains to rise up in between. As with other Native American communities, the Cherokee told this story of how their lands came to be through an oral tradition, the spoken words learned, repeated and passed down over generations. These stories explained how everything, from geographical features to the different species of animals, to the Cherokee themselves, had arrived in the world and come to be the way they were. There were simple versions of the stories and more complicated ones, tailored by the teller, according to their audience. People made their living by farming and hunting, even before the Europeans turned up, with their own ideas about democracy and equality. This was a matrilineal society with the women owning their own houses and fields, which were passed down to their daughters. The Cherokee gathered in their wooden houses with thatched roofs, including the central house that housed the sacred fire, and was large enough to hold the whole community. There they made joint decisions about their future. They held the Earth sacred and believed that every living thing was imbued with a spirit that made them all part of the same family.

When the Europeans did turn up towards the end of the seventeenth century, the Cherokee held their lands to be among the Great Smoky Mountains, the southern tail of the Appalachian mountain range that runs from north to south in the eastern half of North America. These lands are now part of the states of North Carolina, Tennessee, Georgia and Alabama. For a couple of hundred years, the Cherokee traded and intermarried with the English, Irish and Scottish settlers in the Carolinas and the state of Georgia, fighting alongside them in wars against other groups of Native Americans, in accordance with the alliances they had made. There were cultural exchanges between the Cherokee and the Europeans as well, although these mostly seem to have been in one direction. It was during this time that the Cherokee came to be known as one of the Five Civilised Tribes. They held this title along with the Chickasaw, the Creek, the Choctaw and the Seminole, all of which are now nations in Indian Country, in the state of Oklahoma, which is roughly a thousand miles away from where they started out in the

American south-west. Today the dedicated road tripper can make the journey from the western end of the continent to its centre in about five days' drive, but, of course, when they made the journey the five tribes did not have cars. When the time came, they were forced to make the journey on foot, carrying what they could, falling sick and dying in great numbers on the way. The story of how they came to be there, so far away, provides us with a cautionary tale about the nature of Western civilisation – as civilisation, it turns out, has its limits. Especially if you are not white.

The Cherokee Nation was avid in taking on Western culture and ways of living. Over the latter part of the eighteenth century and into the nineteenth, they took on plantation-style farming and, like the English settlers, profited from the free labour of enslaved Africans put to work on those plantations. Portraits of leading figures in the Cherokee Nation from this time show handsome men dressed in the height of Georgian fashion, with high-collared shirts, waistcoats and frock coats. They look like they would be perfectly at home in scenes from *Bridgerton,* or the latest Austen adaptation. In what should have been a surefire shortcut to being civilised, the Cherokee were especially enthusiastic in taking up the written word.

By 1822, Cherokee hero Sequoyah had developed an alphabet, making the Cherokee one of the first North American tribes to ever have a written language, and one of the few to develop a system of writing from scratch. Sequoyah had close relations with English settler colonists through his work as a silversmith, and he took on the belief that writing allowed for greater communication and development of knowledge. On 26 July 1827, the Cherokee Nation adopted a written constitution. It was much like the US Constitution, in that it defined and framed the roles of legislative, executive and judicial branches of government. The Cherokee Constitution also signalled the Nation's adoption of Western civilised values, stating in its preamble that the people of the Cherokee Nation, 'in convention assembled in order to establish justice, ensure tranquility, promote our common welfare, and secure to ourselves and our posterity the blessings of Liberty'. The following year, in 1828, they founded the *Cherokee Phoenix*, the first Native American newspaper, printed in both Cherokee and English, established under the principle of a free press.

Many of these developments in the history of the Cherokee Nation were down to Principal Chief John Ross. From a Western vantage point, Ross would read as something of a hero figure were it not for his firm belief that the Cherokee Nation would sit alongside the new nation of the United States as equals, not subordinates. On paper, Ross embodied all of the virtues of Western civilisation: he was an elected head of state who held firm to republican ideals of a nation-state governed by the rule of law. In reality, for a newly formed nation that similarly held firm to the imperial ambitions of the British Empire, Ross was a liability. By the 1820s, through various treaties, the Cherokee Nation had substantial land holdings in Appalachia. Along with Ross's gleaming new capital at New Echota, home to the *Cherokee Phoenix*, in the modern state of Georgia, they were a considerable obstacle to US expansion. The situation became more tense when gold was discovered in Georgia in 1828. As new white settlers moved further south to capitalise on the gold and fertile farmland, they trampled over Cherokee territory, stealing the land and treating the people in an outright barbaric manner. The US federal government looked on and did nothing to stop them.

How was it that despite their adoption of civilised ideals and ways of living, the citizens of the Cherokee Nation found themselves in such a precarious position? The answer lies in some aspects of the legal history of the newly formed United States. It also lies in nineteenth-century concepts of race. While Native American tribes like the Cherokee were deemed to be the legal and proper owners of the lands they lived on, they were limited in what they could legally do with that land. In an 1823 landmark decision, in the case of *Johnson v. McIntosh*, the US Supreme Court determined that Native Americans could only sell their land to the federal government of the United States, and not to individuals. Chief Justice John Marshall said that this ruling was a natural extension of 'the discovery doctrine', a legal principle originally established in Europe that stated that a European nation gains sovereignty over any land that it 'discovers'.

One of the earliest incarnations of the discovery doctrine was the 1494 Treaty of Tordesillas, signed between the Spanish and the Portuguese. Two years after Christopher Columbus 'discovered' the New (to Europeans) World, Europeans were united in their belief that non-Christian land could be colonised by dint of its discovery. Put simply the Treaty of Tordesillas was a legal document that effectively said: finders keepers. While the English, later the British colonies did not pay much attention to the Treaty of Tordesillas itself, the discovery doctrine was nonetheless a useful legal principle to have in place. Through *Johnson v. McIntosh*, the Supreme Court held that discovery was a transitive property. It had now passed from the British to the US itself as an independent nation (despite being nullified in the 1530s and again more recently by Pope Francis in March 2023).

How is it possible to discover new land if there are already people, like Native Americans, living there? Part of the answer came from the work of John Locke, an Enlightenment thinker famed for his philosophy that all people are born 'free, equal and independent'. In Locke's summation, though, in line with the race science of the time, Native Americans weren't people, exactly. For one thing, they did not make the best use of the land. According to Locke, hunting and gathering were inherently less valuable and inferior modes of economy compared to tilling and farming the land. (Plenty of Native American peoples did practice farming of course, but like so many Enlightenment thinkers, Locke had never been to the Americas, and, in any case, why let the facts get in the way of a useful theory?) Locke argued that America was in a natural state – that is, it was empty. As such, anyone (European) who laboured on the land gained rights to it as property there.

The Supreme Court had another answer for the problem of Native Americans, and its language is telling with the frame of civilisation in mind. 'The potentates of the old world,' wrote Chief Justice Marshall, 'found no difficulty in convincing themselves that they made ample compensation to the inhabitants of the new by bestowing on them civilization and Christianity in exchange for unlimited independence, asserting a right to take possession notwithstanding occupancy of natives, who were heathens ...' As a South Asian Indian, I am more than familiar with this argument. In the case of the Raj in India, it goes that the British Empire was beneficial to Indians through its gifts of the railways and the English language. Marshall went on to say that it was normally the case that conquered peoples became absorbed into a conquering nation and gained the rights of equal citizenship. In the case of the Native Americans, though, this was not possible, because, as he stated:

... the tribes of Indians inhabiting this country were fierce savages whose occupation was war and whose subsistence was drawn chiefly from the forest. To have them in possession of their country was to leave the country a wilderness; to govern them as a distinct people was impossible because they were as brave and high-spirited as they were fierce, and they were ready to repel by arms every attempt on their independence.

Reading this as an outsider, the actions of the Native Americans seem entirely reasonable in the circumstances. Marshall's logic seems to be that Native Americans could not be treated as equal citizens because they refused to do the civilised thing and be conquered. Instead, they continued in their traditional ways of life. When their game moved, they followed and so, according to Marshall, they could not be deemed responsible enough to be in charge of their own land. What is so interesting about this is that it is not the Native Americans' title to the land that is in question – Marshall actually refers to it as 'their country' – but literally the character of the people as to whether or not they could be governed. This judgement in its entirety is about who is civilised and who is savage. As a judgement, it proved remarkably useful to the federal government of the United States who, over the course of the nineteenth century, was able to acquire vast tracts of land at knockdown prices and then make significant profits by selling that same land to white settlers.

With this context in mind, the efforts of Chief John Ross to build the Cherokee Nation in the eye of the civilised US beholder – in the hopes that this would mean he and his people would be seen as equal to Americans under the law – makes perfect sense. To a degree, his efforts were rewarded. When a Christian missionary living on land he had rented from the Cherokee sued the state of Georgia for trying to get him to pay them instead, the Supreme Court came through for the

Cherokee. In another landmark ruling, this time in the case of *Worcester v. Georgia*, the US Supreme Court ruled that the Cherokee Nation was a sovereign state in its own right. The Cherokee were an exception. They could buy, rent and sell their land to whoever they pleased. In a 2020 interview with the *Code Switch* podcast, Mary Kathryn Nagle, a playwright and legal advocate for the Cherokee Nation, described this ruling as nothing short of a miracle. 'It's almost like I carry that moment with me, still, somehow in my DNA. Even Hollywood couldn't make up something more miraculous. You've got a president who just won a national campaign on a platform of completely obliterating your people, and somehow you find solace in the court.' The president in question was the seventh, Major General Andrew Jackson, a hero of the War of 1812, and the worst thing ever to have happened to the Cherokee.

Of all the US presidents, Andrew Jackson is the one most likely to appear in a Tim Burton film – he was tall and lanky with sunken features, a lantern jaw and a shock of vertical white hair. If you never came across him in history class, you may recognise Jackson's face from the twenty-dollar bill, or you may have heard about him from a more recent US president, Donald J. Trump, who often said that Jackson was his favourite president.

As far as Andrew Jackson was concerned, the law was very much something that happened to other presidents. He had built his reputation on a flagrant disregard for any kind of regulation that stood in the way of getting the job done. During his campaigns in the War of 1812, something of a second American war of independence fought between the US and the British over North American land rights, he suspended the writ of habeas corpus. Harking back to Magna Carta and the English Bill of Rights, this was a constitutional privilege that ensured any prisoner could have their case looked at by a judge. Jackson's actions forced the new nation of the United States to reconsider its legal definition of martial law. He also censored a newspaper, nearly executed two of his soldiers for desertion and had a state congressman, a judge and a district attorney thrown in jail. Despite all this, what happened next reads a bit like a rerun of the English king and his barons. When it came to their own affairs, the various states that made up the US had some concerns that Jackson was a tyrant. When it came to their relations with the Cherokee Nation, however, they were happy for him to behave as such. With Jackson as president, they were going to fall from the civilised heights of *Worcester v. Georgia* back into the savage depths of *Johnson v. McIntosh*. And worse.

Andrew Jackson had made it clear from the start that the only option he would leave open to the Cherokee would be for them to be elsewhere. He had run his presidential campaign on a platform of Indian removal. Having heard the Supreme Court ruling in *Worcester v. Georgia*, the gist of Jackson's position is an apocryphal line: 'Chief Justice John Marshall made his decision, let him enforce it.' Much of the efforts of Jackson's presidency were directed towards convincing the Cherokee to give up their lands in the south-west and move over to the US's newly acquired territories in the middle of the North American continent.

In March 1835, Jackson wrote an open letter to the Cherokee Nation, saying, 'Listen to me ... while I tell you that you cannot remain where you now are. Circumstances that cannot be controlled, and which are beyond the reach of human laws, render it impossible that you can flourish in the midst of a civilized community.' As far as Jackson was concerned, whatever the Supreme Court said could not legislate to make the Cherokee fit for civilisation. They were born savages, savages they would remain, and they should act accordingly by agreeing to the removal to the new Indian Territory.

While Chief John Ross was adamant that the Cherokee were staying put, his friend and mentor Major Ridge was becoming more and more concerned about the growing number of white settlers moving to Georgia. For Ridge, if the Cherokee stayed put, they risked becoming second-class citizens, swallowed up as an increasing racialised United States expanded and overtook their territories further south. As discussions between the two nations continued, Major Ridge and a small group of Cherokee secretly signed a treaty with the US government at New Echota on December 29, 1835. They committed to making the move West in the next two years in exchange for five million dollars, new land rights and various other compensations, including the promise of having a Cherokee representative in the US government.

When word of the signing of the Treaty of New Echota reached Ross he was distraught. He immediately swung into action to try to stop the US Senate from ratifying the treaty, riding thousands of miles from house to house, collecting signatures for a petition. Records of the number of signatories on Ross's petition vary, but he seems to have managed to get at least twelve thousand, a substantial majority of the population of the Cherokee Nation. Sadly, a petition with thousands of Cherokee signatures was not going to convince Andrew Jackson to treat Native Americans as civilised equals any more than their written constitution, their free press or, indeed, the judgements of his own Supreme Court. Jackson wasted no time in signing the Treaty of New Echota into law and, when the two years' notice was up, he sent in his troops.

Over a period of twelve months during 1838 and 1839, the US Army ripped sixteen thousand Cherokee people from their farms and homes, corralled them into stockades and forced them to march halfway across the continent to the US designated 'Indian Reservations' in Oklahoma. Four thousand of them died along the way, from starvation and the freezing cold. Their fatal journey is commemorated in US history as the Trail of Tears. It was an act of violence that has echoed down through the generations. In her one-woman play *And So We Walked*, DeLanna Studi, a member of the Cherokee Nation, sums it up this way:

> Twenty Cherokee traitors signed the Treaty of New Echota, going behind the backs of Chief John Ross, his second Chief George Lowry – my fourth great-grand-uncle – the Cherokee National Council and basically the whole tribe. Selling all our land to the US government for five million dollars. This treaty is why there is a Trail of Tears; why we lost everything we knew; why we buried a fourth of our people in hostile territory; why we live in Oklahoma in tribal housing, eat commodity cheese and have diabetes. This is why my father was ripped from his family and sent to a boarding school. Why he never talks about our life before we got to Oklahoma, and why I feel like a traitor. Because we keep betraying each other, and we're not supposed to talk about it.

Today the Cherokee, along with many other Native American peoples, live out Major Ridge's worst fears: at best they are treated like second-class citizens. Their lives are a stark reminder that, try as much as you like, for most non-Westerners, the promise of civilisation is always, tantalisingly, out of reach. The Five Civilised Tribes were so called because they did civilised things, even to the extent that they were enslavers. This may seem patently obvious, but it's important to remember that who does or does not get to be called civilised is seldom a straightforward or just process. It's likely that how the Cherokee managed to last in their homeland as long as they did was down to their acceptance and performance of civilised ways of living. Nevertheless, the line in the sand between civilised and savage can easily shift depending on which way the political wind is blowing. What happened to the Cherokee, civilised as they were, merely goes to show that you can only be as civilised as your nearest Westerners allow you to be.

Writing about his experience as a law student being taught about *Johnson v. McIntosh*, Matthew L. M. Fletcher, a member of the Grand Traverse Band of Ottawa and Chippewa Indians, said it even more plainly. In an article published in the *Michigan Journal of Race and Law*, he wrote: 'Maybe you *can* kill people and destroy what they are and call it legal and fair play.'

*

In his 1971 book, *A Theory of Justice*, American philosopher John Rawls defined justice as a set of principles that, 'free and rational persons, concerned to further their own interests would agree to in a position of liberty and equality'. As Rawls saw it, lawmakers should very clearly not be barons. Rawls proposed a thought experiment based on what he called 'the veil of ignorance'. What laws would people make and agree to if they were kept unaware of their status within a society? The key to a fair and just legal system, according to Rawls, was one in which an enlightened self-interest plays to the benefit of all concerned. Standing a few decades into the twenty-first century and looking at our own social ills all the way back to Magna Carta, John

Rawls' idea has tremendous appeal, mostly because it doesn't pretend that things are perfect. Rawls acknowledged the inequalities and injustices already built into our system. There is no level playing field here, and those inequalities are simply perpetuated and made worse by those in power.

Rawls' theory of justice can be described as 'fairness to everyone'. The degree to which this can work depends, as we have seen, on how you define 'fairness', and also, critically, how you define 'everyone'. For the barons who demanded King John set his seal on Magna Carta, the definition of 'man' as it appears in that document was limited to themselves – a hugely wealthy and highly privileged elite. For the Parliamentarians who passed the various petitions of the enclosure movement, it was much the same. For President Andrew Jackson, the Cherokee didn't really count as people at all, and so he felt justified in treating them like animals, rounding them up and marching them off their homesteads, off into further centuries of marginalisation and discrimination. The abstract nature of the law, however useful or flawed it may be, makes justice seem like something in the abstract – as something that happens to other people, elsewhere. The reality is that our systems of justice in the West are only as good, or more often as bad, as those in power have made them. It remains the case today. And it's a situation that's unlikely to change unless we wake up and do something about it.

Chapter Five

POWER TO THE PEOPLE

If memory serves me, the fall of Western civilisation dates back to a year in the late 1990s. It all happened when democracy – one of Western civilisation's key principles – failed to live up to sustained scrutiny in the public forum. The event had been publicised for weeks beforehand. Banners lined the high school hallway and other communal spaces, screaming in brightly coloured capital letters: 'Democracy or Monarchy: which is best?' This was going to be a high school debate in the old tradition: a pitched battle of ideas, with thesis statements and rebuttals lobbed across the aisle like verbal grenades. The Advanced Placement senior history class, who were studying European history that year, would go up against the matching junior class, who had been studying US history. Of course, a classic historical distinction between the two was their system of government. The Old World had its old ways, with absolute monarchy, the divine right of kings and the historical power of the Catholic Church. Across the Atlantic, fuelled by revolutionary ideas and ideals was a new vision: *democracy*.

I have never liked debates. Still, like badminton, as a nerd in the nineties, it was one of the few public sports available to me. I also didn't have much choice as we were being graded on it, and, as our teacher always enjoyed reminding us, his classroom was *not* a democracy. As things stood, I wasn't too worried about my grade because my team were clearly on to a winner, being on the side of democracy. Even without referring to philosophical notions like freedom and equality, we could fall back on the undeniable truth that, in the civilised West, democracy rules. That was until, stood at a podium in front of the rest of the high school and a lot of their parents, one of my best friends from the year above asked me why I was siding with Adolf Hitler. When I pointed out that Hitler had been a dictator, naively thinking simple definitions would suffice here, this seemed to flip a switch, and she let loose a tirade about all the things that were wrong with democracy as a system of government.

First of all, as had been the case with Hitler, it was perfectly possible for dictators to be elected by democratic means. Beyond the fact that the voting public clearly cannot be trusted not to bring dictators and demagogues into a position of power where they are then free to wreak havoc, their general ignorance results in short-term thinking and instability, or worse, oppressive majoritarian rule. While my teammates did their best to counter with examples of democratic successes – the abolition of slavery, the benefits of a free market economy and the advancement of human rights – it was as nothing to what our colleagues could throw back at us, having studied the whole of US History the year before. There was the American Civil War, when states unable to agree on the abolition of slavery had taken up arms and spent four years steadily slaughtering their fellow countrymen. There was McCarthyism, under which attempts to smoke out undercover communists came with heavy Salem witch trial overtones. There was, of course, the Watergate scandal, where the incumbent Republican President Richard Nixon was forced to resign, having been caught out for illegally surveilling his political opponents. And even before all of that, there was the genocide of Native Americans and the systematic oppression of enslaved Africans, all of whom had to fight to convince the white Americans in sole charge of the government that they even deserved the right to vote. Looked at in this light, it seemed like the whole of the history of the United States was a series of cautionary tales demonstrating why democracy does not make for good government.

When the judges announced their verdict, we saw the blow had been a fatal one. As with so many other times in history, monarchy had emerged victorious.

When I had eventually stopped crying, I looked up to find not only my teammates, but many in the audience, looking dazed and confused. This was as nothing compared to the faces of my history teachers, who looked like men who had rented super-soakers for a kid's birthday party, only to have had water cannons delivered by mistake. Someone had blundered. Open debate was all fun and games until one of the pillars of Western civilisation had cracked, crumbled and collapsed in front of our very eyes. As the dust began to settle, a friend of mine who had been in the audience said what was on everyone's minds: 'But how could they lose? They were right.' The reply came back, as it always does: the winner in a debate is not the side with the best idea, but the side with the best argument. *That* is why I don't like debates. To reduce a complex and nuanced issue to two opposing viewpoints with each trying to win over the other does nothing to help consensus, all it does is polarise. Even so, looking back at that particular debate and its devastating outcome, something about that crude reality doesn't ring true. Democracy *is* a great idea. That being the case, why does it keep going wrong?

Democracy is supposed to be a place where two other great Western ideals intersect: equality and liberty. We've already seen in the previous chapter how equality has something of an illusory quality and how, bound up in the notion of justice, equality for all under the law remains something of a pipe dream in the West. In the final chapter of this book, We're All In This Together, we're going to explore in greater detail exactly what we mean by individual liberty. Democracy, though, with its combined notions of individual political equality and freedom is worth exploring in itself. Particularly because, in the West, democracy is a strong brand.

Ask any US high school graduate like me to define democracy, and they will probably reach for the well-worn phrase that democracy is 'government of the people, by the people, for the people'. They may even remember that this comes from one of the most famous speeches in American, if not world, history: the Gettysburg Address, delivered by President Abraham Lincoln in 1863. Lincoln was speaking at the consecration of a cemetery built to honour the dead who fell at the Battle of Gettysburg.

On the face of it, Lincoln was on the winning side, as Gettysburg would soon prove to be the decisive victory that guaranteed the future of the United States as a single union. It was also, though, the battle with the greatest number of American casualties in the context of a war where the greatest number of Americans died (statistically unsurprising, given they were fighting on both sides). Lincoln's brief and astonishingly moving speech accounted for the loss of life and recommitted the American people to the cause of democracy. 'These dead shall not have died in vain,' he said, before bringing it home with, '... This nation, under God, shall have a new birth of freedom – and that government of the people, by the people and for the people, shall not perish from the earth.' In this one, brief speech, Lincoln enshrined an idea of American exceptionalism and superiority, stemming from the sacrifice of its citizens in the interest of a greater ideal of democracy.

While, as with everything, Western democracy claims its roots lie in ancient Greece, it is a much more recent development in the modern West. It all started with the formation of the United States of America. From there, in relatively short order, the rest is history. The poet Ralph Waldo Emerson described the first moments of the American Revolutionary War as 'the shot heard round the world', turning what started out as a domestic dispute between Britain and one of its settler colonies into the poster child for enlightened, rational government. The French took up the cry and responded with one of their own: liberty, equality and brotherhood! In Britain, progress on the road to democracy was more gradual. We, it must be remembered, don't like to make a fuss. A series of reforms over the nineteenth century extended suffrage – the right to vote – to ever-larger portions of the population. Universal male suffrage in Britain dates to 1918, and the nation could count itself a fully representative democracy when universal female suffrage was enacted in 1928. The period between the two world wars (1919–39) saw the blossoming of new democracies all over the world. Their success was immediately threatened by economic failure. Following the financial crashes of the late 1920s and economic depression, it seemed, in fact, what was needed was that strong man authoritarian leadership of old – and fascism was duly on the rise in the 1930s.

Bloody and long drawn out as it was, the Second World War, fought between 1939 and 1945, was a victorious battleground for democracy, with the democratic Allied powers defeating the fascist Axis, and with both post-war Germany and Japan adopting democratic modes of government in its aftermath. In the years that followed, the United States took up democracy as a moral ideal, it being handily married to human rights in the charter of the newly formed United Nations. Almost a century after Gettysburg, another famous speech was made by a man who was to be an equally famous US president, then in the midst of his election campaign. In 1961, John F. Kennedy set up the US stall as a beacon for the world, based particularly on the idea of democracy. Referring to a sermon by John Winthrop, the Puritan first governor of the English settlement at Massachusetts, Kennedy said, 'Today the eyes of all people are truly upon us – and our governments, in every branch, at every level, national, state and local, must be as a city upon a hill – constructed and inhabited by men aware of their great trust and their great responsibilities.'

In such an analogue view, it was natural that, after the Second World War, the democratic West's next great opponent would be the spectre of communism. While the war may have been cold, the ideological conflict was heated. For the US, in particular, with its core belief that communism as practised in the Soviet Union and China should not be allowed to spread to other countries, this became a matter of managing political priorities. The US supported autocratic states like Franco's Spain and Pinochet's Chile if it meant they could keep communism at bay. For the most part this strategy worked. Following the landmark conversion of Portugal to democracy in 1974, the process was repeated across a range of South American countries in the first half of the 1980s and Asian nations in the second. There were imperial overtones to this change, of course. While Europe, having bombed itself to bits, was no longer the imperial powerhouse it had been in the nineteenth century, it still had both money and influence in the international sphere. The West might no longer directly govern its old colonies, but at least it could influence how they governed themselves.

The final act in the ascendency of democracy (at least the way this particular story is being told) came with the fall of the Berlin Wall in 1989, followed soon after by the dismantling of the Soviet Union, which, ironically, voted itself out of existence. The release of the communist political pressure valve made room for several African countries to fall into line, adopting representative democracy. And voilà! We can now zoom out on the map of the world and see many of the nations of every inhabited continent demonstrating democracy, to one level or another.

The prolific spread of democracy in the twentieth century seemed so progressive and so monumental that it led a young American political scientist called Francis Fukuyama to declare, in the 1990s, that this was the 'end of history' (as had been described by the German philosopher Georg Wilhelm Friedrich Hegel in the nineteenth century). While, of course, things would still continue to happen, Fukuyama held that, as far as political evolution was concerned, we were done. He referenced Hegel who believed there would come a time when a perfectly rational form of society and the state would be victorious. And here it was. Fascism and communism had been vanquished, and even nations that did not openly embrace democracy, such as China and North Korea, declared themselves to be 'people's republics', that is, they acknowledged the ideal that a government is answerable to its people. Here it doesn't really matter what those countries are doing, provided they are seen by the West to be doing it 'right' – that is to say, doing things the *Western* civilised way.

I would say this is the view of the history of democracy we are most familiar with. Beyond a system of government, democracy as an idea has its own moral authority. At the same time, it is a progressive, even an evolutionary ideal. Bound up in our ideal of democracy is that, given its historical development and as Fukuyama had it, it is the natural end point of Western civilisation. Just as J. G. Frazer posited a transformation from superstition to religion and finally to rationality, or the English archaeologist John Lubbock considered the so-called progression from hunter-gatherer economies to agriculture and state-development, so too is the idea that the barbarism of absolute monarchy, oligarchy or theocracy was a passing and necessary phase towards the final end point: civilised democracy.

By its nature, democracy is portrayed as the linchpin of a civilised society, keeping the wheels of all the other civilised ideals from falling off: a free market economy, a meritocratic society with freedom of social movement, all governed by the rule of law. It's a system of government that guarantees social care, universal education and political participation and provides space for cultural activities like the performing arts. The consensus remains that you're not doing civilisation right unless you are doing democracy, however shaky its hold might be. High school debates notwithstanding, democracy is a winning option.

Democracy Rules OK.

Except, of course, it doesn't.

Not even close.

The real ideal that holds Western civilisation together – as we've seen in previous chapters – is the notion of social hierarchy, and hierarchy is the antithesis of true democracy. Philosophically speaking, democracy is where equality and liberty intersect.

Historically, though, it's the place where those ideas have consistently failed. Social hierarchies of race and class, along with inequalities based on gender and disability, are so deeply ingrained in Western society that, in fact, neither liberty nor equality are actually possible. By extension, then, it stands to reason that democracy itself is fundamentally impossible in the West. That being the case, it raises a number of questions. How does democracy continue to be such a strong brand? How is it that so many people continue to put their faith in an idea that doesn't actually exist? Where does the strength of the brand of Western democracy actually come from? And what are the real ideas that shape our Western systems of governance? To find the answers to all these questions, we need to go all the way back to the beginning.

*

Original recipe (i.e. classic) democracy dates to a very particular time and place in the history of the Western world: the city-state of Athens in the fifth century BCE. How would the Athenian democrats feel about the triumph of democracy in the twentieth century? The truth is, they probably wouldn't recognise it. Whether in the United States, which has been gently sliding down the rankings of the Democracy Index for over a decade, or in the United Kingdom, where every prime minister to win an election since the Second World War (with the notable exception of John Major) went to the same university, an ancient Athenian would be appalled to see how political power in Western democracies is consistently and seemingly inevitably, devolved into the hands of a privileged few. That wasn't how they did things at all.

The ancient Greek city-state of Athens was the original city upon a hill. For a couple of hundred years, starting from around the beginning of the fifth century BCE, the Athenians governed themselves in a manner that has never been repeated since. In order to experience what that democracy was actually like, as practised by the people who invented the idea, we need to travel those two and a half thousand years into the past in the heyday of the Athenian city-state. Here, as the rosy-fingered dawn creeps up the skyline heralding the arrival of a new day, we can follow the crowds through the city's streets. Over to our right, you may recognise the Acropolis, Athens' fortified citadel, adorned with the Parthenon — the monumental temple dedicated to the goddess Athena that survives to this day. This is not the hill we are interested in today, though. Today, we are turning left and heading to a less famous landmark on a less famous hill. This would bring us to the Pnyx, half stadium, half polling station at the top of the hill that was the beating heart of Athenian democracy.

It's important to point out that even by our flawed contemporary standards, Athenian democracy left much to be desired. Here, citizen women, the enslaved and foreigners were all denied the vote. Despite this, archaeologists have worked out that the Pnyx seated between six and seven thousand people — about a quarter of the population who were eligible to vote at the time. Alongside this, historical records suggest that by the fourth century BCE this substantial number of people met at the Pnyx every nine days. Here they debated the actions the state would take and made decisions via referendums. While today, the mere mention of the word 'referendum' is enough to freeze the blood of everyone who lived through the 2016 Brexit vote, back in the day in Athens it was the sole means of deciding whatever needed deciding. This included everything from going to war and equipping the navy, to appointing someone to ensure the streets of the city's port, Piraeus, were clear of dog shit. For the Athenians, government was a system of everyday things, enacted by everyday people, pretty much every day.

The Athenians did have elected political and civil leaders, but they treated them very differently from how we treat ours. No fancy houses, private cars or jets or corporate retirement plans for these folks. They were chosen by a process of sortition, or lottery. Prospective candidates would put themselves forward for office and, if their bronze token was the one that was picked by the selecting machine, they got the job. To say that the people appointed to these positions were held to a high standard of conduct is putting it mildly. Failing to do the job, being corrupt, or even just generally useless could be punished by ostracism, that is, exile from the whole of the city-state for a period of ten years. Bad leaders could also be tried by jury for their ill actions or bad decisions, and, if found guilty could be executed. If all this sounds too good to be true, rest assured that on occasion it was, particularly the one time the Athenian democracy managed to vote itself out of existence (they managed to come back together and wrote up a new law to prevent this from happening again). All told, though, it was clearly a highly involved and effective system of government that lasted for two hundred years, stopping only when the city of Athens fell victim to the imperial ambitions of its neighbour, Sparta.

The 'triumph' of democracy was never a surefire thing. The word itself, combining the Greek words for 'people' and 'power', was first used by people who found the idea of it unconscionable. Throughout its history, opponents of democracy have returned again and again to a single criticism, turning on what they see as democracy's fatal flaw. Their argument, simply put, is that democracy depends upon its people being able to govern themselves. In other words, democracy depends on not just one, but a whole society of rational voters, working together for the benefit of their collective best interests. The big problem here, of course, is that people are just the worst. Socrates, as portrayed in Plato's *Republic*, had no faith whatsoever in the average ancient Greek citizen:

> Sometimes he drinks heavily while listening to the flute; at other times, he drinks only water and is on a diet; sometimes he goes in for physical training; at other times, he's idle and neglects everything; and sometimes he even occupies himself with what he takes to be philosophy.

I don't know about you, but I feel seen.

All told, Socrates' view of democracy was that it was little more than glorified mob rule. The collective, uneducated and poor citizenry having the power to rule over the wealthy and learned minority would be a world turned upside down, a case of the savage ruling over the civilised. Ancient Greeks in the know, that is, wealthy and educated members of the leisured elite, like Plato and Aristotle, were troubled by how it would be possible for the poor majority to rule over the rich minority. Why, they wondered, should anyone want government by the *people*? As a rule, the people tended to make bad and ill-informed decisions. While Hegel, centuries later, may have said that democracy was the most rational form of government, this did not account for the fact that throughout all of its history, the main concern with democracy was that the people themselves cannot be trusted to be rational. For millennia, the consensus of the ruling elites has been that there is something naturally dangerous – barbaric or savage, even – about the electorate.

According to the greatest philosophical minds of their – and arguably our – age, any decent city should be run by a knowledgeable few. By the time of the Age of Reason (also known as the Enlightenment), when ancient Athens was being transformed from a lost memory into a model civilisation, little had actually changed. Influential eighteenth-century British thinkers – who were writing in the aftermath of the bloody French Revolution, and through the ignominy of the loss of some of their American colonies – thought democracy was a downright dangerous idea that any civilised society would do well to avoid. So, how did this controversial idea, based on an experiment for how to run an ancient Greek city, become a bulwark of Western civilisation? The answer, in part, is that it didn't.

*

If the Athenian experiment of direct democracy has never been repeated since, what, exactly, do we in the West mean when we say, 'democracy'? This time, finding the answer involves going back only a few centuries where, it turns out, the pioneers in the system of government that we now think of as democracy came up with a handy workaround for what to do with the problem of having to entrust and share power with their fellow citizens. Instead of letting the voters run the show for ourselves, our systems of democracy involve voting for other people to do it instead.

It was the foundation of the United States of America towards the end of the eighteenth century that saw the return in the West to democratic ideals. Or at least it seemed that way. It all started when, in the run-up to the Declaration of Independence in 1776, the revolutionaries living in the thirteen British colonies in North America had been faced with a challenge.

Originally strident monarchists, they had been sorely disappointed when King George III had failed to intervene on their behalf when they had protested the new taxes being imposed on them by the British Parliament, where none of them were directly represented and over which they had no say. The king's betrayal had raised the battle cry of 'no taxation without representation!', along with the idea that what was needed here was an entirely new system of government. This system would need to reject the tyranny of monarchy, and also maintain the relative freedom of the individual colonies to sort out their own, internal affairs as they pleased. The solution they cottoned on to was democracy. Power and authority would not sit with the king, but with the people. For inspiration, they looked to that other great bastion of the ancient world: Rome.

In building their democracy, these new Americans branded themselves with the Greek word democracy, but they looked to the Roman Republic for the details of how to carry this out. Things here were rather different, although their beginnings were much the same. Through its own self mythology, the Republic of Rome also claimed to have sprung from the rejection of a tyrannical leader. According to the Roman historian Livy, the Roman Republic was founded in 509 BCE when Lucius Junius Brutus drove the king of Rome, Lucius Tarquinius Superbus, out of the city in retribution for the death of a noble-woman named Lucretia, who had publicly killed herself after the king's son had raped her. In doing so, Brutus is said to have vowed, 'I will suffer neither them nor any other to be king in Rome!' The story speaks to the forming of the republic as a family dispute rather than a social revolution, used to legitimise the power of Brutus and Lucius Tarquinius Collatinus (Lucretia's widower) as Rome's first consuls. The two consuls replaced the king and, in order to stave off tyranny, they served limited terms, holding the office for a single year. The consuls were appointed by magistrates, holders of high Roman political office who were also the Roman nobility, known as the patricians. We are very much back in the territory of Magna Carta and the twenty-five barons here, in that the Republic seemed to be a whole new system of government, but really it was still the same old, rich families in charge. Over the centuries, the system changed to admit plebeians, or non-nobles, to government roles, but for the most part the power stayed exactly where it had been. All told, the Roman Republic distilled the idea of a representative government. The Romans travelled under the banner SPQR, which stood for Senatus Populusque Romanus – the Senate and the People of Rome – two united but ultimately separate groups of people. Throughout the five hundred years of the Republic's history, it was this limited group of people in charge.

The idea of a representative government as practised by the Roman Republic solved a big problem for the founding fathers of the nascent United States. It dispensed with a monarch while at the same time fending off what they saw as the mob rule of direct democracy. This was the model the US adopted along with other aspects that hark back to the Roman Republic. The business of government in the US is carried out in a building called the Capitol, a name insisted on by Thomas Jefferson, and evoking the Temple of Jupiter Optimus Maximus on the Capitoline Hill, one of the seven hills of the city of Rome. The US have their own Senate, as did the Romans, and the US president shares many of the powers of the consuls, such as being the head of the armed forces, and having the power to veto government proposals. The Americans had one further requirement of their new government. As mentioned, they wanted to maintain the relative freedom of the individual colonies to sort out their own internal affairs as they pleased. As luck would have it, just such a system was operating close to hand.

The Haudenosaunee (called the Iroquois League by settler colonists) was a federation of different Indigenous nations in North America – first the Seneca, Cayuga, Onondaga, Oneida and Mohawk and then later the Tuscarora – that had banded together in their common political interest. The members of the Haudenosaunee, who lived according to the Great Law of Peace, proved inspiring to the English colonists in search of a new way of governing themselves. The Haudenosaunee was also a representative government. Each nation was represented by a number of officials called sachems, fifty in total, who met in a council to collaboratively make decisions which had to be unanimous. The Great Law was made up of 117 codicils, many of them involved in limiting the powers of the council and also making provision, in the case of more important or urgent matters, for decisions to be made by general referendum. The male sachems were chosen by the women clan leaders, and while the role could be passed on to the next generation of the same family, it could just as easily be revoked if the new sachem wasn't up to scratch. Through a combination of traditional record keeping and archaeological investigation, we can safely say that the federation of the Haudenosaunee dates at least as far back as 1150 CE, making it the world's second oldest continuous existing parliament (second to Iceland's Althing, which dates to 930 CE). According to a Dutch lawyer named Adriaen van Der Donck who had moved to the settlement of New Amsterdam in 1641, the Haudenosaunee were 'all free by nature, and will not bear any domineering over them'.

The Haudenosaunee provided the English colonists with a practical, working example of a federated union of nations where, for them, only political philosophy had existed before. While the English philosopher John Locke had said that there was a natural law that guaranteed all people certain rights from birth and that people enter into a social contract with the government to maintain these rights, he had unhelpfully written nothing about what this would actually look like in practice. The same goes for the French philosopher Montesquieu, who argued for a balance of power to be maintained by the separation of the judicial, legislative and executive branches of government. Here again, was a theory with no real life European practice to refer to. While the Haudenosaunee was not the sole influence on the newly rebellious European American colonists, there can be little doubting it was a significant influence all the same.

There was, though, the question of whether this new system was the civilised thing to do. On a practical level, it certainly seemed achievable. As early as 1751, that old charmer Benjamin Franklin had written, 'It would be a strange thing if six nations of ignorant savages should be capable of forming a scheme for such a union ... and yet that a like union should be impracticable for ten or a dozen English colonies, to whom it is more necessary ...' This left the problem of how this new government could be seen as an improvement on what had come before. For settler colonists like Franklin, Thomas Jefferson and John Adams, the societies surrounding them were by definition less advanced. To the settlers, Indigenous Americans were a living version of what government would have looked like before the development of monarchy. To a certain degree this was useful. As Thomas Paine, a recent English immigrant and arguably the most influential thinker behind the American Revolution put it: 'To understand what the state of society ought to be, it is necessary to have some idea of the natural and primitive state of man; such that as it is at this day among the Indians of North America.' While the Indigenous system of government and ways of living were undeniably appealing, they also had their limits. It would be impossible, Paine believed, for advanced Europeans like himself and his fellow settler colonists 'to go from the civilised to the natural state'.

For modern Western democracy, the solution to this quandary turned out to be a philosophical compromise. Where direct democracy was not fit for purpose on account of all the people involved, a representative, liberal democracy could be brought in to do the job instead. In the US, the founding fathers were happy to leave much of what they saw as the 'savage' aspects of the Haudenosaunee democracy behind. They ignored the clan-based system, with its associated female power and accountability, in favour of a classical model. The one thing they did take from the Haudenosaunee was the idea of federalism – independent and self-governing states within a state that send their representatives to form a central government when collective decisions needed making. Here, though, they applied a sleight of hand, through what they called 'the miracle of representation'. This goes as follows: the represented will of the people equates to the actual will of the people. And it seems to make perfect sense until, in comparison with the Athenian model, we can see that the US was a federal republic, not a democracy. The governments of the individual states were accompanied by an overarching national government. Rather than wielding the power directly within either of these bodies, the people elected officials to exercise it on their behalf.

The US model of government gave its voters all the trappings of decision-making without the trouble or, indeed, benefit of having any real authority themselves.

The development of British democracy, while a different story, ends up with pretty much the same result. Britain claims to have a special place in the history of democracy on account of having arrived at it not through revolution, but through a creeping series of reforms which all happened while the British state was trying to accomplish other things. We've seen this story before, starting with Magna Carta, moving on to the English Bill of Rights and a series of reforms in the nineteenth century, with the definition of 'free men' becoming wider and wider until it went so far as to even include women, and we get to universal suffrage in 1928. As a result, the British ship of state is something of a chimera, a bunch of laws and reforms variously cobbled together at different times and speaking to different priorities and ideologies, put together in the shape of a democracy, again without actually being one. Even putting aside the fact that Britain retains a monarch – and it is a well-known fact that kings and democracies do not mix, even the Romans knew that – the British state, like the US, more closely resembles the republican model than the Athenian one.

The Athenian model of government was what is called a direct democracy. This is as opposed to representative democracy, where the people appoint political leaders to represent them in government through a process of elections. In the modern West, and in Western-style democracies more broadly, it's this representative model of democracy that has taken hold. Rather than make all the decisions directly by and for ourselves, we devolve power into the hands of an elected few whom we entrust to make the big and important decisions for us. In a liberal democracy, things are kept in balance through a separation of powers between different branches of government. What those branches are depends on the time and the democracy in question. In the US, the power is divided between the legislative branch (where the laws are made), the judicial branch (which enact and interpret the laws) and the executive branch (the president). By contrast, at the beginning of British democracy, following the Glorious Revolution of 1688, power was divided between the monarch and Parliament, made up of the aristocracy in the House of Lords and everyone else, as represented by the House of Commons.

While it may be the case that the power of the monarch is not exercised with the force it once was, one look at the UK Parliament and the way we run our government would be enough to make an ancient Athenian throw up all over their tunic. They would be astonished that we say we have a government where the power lies with the people when the reality is that power is continuously and inexorably devolved into ever more limited sets of hands. While we do elect members to the House of Commons, the electorate as a whole has no direct say in who gets appointed to the other half of our government, the House of Lords. Then, within Parliament itself, power lies with the governing party, where it is devolved to the cabinet and then, ultimately, to the prime minister. Ancient Athenians were suspicious about elections, which they believed to be innately and inherently divisive and biased in favour of social elites and the already powerful. In other words, when it comes to our Western-style representative government, ancient Athenians saw our problems coming two-and-a-half thousand years ago and did everything they could to avoid them.

Their suspicions seem well-founded when we see who gets elected to political office. Today it's most usual to see the word 'oligarch' preceded by the word 'Russian', but really, neither now nor historically has the idea of rule by a limited few been the monopoly of a single state, nation or civilisation. Increasingly, it's becoming clear that being able to win an election and being able to actually run a country are two very different skill sets. In recent years, political parties on the right have made it clear that they are willing to embrace more extreme positions if doing so can guarantee them a winning share of the vote. There's also clear evidence of an embedded political class, with successful politicians better placed because of their education or because of their success in a particular walk of life. Western democracies are also well-versed in dynastic power, from US father-and-son presidential combos like John and John Quincy Adams and George H. and George W. Bush to political dynasties like the Kennedys, the Roosevelts and the Trudeaus.

The philosophical concerns about the rational fitness of every-day people have, of course, been useful in oppressing those people and quelling dissent, particularly those people who for centuries were deemed less than human. In the US, this took the form of intelligence and literacy tests that were designed to deprive people, particularly African Americans and Native Americans, of their right to vote. Different arguments were used to the same effect regarding women, who for most of human history were denied the franchise because they were considered too ill-equipped, both socially and intellectually, to carry it out. Combined with other things like the need to present ID cards, inaccessible polling stations or limited polling hours, it turns out that concerns about oppressive majoritarian rule, such as those voiced by the nineteenth-century French diplomat and scholar Alexis de Tocqueville, were very real indeed. The systems of a representative democracy seemed almost designed to replicate themselves, including reproducing and reinforcing existing inequalities.

All of this leads us to an existential question: is democracy inherently flawed?

Was Winston Churchill really just being pragmatic when he said: 'it has been said that democracy is the worst form of Government except for all those other forms that have been tried from time to time'? What if it turns out, governmentally speaking, this is the best we can do? Life can't all be about ideals, some practicality is necessary, after all. Well, when it comes to Western civilisation, you'll forgive me if I sound like a politician when I say this is the wrong question. The real question is: in the modern West, particularly in Britain and the US, has there ever been democracy in the first place? And if you ask the people who originally came up with the idea, the answer, quite clearly, is no.

The problem with Western democracy, for all its vaunted popularity as a modern, civilised ideal, is that it has never really existed. In a representative democracy – as all modern democracies are – our choices are limited to deciding who gets to be in power, not what they actually do with that power. All of the concerns for the efficacy of democracy relate to the people not being capable of making the right decisions. This, though, takes no account of how, in a representative democracy, the decisions we are allowed to make are limited to choosing who will govern us and not, as it should be, how to govern ourselves. We choose our representatives and leaders and relieve ourselves of any say in any of the decisions that may result.

All of this, of course, is even before we get to the huge potential for corruption in democracies. Ancient Athens wasn't impervious to this, given that one of its great leaders, the military general Pericles, owed his unimpeachable reputation to the fact that it was widely known he didn't take bribes. The implication being, of course, that lots of other Athenian politicians did. Fast forward to today and there are days I yearn for news of a little quiet bribery or some gentle sleaze. Instead, the newspapers and social media feeds are full to overflowing with stories of unelected political advisors, lobbyists and cronies exercising undue influence on our elected representatives. Some of those representatives themselves are clearly more demagogue – playing on their personal charisma for their own personal benefit – than they are democrat. With all of this going on, keeping the electorate from getting involved, particularly getting involved to the degree that they may be able to bring about sufficient political reform to govern themselves, is not only the easy option; it's absolutely vital for the powerful, if they want to keep themselves in power.

Accountability counts for nothing in this scenario. When the maximum penalty for having won an election by rigging it is £20,000, rather than immediate execution (which, I'll concede, is a little bit extra), it's small wonder that allowing the shocking 2017 Grenfell Tower fire in London to gently fade into oblivion is what a modern Western government considers to be business as usual. Rather than guaranteeing the safety of and justice for the most vulnerable people in our society, our system of government is set up in such a way that those in charge get to keep the profits of the deals they make with their friends to themselves, even – and you could even say often – at the expense of other people's lives. Who are our elected leaders really accountable to? Democracy may have gone global, but it hasn't been for everyone. It just isn't what it said on the tin.

★

Ever since the Cold War, the period of political tension between democracy and communism in the aftermath of the Second World War, the US government has carried out a strange ritual, aligned with key moments in the political calendar. Whenever a presidential inauguration or state of the union address rolls around, a single member of the government is split off from all their colleagues and taken to a secret location for the duration of the event. Instead of listening to the speeches or playing up to the news cameras (or, more usually, both), this individual is provided with their own security detail so that they can wait out their time until the party is over and the coast is clear. This person is known as the 'designated survivor'. The reason this political Cinderella cannot go to the ball is because it will be their job to take over the whole business of government in the event that all of their colleagues are somehow wiped out in a single accident or attack. The birth of this tradition during the Cold War is not surprising, given the precarious nature of US and, indeed, all of our politics in a world where things have the potential to go nuclear.

The idea of a designated survivor is the lie of representative democracy played out to its natural and ridiculous conclusion. In a representative democracy, political power is a transitive property – we are able to give it away to our elected government officials and it becomes concentrated into ever smaller hands. The idea of a designated survivor shows the importance of keeping this process and of going through the motions of a democracy, if only for appearances' sake. All of this in spite of the fact that, should the whole of the US government get wiped out in one fell swoop, surely there will be bigger problems than who gets to be in charge?

Democracy is the ultimate in ideas worth spreading, but the idea that has spread isn't really democracy. In the modern West, the power has never been with the people, it has always been with the barons. From the king and the barons who came up with Magna Carta to the elite political ruling classes in the West today, government is exactly where it has always been. Not by the people for the people, but through power exercised over the many by the few. One well-placed nuclear warhead and there goes our democracy.

Chapter Six

TIME IS MONEY

I remember a seminar on the subject of time during my archaeology master's course. Our tutor began by saying that for archaeologists, time was like a navel. Time sits at the centre of our being. Everything we do revolves around time: interpreting the past in the present in order to better inform the future. But we barely pay any attention to it at all. So, he asked, with that in mind, what exactly is time? With that began the traditional ritual that plays out at every university seminar when a question is asked at the room in general: for a full minute or so, no one spoke. Those of us who hadn't done the required reading looked down at our shoes pretending not to exist. Those who had looked contemplatively around the room, pretending to think. After what felt like an eternity of thick silence, I caved and said the first thing that came to mind.

'Time,' I said, 'is a measure of stuff happening.'

Not Shakespeare, I grant you (it wasn't even Shelley) but I had chosen one word in that sentence with some care. Spend three-and-a-half years as an archaeology student and you too will have learned not to carelessly throw around the word 'things'. 'Stuff' is inevitably kitsch and, now in my forties, seems like a vain attempt to sound young, but it does cover all the basics. 'Stuff' contains multitudes in the context of time. Things, that is to say physical objects, are made, used and destroyed. Beyond that, events occur, people change, life begins, grows, dies and, depending on your point of view, is reborn.

For a first attempt, I still maintain it was pretty decent. It turns out the same idea had occurred to St Augustine of Hippo, the theologian, philosopher and Berber bishop of Numidia in Roman North Africa (modern-day Algeria). Most famous as the author of *Confessions*, his idea was considerably more nuanced, of course. Augustine was one of the first people in the West to write about how we conceive of time as something that people experience, that is, as an embodied idea, rather than an external, physical one.

'There are three tenses or times,' Augustine wrote, 'the present of past things, the present of present things, and the present of future things.' (Augustine clearly had not trained as an archaeologist, and this is to his credit.) For Augustine, his experiences of the world travelled through his mind, leaving behind an impression of themselves. 'Either time is this impression,' he concluded, 'or what I measure is not time.' Augustine wasn't alone in thinking this. For much of the history of the West, the reality of time has been a subject that's up for debate.

If all of this seems unnecessarily esoteric, this is only the beginning. For the last hundred years or so, our understanding of time has been very different, albeit equally abstract. When, in the early decades of the twentieth century, a German Jewish theoretical physicist called Albert Einstein came along with his ideas about relativity, it helped us to conceive of time as something that had a real, direct effect on our physical lives. Before this, time was something that happened independently of us. Time passed and that was pretty much that. With Einstein, time was relative to the observer. Time, according to Einstein, is relative altogether. Suddenly, our world came into view in four dimensions, not only three, with space and time woven together in the fabric of the universe.

Even so, the embodied reality of physics is well beyond what most of us are able to conceive of as we go through our day to day lives. While it is the case that when we sit on a chair, for example, what is happening is that the chair, the floor that the chair is on and the planet that the floor is on are all accelerating through space, and therefore pushing against our body and holding it in place, that's not how most of us see it. Most of us simply feel that we are sitting in a chair. Nevertheless, when it comes to humans and the ways in which we experience it, time is a construct. As is only to be expected, the nature of that construct varies from place to place and from people to people. This chapter is a story of how the Western Enlightenment construction of time turned out to be a trap, one that we are still stuck in today.

*

At the Science Museum in London, on the first floor in the south-eastern corner, is a gallery of clocks and timepieces. Originally the collection of the Worshipful Company of Clockmakers, displayed at the Guildhall, its exhibits date from 1600 to the modern day. As you walk through the displays, you can learn about how timekeeping technology developed in the West over the eighteenth century, and how these developments were vital to British imperial success during the Age of Exploration. A good example of this is Captain Cook's mission during his famous 1769 voyage (which we briefly discussed in Chapter Three), when he and his crew set out to measure the transit of Venus. They did this by using a cutting-edge, state-of-the-art astronomical clock designed and built by the British clockmaker John Shelton. This observation and other measurements like it helped to establish the size of the solar system, which in turn helped to govern navigational techniques back here on Earth. The techniques of navigating great swathes of ocean without getting lost were, of course, not a uniquely Western invention. Cook and his crew met many Polynesians who had successively been navigating Oceania for generations, including their navigator Tupaia, who was able to draw them a map of an area the size of Europe (including Russia) that included seventy named islands. It was Westerners, though, who over the course of the nineteenth century took their preoccupation with time to a whole other level.

If we walk a little further through the gallery we can see the fruits of this. To an untrained eye like mine, one clock – be it a tall case clock, a pendulum clock, a carriage clock, a wristwatch or a pocket watch – is much the same as another. There is, of course, more to this story than simple appearances, mostly variations on a theme of improving accuracy over time. Developments in the history of timekeeping span the whole of human existence, from calendars inscribed on bones, to sundials, water clocks, hourglasses and, in the modern era, the mechanical clocks we in the West are more familiar with. Advances in technology led from clocks being powered by gravity to using springs and balance wheels, which in turn were replaced by quartz crystals, which vibrated by means of an electric current. By the end of the twentieth century, atomic clocks were so accurate, we could calibrate the movement of the Earth to the clocks and not the other way around.

As time is a construct, the ways in which we have gone about measuring and apportioning the time reflect our changing priorities. Historically, there had been important delineations of time for prayer and it was important to know your Shacharit,

Lauds and Fajr from your Marriv, Vespers and Maghrib (morning and sunset prayers in Jewish, Christian and Islamic traditions). Coming into the modern era, public clocks guided the times when, for example, the doors to a city would be opened, when markets opened and closed and when auctions ended. The Navy had its own arcane system of timekeeping, based on a system of bell-ringing. Officers and crew aboard a naval vessel were specially trained to the point where they knew, seemingly instinctively, that if it was five bells in the first watch, that meant that it was ten-thirty at night.

None of this, of course, applied on land. The development of the railways and the potential for extensive rail travel is usually seen as the reason behind the growing need for standardised time. When the time came that more and more people were travelling further and further by train, individual travellers and the places to which they travelled were forced to account for more than just themselves. As the train schedules developed, time became systematised, first across nations and then between them. Even with this great social advance, outside of rail travel, people still kept their local time themselves, as far as they were allowed. As the historian David Rooney has pointed out, 'local time passed into history not because the railways used it, but because 1870s anti-alcohol reformers wanted to use clocks to police their moral crusade'. Those Victorian do-gooders really do have a lot to answer for. They lobbied for licensing hours, ensuring that people needed to know exactly what time it was so they knew when to stop – or probably more importantly, start – drinking. Still, time waits for no one, and on 18 November 1883, time zones in the United States were brought into line with Greenwich, and we were on our way to creating the global, universal time by which we all live today. Greenwich Mean

Time, which practically places that London borough at the centre of the known universe, was established the following year in 1884.

Along with all of these technological advances in the field of watchmaking, the Clockmakers' gallery at London's Science Museum also contains a number of historical objects that help to illustrate the history of timekeeping. It's one of these that we have come to see. Made in 1794 and bequeathed to the Clockmakers' Museum in 1943, it's a large, solid-looking silver pocket watch, with a plain white face and elegant, elongated black Roman numerals circling around its edge. Named 'Mr Arnold' for its makers, John Arnold & Sons of London, it had originally been made for the Duke of Sussex who found the watch a bit of a beast, so rehomed it at the Greenwich Observatory, where it came into the hands of John Henry Belville. Originally a meteorologist and astronomer, Belville found himself uniquely placed to take on a new profession with Mr Arnold in hand, and fill a gap he had spotted in the market.

Belville's higher-ups at the Observatory found themselves constantly distracted by the watchmakers, clockmakers and chronometer-makers who made their living in London, the crews of ships moored on the Thames about to set sail, along with the odd amateur astronomer, all of whom were flocking to Greenwich in order to ensure their record of the time was as accurate as possible. When it came to timekeeping, Greenwich was the real deal. The Greenwich Clock was one of the most advanced in the world, and it was kept accurate by daily calibrations made in line with the astronomical sightings made at the Observatory – sightings that determined what time was in the first place. This was a marked step up from the kinds of personal timepieces everyday people owned, which either gained or lost time every day. With help from Mr Arnold, John Henry Belville could take the time to them. Every day, Belville would synchronise the pocket watch in time with the Greenwich Clock before travelling to visit any one of his nearly two hundred clients. This freed up the Observatory and set up a unique model for a family business. When John Henry died, his wife, Maria Elizabeth, and then their daughter, Ruth, carried on this work, under the romantic title of 'the woman who sold time'.

Mounted behind Mr Arnold in the museum's display is an enlarged black and white photograph, taken on Monday 9 March 1908. It would have been a Monday, because that was the day of the week that Ruth made the journey from her home in Maidenhead to Greenwich in order to have Mr Arnold synchronised with the Observatory's master clock, the standard bearer of Greenwich Mean Time. She would then take Mr Arnold, along with a certificate issued by the Observatory, on an elaborate route through the city of London, selling the time to those businesses whose profits and livelihoods depended on an accurate record of the time. As you might expect, this included rail stations, banks, newspapers and factories, along with pubs and taverns whose owners needed to stick to licensing hours. Then, of course, there were all the London clock, watch and chronometer makers whose works now sit alongside Mr Arnold at the Science Museum. I get the impression Ruth was not keen on having her photograph taken. While the liveried attendant who is handing Mr Arnold back to her seems game for a laugh, Ruth all but has her back to the camera, her face little more than a shadowy profile. Maybe when your business is selling time, there is little appeal in getting stuck in a moment yourself.

The story of the woman who sold time crops up fairly regularly in books and magazine articles. On the face of it, this is understandable – it's incredibly endearing. Also, standing in the Science Museum, with Mr Arnold right there in front of us, it taps into that voodoo that museums do so well, collapsing the past and present into a single spot, carefully contained in a glass case. But this story's appeal goes way beyond that. The story of the Belvilles and their unique, quirky profession is a modern-day fable. It literally embodies something we believe to be metaphorically true: that, in the West, as Benjamin Franklin put it, 'time is money'.

For us, it makes perfect sense that time should be a commodity, it's dotted everywhere throughout our language. We spend time, we waste time, we save time, we lose time, we have time to spare. This kind of time is something outside of ourselves. It progresses independently of us, but nonetheless we can move and manipulate it to suit our purpose. For the last couple of centuries, that purpose has been much the same: the making and the maintenance of wealth. Time is not just money, though. Time is also a trap.

For a society that has devoted so much energy to perfecting the accuracy of how we read time, it turns out we that we in the West also treat time as something wonderfully malleable. We have played – and continue to – play with time, first in the interests of saving it, and then of making money. When, in 1784, the eminently quotable Benjamin Franklin had suggested the Parisians change their sleep cycles so as to be able to save on candles, he had meant it as satire. A century on, though, and the idea was a reality in the extensive tea gardens of the Raj, where 'chai bagan' or 'tea garden' time put the eastern state of Assam an hour ahead on the clock to the rest of British India, all in the interests maximising tea picking during daylight hours. To the distress and dismay of many pet owners and parents, Daylight Saving Time is now a common part of our reality, with the clocks turned an hour ahead in the spring, and an hour back in the autumn. It was the Germans and then the British who started the practice in 1916, in order to save fuel during the First World War. When the Americans cottoned on to the idea a few years later, it was ostensibly for the same economising reason, although it was also certainly the case that extended periods of waking daylight made for greater opportunities for people to spend money during their leisure time, whether by shopping or playing sports. Daylight Saving Time apparently did wonders for bringing more people out to play golf, which, if you were conflicted about whether or not it is a good thing, should help you make up your mind.

As with the ideas do with 'nation' and 'democracy', our understanding that time is something that can be played with is a relatively recent one. We can date it to the advances of the Industrial Revolution, specifically in the nineteenth century, where in Britain, for example, large numbers of people abandoned farming and village life in the countryside in favour of urban living and industrial work that, to start with, paid much better. Industrialisation was a key historical development in the West, made possible in no small part by the profits from slave labour and colonies all over the world. Colonial subjects were first the labour force that enabled access to the raw materials needed to feed manufacturing, and then the markets for the finished goods. It's a neat trick, guaranteeing a never-ending supply of profit and development, provided, of course, that you don't run out of colonies (and, as we have been slow to admit, provided that you don't run out of raw materials).

The manufacturing industries that emerged in the form of the factory system didn't simply revolutionise Western economies, they completely changed the ways in which people worked. Before industrialisation, people had some flexibility in how they managed their work and, by extension, their leisure. Work was seasonal, dictated by the weather, the harvest and daylight hours. People could use their time as they wanted, even breaking up their nights with a few waking hours in between two shifts of sleep. As the factory-based systems of manufacturing became more established, people were expected to work around the clock, so to speak. And while we're familiar with the history of people being exploited by this system, of industrial workers, many of them children, being worked into the ground, losing fingers and arms, sacrificed to the machinery and the hunger for profit, working people lost something else here too: the freedom and ability with which to govern their own time and, by extension, to govern themselves.

Over the late nineteenth and into the early twentieth centuries, workers and the time in which they worked were squeezed ever further in the interests of efficiency and profits. Much of this was enabled by the work of a man who, in the 1920s, held factory owners, first in the United States and later all over the industrialised West, in his thrall. His name was Frederick Winslow Taylor and he was one of the first ever management consultants. I appreciate this is pretty damning in itself, but brace yourselves, it gets a whole lot worse. Like John Henry Belville, Speedy Taylor, as his industrialist employers tagged him, had carved out a novel career for himself with the help of a clock. He would turn up at a factory and spend many hours carefully watching the workers go about their day. The main tool of Taylor's trade was the stopwatch, and what he was doing was measuring, to an exacting degree, the amount of time it took people to carry out the individual components that made up their work. From hauling pig iron to designing the perfect shovel, no physical aspect of the work process escaped his scrutinising eye. Taylor worshipped at the altar of efficiency. His goal was to find the best way to get the job done in the least possible amount of time. His innovations in the field of studying and managing work gained him the title of 'the Father of Scientific Management'.

In a nutshell, scientific management is a rational approach to measuring — and through measuring, improving — worker productivity and efficiency. Taylor's work formed the 'time' element of the famous 'time and motion studies' of the early twentieth century. A husband and wife team of scientists, Lillian and Frank Gilbreth, provided the 'motion' element, filming workers and breaking down how they moved in the interests of discovering and implementing the most efficient ways of moving to get a particular job done. As with Taylor's focus on time, the goal was to cut out wasteful movements and arrange tasks in such a way as to yield the most efficient result. Together the influence of time and motion studies went well beyond the manufacturing industries to, scarily, the work of hospitals, and the so-called white-collar industries, like banking. To say that Taylor was worshipped as a management consultant god in the twentieth century is no exaggeration. His 1911 book, *The Principles of Scientific Management*, was the best-selling business book of the first half of the twentieth century. The management doyen Peter Drucker called it, 'the most powerful as well as the most lasting contribution America has made to Western thought since *The Federalist Papers*' (the collection of essays written to persuade the founding fathers to ratify the US Constitution).

And Taylor's ideas formed the metaphorical foundations of every business school from his time to ours. As with so many other things in the West, whatever the problem, science is the solution.

This itself was, of course, not without its problems. While Western imperialism treated colonised people as the source for raw materials and new markets, Taylor's paradigm of efficiency treated working people everywhere as if they were machines. Working people cottoned on to this pretty quickly. In the same year his book was published, Taylor was giving a speech at the Boston Central Labour Union, when one of the members called him out. 'You can call it scientific management,' she said, 'but I call it scientific driving.' Taylor's methods may well have been increasing efficiency and productivity, but they were doing so by driving people into the ground. By the time anyone in a position of power had thought to mobilise themselves to protect working people from this kind of exploitation, it was too late. Scientific management had and continues to infiltrate mainstream Western consciousness. Efficiency is our constant obsession, whether we are trying to better achieve it, resisting it or trying to break free from it.

Also inherent in Taylor's thinking, as was the case throughout colonised places, was the idea that some workers were superior to others. Those who did not fit the system, showing it up for the flawed, exploitative thing that it was – were deemed unfit altogether. In the history of Western civilisation, this is an idea that has extended over space and time. In order to find out more, we need to travel back a couple of hundred years, and all the way over to the other side of the world.

★

Plenty of European explorers and settler colonists had written about First Australians before Charles Darwin, but, given how important his ideas would turn out to be for their future, it's worth our looking at what he had to say. Darwin met First Australians (Aboriginal and Torres Strait Islander peoples) during his journey around the world on HMS *Beagle*. The *Beagle* was a British survey ship, and its main mission was mapmaking, particularly drawing more accurate maps of the South American coastline. Darwin came on board as a companion for the *Beagle*'s captain, and he made good use of his time by going ashore whenever possible and gaining first-hand experience of the animals and plants in the neighbourhood. For Darwin, this involved observing them in their natural habitat – as well as killing them in great numbers. It was these observations, along with the thousands of preserved specimens, fossils and minerals he brought home to England, that formed the foundations for his theory of evolution by natural selection.

Having first visited New Zealand at the end of 1835, the *Beagle* anchored in Sydney Cove, Australia, in January 1836. A landing party, including Darwin, made their way to Bathurst, stopping at Parramatta, now a suburb of Sydney, along the way. On 16 January 1836, Darwin wrote in his journal: 'At Sunset by good fortune a party of a score of the Aboriginal Blacks passed by, each carrying in their accustomed manner a bundle of spears & other weapons.' He described how members of the group threw their spears to amuse the white visitors, and he marvelled at their abilities and tracking skills. He was so impressed that he even went on to say, 'they appear to me to stand some few degrees higher in civilization, or more correctly a few lower in barbarism, than the Fuegians'. The Fuegians were inhabitants of Tierra del Fuego – at the southernmost end of South America

– that Darwin had encountered a few months earlier in the voyage, and they were another group of Indigenous peoples that he would go on to form opinions about.

Even while his research had the makings of a revolution in scientific thinking, Darwin nonetheless conformed to many of the hierarchical and reductive ways Western scientists thought about other 'races' of people, particularly the idea that dark-skinned people from Africa, South Asia and Australia sat on the bottom rung of the ladder of humanity. This is a far from straight-forward story: Darwin was raised in an abolitionist family and was famously strongly opposed to slavery. In fact, this was one of his main motivations for wanting to prove that all humans, however different they looked, descended from a common ancestor and were part of the same human family. Slavery, according to Darwin, was far from the natural order of things. Despite this, Darwin used ideas to do with race to argue for and support his ideas about natural selection. The Fuegians he mentioned in his journal were, in his view, so little removed from orangutans in the arrangement of living things that it helped him build his view that humans were descended from apes.

For all that Darwin believed in the idea that all humans descended from a common ancestor, he was also perfectly happy with the idea that some groups of people were less developed and, by that definition, inferior to others. He also believed in the importance of the British imperial project, and the idea that European Western civilisation was at a considerably more advanced stage than the rest of the world.

When the *Beagle* went on to Tasmania, then known as Van Diemen's Land, Darwin wrote that the place 'enjoys the great advantage of being free from a native population'. The reason for this was that, during the previous five years, British colonists had moved what little was left of the local population to neighbouring islands in the Bass Strait. Most had either succumbed to new diseases for which they had no natural immunity or had been murdered by British settler colonists, who were paid bounties for the numbers of local people they were able to shoot. While Darwin himself appreciated the politics at play in Tasmania, his work set the scene for a Social Darwinist assumption many Westerners would make for more than a century: that First Australians, along with the Maori in New Zealand, and other Indigenous peoples all over the world, were so primitive, uncivilised and backward that they were sadly destined to become extinct.

There is another part of the entry in Darwin's diary from January 1836 that's of interest to us here. Having noted that they were surprisingly less barbaric than he had been expecting, Darwin went on to write of the First Australians: 'They will not however cultivate the ground, or even take the trouble of keeping flocks of sheep which have been offered to them; or build houses or remain stationary.' Remaining stationary, in space if not in time, was an important step up the ladder towards civilisation. Wandering around without many clothes on and turning your nose up at proffered sheep, by contrast, wasn't going to get you anywhere. What Darwin and many other Europeans did not know when they first caught sight of Australia – in fact, what they completely failed to fathom – was that there is more than one way to gather produce from the land. Settler colonists had very specific views as to what constituted agriculture, specifically planting and growing crops and keeping and grazing animals. The colonisers view of themselves as civilised people and their related view that First Australians were barbaric, meant that they missed what was in front of their very eyes. The conception of First Australians as throwbacks, somehow frozen in time, was something Darwin himself had noted elsewhere. Writing of the Fuegians, 'Although essentially the same creature, how little must the mind of one of these beings resemble that of an educated man. What a scale of improvement is comprehended between the faculties of a Fuegian savage and a Sir Isaac Newton.' Of course, when it comes to some things, like understanding the nature of time, you don't need a Newton. What you need is an Einstein. Newton had concluded that things fall to Earth because of the pull of gravity. Einstein worked out that things don't fall at all. Instead, he conceived of the universe as a place where everything is moving through the fabric of spacetime, which itself is shaped and warped by the mass and energy of those things. Time, in its infinite complexity, can be conceived of in myriad different ways.

For First Australians, time is not money. It is not a commodity, but a way of building community and managing the surrounding environment to best effect. The English name given to this world-view is the Dreaming, a name coined by the anthropologist W. E. H. Stanner in 1953. For European Enlightenment thinkers, time was fixed and linear, that is, it only travels in one direction. In that frame, crucially, time is also measurable. And when it comes to time as measured out in discrete units of production, or time as a measure of progress, be it the progress of human technology or human ideas, it is a distinctly Western construction. By contrast, the Dreaming, if anything, seems to resist or possibly even reject time in that, in part, the idea is to prevent things from changing. The Dreaming is everything, everywhere, all at the same time. Contrary to what the name suggests, the Dreaming is very real indeed. The Dreaming fixes

First Australians in space – on the Australian continent – since the beginning of time. It is a practice that is composed of places, stories and songs, all of which describe the creation of animals, plants and humans, the very specific connections and relationships between them, along with historical events. It's a taxonomic system that assigns different families, clans and nations to particular animals and plants as totems, whom they are directly connected to and responsible for taking care of. In the West, we lament the fact that life doesn't come with a book of instructions. In Australia, the Dreaming goes some way towards making up this shortfall.

The Dreaming encompasses some 7.7 million square kilometres including the whole of the Australian continent, the island of Tasmania and the Torres Strait Islands in a single, holistic connection – what the Australian historian Bill Gammage called 'the biggest estate on Earth'. Gammage conceives of the Dreaming using the term 1788, an Australian equivalent to the American 1492. Just as when in 1492 Columbus sailed the ocean blue, bringing civilisation, colonialism and genocide in his wake, in January 1788 Captain Arthur Phillip led a fleet of 11 British ships to establish a penal colony in the place his fellow colonists had called New South Wales. As well as marking out the moments in time when these places were free of European colonists and settlers, these dates also embrace ideas, world-views and ways of life. The year 1788 and the stories and songs of the Dreaming are the frame for active land management of the estate.

Central to these techniques is the use of fire, and a detailed appreciation of which of the many types of Australian trees responded to fire and which didn't. First Australians knew what time of the year to set fires, and how long and how hot to let them burn to best effect. This strategic burning allowed First Australians to manage the distribution and types of tress in the landscape, as well as encouraging the growth of new grass, which had the benefit of attracting grazing animals, like kangaroos, which they could then hunt. Why chase after your dinner if you can clear a path to it or, better still, arrange for it to come to you? These highly effective and efficient systems were centuries in the making. Under the banner of 1788, there is no such thing as the wilderness. All the land needs managing and for millennia people did just that.

All of this knowledge is collected and communicated through a complex oral tradition. Just as with the Inka khipu in South America, Westerners tend to dismiss forms of communication that aren't written down as being primitive and inaccurate. Far from it. The knowledge of the Dreaming is both specific and universal, with song lines stretching the length and breadth of the Australian continent. The traditions are so well developed and sophisticated that these songs – the instructions for how to best manage a continent – maintain their accuracy over both space and time, even when traversing the continent and being translated into different languages.

If Frederick Winslow 'Speedy Taylor' had rocked up in the outback with his trusty stopwatch, it's unlikely that he would have marvelled at the astonishing efficiency of this ancient land management system. Gammage makes the point that the methods and techniques inherent in the Dreaming all involve active management of the land, albeit in ways that are neither labour nor time intensive. In Taylorian time management terms, they were so efficient that Westerners almost completely failed to notice anything was happening at all. The few that did were confused. The reason, though, that most non-Australians failed to comprehend what was going on in Australia is not because they simply didn't understand about how landscape management worked, it's because their idea of what savages, compared to what civilised people could do, was so limited that they could not see beyond this frame to acknowledge the reality that surrounded them. They refused to believe what they could see with their own eyes. Once again, as some European scientists had done when coming up with their racial typologies, settler colonists looked at the world around them as what they saw to be a natural outcome, not one that had come about through human intervention.

Everyone from Captain Cook on down had spotted that the land in Australia was clear under trees, and that the trees themselves seemed deliberately placed and well-spaced apart. Describing the country inland from Port Stephens, an English settler called Robert Dawson wrote, 'in Australia, the traveller's road generally lies through the woods, which present a distant view of the country, combined with the pleasurable associations of civilised society.' Europeans like Dawson consistently described the landscape as 'parks', a word that, at the time of the growing enclosure movement, only had one meaning – land deliberately managed and, habitually, belonging to rich people. The fact that you could have parks without having fancy rich people to own them was more than the European mind could fathom. It was also remarkably convenient. As we've seen, according to the rational principles of the Enlightenment, land could only be owned if it was actively being managed. In Australia, then, white settlers could revel in an entire continent where, as far as they could see, nothing was being done with the land and, as they also saw it, there were no real people to get in the way of their colonising settlement.

This conception of First Australians as something less than human would go on to, and in many ways continues to, have a devastating effect on both the land and the people themselves. Following on from Darwin, archaeologists and anthropologists conceived of First Australians, particularly those that lived on the island of Tasmania, as more akin to fossils, rather than living humans. Some suggested Tasmanians were the missing link in the evolutionary chain that they saw as connecting modern humans to our earlier ancestors. As such, they became frozen in the Western scheme of things, a sort of timeless ethnographic present. This is what some academics call the historicising of people, that is thinking about a group of people as trapped in a particular moment in time and, by extension, at a particular stage of development along the civilisational scale.

Over the following century, Western views of First Australians changed in relation to the prevailing academic ideas of the time. With the growing popularity of eugenics in the early twentieth century, they became the focus of what was termed 'the half-caste problem', in short, what to do with those few recent generations of people with both Aboriginal and white settler colonist parents. The attitudes of the settlers (whose views were the ones that counted) were divided between those who believed they should be incorporated into the white population, with others believing they should be an independent community and supported with government money. Eventually, concerns about racial degeneration won out, the result being children ripped from their families, brought up in isolated schools and camps, all in the interests of 'breeding out the black'.

In early 2020, before the COVID-19 pandemic took over the headlines and, seemingly our whole existence, the greatest natural disasters were wildfires burning out of control across the

Australian continent. Much of this was down to the damage wreaked by settler colonists and Western agricultural practices, particularly the fact that vast tracts of Australia are now used for grazing sheep. The sheep may have been the civilised option, but it was the sheep, along with the lack of traditional fire regimes, that have contributed to ruining the land.

The result has been the loss and erasure of vast quantities of knowledge. It took Western scientists eighty-five years to accept the fact that platypuses do, in fact, lay eggs – something First Australians had been telling them from the start. Collaborative research means that it is also now commonly acknowledged that First Australians lived alongside species of now extinct megafauna in the deep past. First Australians were only granted full citizenship rights in 1984. There is a longstanding myth that, until a historic referendum in 1967, they were classified as part of the local flora and fauna. While this wasn't the case, the fact that so many people continue to believe and repeat this idea speaks to a wider truth. As Professor Marcia Langton, one of Australia's most respected Indigenous academics, put it: 'We were not classified under the flora and fauna act, but we were treated as animals.'

Modern Australia is clearly part of the West, being one of the settler colonies that hark back to the ascendancy of the British Empire. In a process that seems excruciatingly slow, ideologies like the White Australia Policy are giving way to integration in the interests of greater social justice. But modern Australia is the blink of an eye. First Australians have been there for millennia, and they made an impact whether we have chosen to see it or not. First Australian conceptions of time, the universe and everything, as with so many Indigenous and colonised people all over the world, were diminished, dismissed and ignored by dint of their association with people who, supposedly, could never be civilised. Their ideas are, of course, unwritten ideas, which, as we saw in Chapter Three, diminishes them in the eyes of the West even further.

Earlier in this chapter, I talked about how time is a construct. That being the case, we need to keep in mind the political implication of time as an idea. The Indian historian Dipesh Chakrabarty has pointed out that in the reality of our lived experience, what time is depends on who is constructing it. The principles of land management that passed across the Australian continent and down through the generations form a complex method for keeping things as they are, for maintaining a system that could comfortably support the people that lived in it. This made no sense in the context of the civilising mission of the West that depended on an understanding of progress, and more-over a view that progress was the sole purview of the West. After all, how can you demonstrate your superiority over a group of other people without making them inferior to you first? Critically, what we lost as a result was the ability to conceive of the world beyond our own narrow, blinkered frame, and to be able to acknowledge that other, non-Western world-views and other perspectives have value too.

*

In the modern, supposedly post-industrial West, the commodi-fication of time during the Industrial Revolution has morphed into something different, something arguably equally damaging to the fabric of our society. That thing is busyness.

We are so busy.

Busy is both a state of being and a status symbol. Busy is a badge of honour. It is good to be busy, even if you are not doing much of anything. Activity is a substitute for achievement, and presenteeism, in place of efficiency, is a necessary route to success. This wasn't where we were supposed to be. The economist John Maynard Keynes had projected that, with advancing technology, people would only need to work for three hours a day. In 1964, *Life* magazine published a two-part series focusing on the looming disaster of excess leisure, including strategies for how best to cope with an easy, work-free life. So what happened? The short answer is that we got stuck. Just as Westerners mistakenly thought of First Australians as living fossils frozen in time, so now we are stuck in a construction of time that reproduces itself in such a way that we feel we must must work ourselves into the ground. Work, as an idea in the West, is inevitably bound up with class. There are blue-collar workers who work with their hands in both skilled and unskilled jobs (how this distinction is made is a job in itself). In addition, there are white-collar workers, whose jobs revolve around desks, paperwork, meetings and management. There are also grey-collar workers working past retirement age and even pink-collar workers who do jobs traditionally done by women.

The odds are, though, that you are working yourself into the ground, whatever the colour of your collar. Every now and again there's a news story about the perils of zero-hour contracts, factory workers and delivery drivers denied toilet breaks, alongside a shocking number of headlines about people giving birth in the toilets at their workplaces before heading straight back to the assembly line for fear of losing their jobs. Well-paid middle management or professional jobs are not immune to this either. A story in the *New York Times* reported white-collar workers at Amazon too scared to move from their desks, petrified of being fired at a moment's notice, reprimanded for not answering their emails at all hours of the day, and crying into their keyboards from the stress of it all. As for the freelance professional, work is the ultimate trap because, remember, time is money. In his book *Four Thousand Weeks*, Oliver Burkeman hits home with the real life implications of this simple calculus, particularly the things we lose and miss out on when our sole focus is efficiency in the interests of making money. Why, we may think, should we spend our time on hobbies, with our friends or family? Why go to a kid's birthday party or on that once-in-a-lifetime trip around the world? Why do anything, really, other than work when all of the precious minutes we can tally up at the end of the day can be directly translated into our bank account?

Whatever the scenario, it's easy to see that these are all traps of our own making. Somewhere along the way, we lost track of time.

'Your so-called boss may own the clock that taunts you from the wall, but, my friends, the hour is yours.' This is one of many aphorisms from *The You You Are*, a fictional self-help book that appears in the TV series *Severance*. The show takes today's white-collar workplace to its next logical dystopian level, where workers agree to split their consciousnesses into a work and a non-work persona. Each is aware of the other's existence, but neither knows what the other gets up to in their time either in or out of the office. The idea that we need self-help books to guide us through our working lives makes complete sense. During working days, my inbox swells with newsletters replete with articles that tell me what my work persona is, how to use it to best advantage, how to prevent or recover from burnout and what to wear to convey that I am a useful, productive member of our society. I read them religiously, of course, because that is what you're supposed to do with things that turn up in your inbox, even if they have nothing to do with the work you are actually doing. Also, I like to look at earrings.

The nature of how we view work in the Western world ties in perfectly with my conception of my working self as almost a completely separate persona. I close the lid on my laptop at the end of my working day, and for a few moments I am completely discombobulated. Just as when waking from a dream, I'm forced to ask the question, who am I again? – then piece myself back together. Luckily, I also have a smartphone to help me do this, and on it is a separate to-do list from the one that lives in my laptop. (I'm kind of kicking myself that I never got on board with smart watches, because that would have made this so much neater, metaphorically speaking.)

The idea that a guide, even a fictional guide in a dystopian alternative universe, would encourage you to conceptually blow up the office is at once liberating and depressing. I'd love to do it. I just don't see how. It means giving up the trappings of a civilised life, everything from the laptop itself to the tip-tapped flowery ideas it contains. Time may well be a measure of stuff happening, but it's all I can do to keep myself standing still. It's not a manual we need, but something like the Dreaming. A useful conception of the world and how to live meaningfully in it.

On a guided tour of the Casa Rocca Piccola, a historic villa dating from the 1580s in the Maltese capital Valletta, I spotted an antique clock hung on the wall like a painting. Set in a gilded rectangular frame, the clock face was a painted pastoral scene surrounded with concentric circles inscribed with Roman numerals marking the hours and embellished with stylised painted flowers. Aside from being a beautiful thing in a whole villa full of beautiful things, the clock had a distinguishing feature: it only had an hour hand. When I asked our guide about it, he explained that, back in the day, for the rich people who had lived in this house, that was as accurate as a clock needed to be. You needed to know roughly what hour of the day it was, and this would let you know when the next prayer or meal was coming. How nice for them, I thought.

Chapter Seven

YOUR COUNTRY NEEDS YOU

Another day, another immigration queue. You join me on the course of my bureaucratic journey to become an Overseas Citizen of India. This is a political status conferred on people of Indian origin – that is, people or their parents who were born Indian subjects – who live outside of India and are not themselves Indian citizens. What I find simultaneously poignant and annoying about this is that I have had to expend considerable effort, and am about to be put to considerable expense, in order to officially become what I was born as: a citizen of the nation of India. But India doesn't allow for dual citizenship with the United Kingdom for what, I assume, are historical reasons. And so, when I was naturalised as a British citizen, I was forced to surrender my Indian passport. As such, I have spent what feels like an unfairly large share of my life standing in immigration queues, and they are all just unspeakably horrible. I am sick to my stomach. It's not a nice feeling when your future life and happiness hangs in the balance of national bureaucracy. It's not a nice feeling when someone other than yourself, your friends and family have the power to tell you where you belong. At the same time, I am extraordinarily privileged to be able to do this. I'm not fleeing a homeland where my life is at risk and, expensive though the whole process is, I can afford it. But still, my leg is jiggling as though it has a mind of its own and I compulsively sift through my papers and grind my teeth.

In my bag are all the documents I need to complete my application, along with self-attested copies and an application form, duly signed to testify that I am who I say I am. Today would be a good day to be one of those characters in a soap opera who suddenly gets amnesia or falls into a fugue state. I have all of the definitive proof of my identity and existence slung over my shoulder. The whole episode would be over in, like, three minutes. I talk a lot when I'm nervous – a character flaw that has served me well in my comedy career, but which in real life is highly unattractive. And it so happened I got to chatting to a lovely, patient, young English man, there applying for a tourist visa. I had done this myself a few months earlier in order to be able to visit my mum, who is now retired and lives in India. The fact of needing a visa to get into the country that some people would like to tell me to fuck off back to is an irony that is not lost on me. In fact, that also makes me sick.

It turned out my new friend in the immigration queue was a historian of music in North India, specialising in classical music in Bengal in the nineteenth century. He spoke Bangla fluently and could read the language too, a fact I forced him to prove to me by making him read aloud from the photographed pages of books my mum had WhatsApped me as part of our ongoing reading lessons. While I read Bangla like a five-year-old sounding out the letters, he read confidently and fluently, as if he'd been doing it all his life. He knew loads of Bengali history, had many Indian friends, both in the UK and in India, and was so well travelled around the country that a part of me wanted to hand him my application and say, 'You know what, take this. You should have it. You're way more Indian than I am ever going to be.' I often say I am the whitest Brown person you are likely to meet and it's at moments like this that the truth of that statement really hits home.

My love affair with the UK started young. Like most things, I blame it on my education. All those books in the library of my English school in the Middle East, from *Topsy and Tim Go to the Seaside* (don't quote me on the title, it's been a minute since I read it), through to the Famous Five and Jeeves and Wooster, all painted such a glorious and attractive picture of pure Englandness that I was completely besotted. And it's a feeling that's lasted to this day. I'll find myself visiting a new place, the Cotswolds, say, or the North Norfolk Coast or the Welsh Borders, and I have to pinch myself because I am giddy with the fact that it looks exactly like the way that it was described in the books. It all looks so British.

Even after living in London for more than twenty years, I still feel, standing on the Hungerford Bridge and looking at the Thames and the Southbank, that I am winning at life. England, and London particularly, with its black cabs, tomato red double decker buses and leafy green avenues was once a place in a dream. And it seemed beyond dreaming that I would ever get to live there. The fact that my dream has come true is nothing short of a modern miracle.

I became a British citizen in 2008. This was the culmination of many years living in the UK, and a whole heap of admin. I applied for an assortment of different visas, passed the citizenship test (with a perfect score!), applied for naturalisation and handed back my Indian passport. When the great day finally dawned, I toddled off to the ceremony in Hounslow Town Hall where the Lady Mayoress listened while I swore an oath of loyalty to the Queen and then presented me with a memorial teaspoon. What was happening here was that I was metaphorically shedding the administrative cloak of one nation so as to be able to wrap myself in another. Physically I felt no different. Practically, everything changed.

While my primary motivation in becoming British had been to be able to stay in the country without the constant, low-level background fear that at any point somebody was going to kick me out, suddenly I could travel so much more easily than I could before (even post-Brexit, a UK passport ranks joint-fourth in the Henley Passport Index alongside Ireland, Denmark and the Netherlands, giving its holders access to 189 countries). In the time since becoming British, the number of countries I have visited has rocketed from eleven to fifty-seven. Certainly, it's the case that I've gotten older and have more disposable income to allow for this, but it's also the case that travel becomes an absolute breeze when you don't need to apply for a visa every time you want to leave the country. A British passport, it turned out, is a ticket to see the world. This is, in no small part, down to the ghost of the British Empire, and how it influenced agreements between nations as to who they were going to let in and who they were going to keep out.

A key question here is: what counts as a 'nation'? What is the nature of nationhood? Given that my parents were both born British subjects, why did I need to go through all this rigmarole to get to the same place? It's worth our looking at the history of the idea of the nation, first to understand what it means, and, perhaps more importantly, to understand how it has come to mean so much. Historically speaking, the idea of the nation as a place with solid borders containing people united by a common identity, is very much a modern one. The development of the nation and the development of different nations into their own senses of nationhood follows much the same pattern in time and space as we saw with the flowering of democracies all over the world. In 1914, before the outbreak of the First World War, the count of sovereign nations stood at fifty. Today it is nearly two hundred. Of course, the conceptualisation of this progress as part and parcel of the rational progress of Western societies continues to loom large. As with democracy, the coming to nationhood is seen as a natural end of the civilising process. Nationhood is the final phase of the journey of civilised people on the road to modernity.

Writing in 1830, the German philosopher Georg Wilhelm Friedrich Hegel declared, 'In the existence of a people the substantial purpose is to be a state and to maintain itself as such; a people without state-formation ... has no real history.' The logic is that any self-respecting society should also have a strong sense of itself. Here again is the idea that different groups of people will progress through various stages of self-awareness and self-governance, and those capable of attaining civilisation would do so through the mastery of their own nation-states. The idea of the nation, though, is a more complex one than the ideas we've encountered so far, because, along with rationalism, romanticism also played a significant role in how Western nations came into being.

It's almost impossible to look into the Western notion of nationhood without stumbling over a book by the political scientist Benedict Anderson called *Imagined Communities*. Anderson's citizenship is listed as Irish, but his life was a cosmopolitan one. Anderson's father was Anglo-Irish, his mother was English and he himself was born in Kunming, the capital of China's Yunnan province, in 1936. He went to Eton, then to Cambridge and on to Cornell, and he spoke several Southeast

Asian languages, including Indonesian, Thai and Tagalog (the national language of the Philippines).

In a move that makes perfect sense to me, having also been born and raised in a culture that was not my parents' culture, Anderson's 1983 work conceived of the nation-state as large groups of people connected by their sense of belonging to a place that isn't real. We're back in social construct territory again, with an idea of unity based on political and cultural solidarity. That is to say that, as an everyday Brit, I have no connection to – I'm not related to and I'm not friends with – any of the people I walk past in the street except through this shared sense of national belonging. (Obviously, I am friends with some of them, but you get the drift.) *Imagined Communities* might be an academic work, but the thing that it is referencing is something that is viscerally real to a lot of people. You may have thought I was being a bit of a drama queen with all my talk of black cabs, Routemaster buses, the Hungerford Bridge and the like, but it turns out I was really on to something. In fact, as is so often the case, I was barely getting started. The package that defines 'Britishness' is not simply the physical space bounded by the coastline of the British Isles and the border of the Republic of Ireland, it is all of the mix of Irish, Welsh, Scottish and English identities, histories and traditions along with their misapplications and misapprehensions. It's fish and chips, endless cups of tea, queuing, red phone boxes, chocolate box villages, rolling green hills, church spires and Morris dancing. It's the Red Arrows, Glastonbury, *The Wind in the Willows*, Elgar's *Enigma* variations, Monty Python, The Clash, 'Danny Boy', 'Flower of Scotland', 'Bread of Heaven', Isambard Kingdom Brunel, the Industrial Revolution, Remembrance Day poppies, the suffrage movement, *Empire Windrush,* pearly kings and queens, the NHS, the Queen (or now King), James Bond, Akram Khan, *Chariots of Fire*, *Mr Bean*, *EastEnders*, *The Archers*, *Bedknobs and Broomsticks*, *Four Weddings and a Funeral*, The Pet Shop Boys, Paul McCartney, David Bowie, and any myriad other things I haven't copied off the list of things featured in Danny Boyle's exemplary opening ceremony for the London Olympics in 2012. The process of building an imagined community is the process of turning geography into friends and family.

Anderson's idea of the nation was imagined on three not altogether flawless premises. The nation, he said, was limited, sovereign and a community (I do like a strong brand, especially when the idea is in the title). According to Anderson, the nation is limited because it is finite. Its boundaries may be elastic and change over time, but a single nation, by definition, will never encompass the whole of humanity – there will always be other nations at its borders. Regarding sovereignty, Anderson dated the rise of the nation-state to the Enlightenment and held that this was a revolution aimed at exploding the hierarchical nature of religious authority. A sovereign nation has the autonomy and the right to make its own decisions. Or, perhaps more historically precisely, the Church can't tell it what to do. Finally, the idea of the nation as a community rests on the imagined connections between people through fraternity bound by common cultural values. The 2012 Olympics' opening ceremony is one manifestation of this. Another literally falls under the banner of what I call 'fools who wave flags' (full disclosure, I have done this myself on occasion, although, in my defence, I was six at the time).

While Anderson's notion of the nation as an imagined community is an influential idea, it's not without its problems, particularly when it comes to the role of the nation in imperialism and colonialism. I think it's interesting that Anderson's idea about the limits of a nation failed to consider the British Empire, which, putting it generously, seemed intent on acquiring and subsuming everything it could get its grubby imperial hands on. He also falls short in his ideas about racism. As a self-avowed nationalist, Anderson insisted that nationalism doesn't breed racism on account of them each having different goals. The dreams of racism, as Anderson saw it, were bound up with ideas about blood purity and hierarchy. He also believed that racism was external to nations, that is one nation could despise another on the basis of race – not internal, as nationalism was. I think this position reveals an unspoken assumption on Anderson's part that he saw nations as racially coherent. For him there is no racism within a nation as all its people are already all racialised in the same way. At the very least, the nation in Anderson's views becomes a proxy for racial cohesion. The reality, of course, is quite different. And by now, it likely won't surprise you to learn that, at its heart, in the West, the nation-state is a project based on 'race'.

*

However imagined the nation is as a community, its physical borders as a nation-state have to be policed. And, as the cultural theorist Stuart Hall put it: 'There is no understanding of Englishness without understanding its imperial and colonial dimensions.' This is because, when it was officially formed in 1707 as a political project, the Kingdom of Great Britain was an imperial project from the start. This newly-formed national identity was forged through the union of Scotland and England. While they had their differences, the governments of both England (including Wales) and Scotland had one clear, shared motive for this union, which was to have a stronger combined political edge in the era of rising empires. Both countries had their own colonies before unification, and, together, went on to become the greatest imperial force in history. At its height, the British Empire encompassed a quarter of the Earth's human population, covering every corner of the globe. This was fine by the British ruling classes, provided all that mass of humanity stayed where it was. As the Empire began to crumble in the middle of the twentieth century, as the expense of administering it became too much and former colonies fought for independence, it became clear that this wasn't going to be the case – increasing numbers of people were relocating in the post-war period – and action needed to be taken.

The history of UK immigration laws is one of ever more restrictive legislation, designed specifically to keep those citizens of the Commonwealth not racialised as white at a safe distance. In this regard, the British Nationality Act of 1948 was a disaster. Originally designed in the aftermath of the Second World War, its purpose had been to foster closer ties between the British settler colonies – Canada, Australia and New Zealand – and the Motherland, making it as easy as possible for those white citizens of the Commonwealth to travel back and forth between Britain and its former dominions. What the civil service bureaucracy in Whitehall had failed to take into account was that all citizens of the Commonwealth had exactly the same rights under the same law, regardless of how they were racialised. When word arrived that some three hundred Jamaicans were making the journey to Britain on a ship called the *Empire Windrush*, the British government was horrified. Prime Minister Clement Attlee described the Jamaicans as 'an incursion', and his government took all kinds of measures to have the ship diverted or turned back. When they failed to do this, it was clear that the law needed changing.

In the decades that followed came a series of government initiatives to try to keep Britain white (well in advance of the racist political campaign of the same name). In the immediate aftermath of the Second World War, this had included actively bringing in Polish refugees and other displaced European people from the Baltic, Balkans, Yugoslavia and Italy, along with former prisoners of war to help replenish the workforce. In other words, the British government was happy to bring in white immigrants, some of whom had recently been members of an opposing military force in the greatest conflict humanity had ever known, in favour of the Black and Brown people who'd actually served in the British Army, and were themselves British subjects. There was a clear understanding, at least as far as the British government was concerned, that these European arrivals were here to stay, and that they would intermarry and become seamlessly absorbed into the British population. In a 1948 letter to a fellow civil servant, the Deputy Permanent Under-Secretary at the Ministry of Labour Sir Harold Wiles wrote that these European Voluntary Workers:

> ... are coming definitely for permanent settlement here with a view to intermarrying and complete absorption into our own working population. Whatever may be the policy about British citizenship, I do not think that any scheme for the importation of coloured colonials for permanent settlement here should be embarked upon without fully understanding that this means that coloured elements will be brought in for permanent absorption into our own people.

Immigrants from other parts of the world, most particularly from the Caribbean, on the other hand, were seen as so irredeemably different – and as such a threat to British racial purity – that the only solution was to keep them out.

Across the Atlantic, the United States carried through overtly racist immigration legislation with a practised hand (a tradition it continues to uphold today). For example, the Immigration Act of 1924, also known as the Johnson Reed Immigration Act, notoriously delineated a 'Barred Asiatic Zone', effectively halting Asian immigration to the US for decades (notable exceptions were Japan, where entry quotas had been limited by a previous treaty; the Philippines, which was an American colony at the time; and China, whose citizens were already denied entry by the earlier Chinese Exclusion Act). Britain couldn't openly be seen to be doing the same thing. There was its reputation as a civilised, free, just and open society to maintain. As such, the approach of Harold Macmillan's 1957–63 Conservative government was to overhaul the immigration system based on the relative skills of the immigrants concerned. Potential immigrants were divided into three categories: skilled; skilled or unskilled with a guaranteed job to go to; and unskilled. The assumption built into these categories was that the last one – unskilled workers – would be predominantly made up of Black and Brown people and more severely restricted by the law. In a memorandum on 'Commonwealth Migrants', then Home Secretary Rab Butler wrote:

> The great merit of this scheme is that it can be presented as making no distinctions on grounds of race and colour ... We must recognise that, although the scheme purports to relate solely to employment and to be non-discriminatory, its aim is primarily social and its restrictive effect is intended to ... operate on coloured people almost exclusively.

The British way, it seems, is that you can discriminate against people as much as you like, provided you don't appear to be doing so.

Despite our journey together in this book, you may still believe that this kind of blatant institutional racism is a remnant of the past, something we can safely consign to history (which, as the British novelist L. P. Hartley informed us, is, itself, a foreign country). Sadly, this is a situation that persists in exactly the same way today. Brexit notwithstanding, it still remains easier for Germans – the biological, if not the philosophical, descendants of the Nazi soldiers who fought against Britain during the Second World War – to enter the country than it is for the descendants of people from those countries who had fought alongside Britain. You can take my word for it – I am one of them.

Earlier I asked a question about why British nationality didn't have a transitive property. If my parents were both born British subjects, why didn't the same apply to me? The answer is: if, as British subjects they had been white, it probably would have.

I got my first big chance to appear on UK television when I was invited to be interviewed on Channel 4 News. I appeared alongside the writer and journalist Afua Hirsch, and the host that evening was that national treasure, broadcaster Krishnan Guru-Murthy. Our three Brown faces appearing together on camera made quite the statement about what it meant to be British before any of us had even spoken a word. We were gathered together to talk about a newly unveiled sculpture representation of Cheddar Man, modelled using new data extracted from his DNA. Cheddar Man is the name given to a ten-thousand-year-old human skeleton discovered during the draining of Gough's Cave in Cheddar Gorge in 1903. Since the discovery, Cheddar Man has been widely acknowledged to be the oldest known inhabitant of the British Isles (they lived here, in fact, several millennia before anyone even called them British). The story was big news because this new model presented quite the break with tradition as Cheddar Man, it turned out, was Black. Or, perhaps more to the point ... he definitely wasn't white.

The model of Cheddar Man was made by a Dutch company called Kennis & Kennis Reconstructions – identical twins Adrie and Alfons Kennis – who specialise in creating reconstructions of ancient peoples. Informed by a recent research project that used the most advanced ancient DNA analysis methods to date, it's the bust of a person with dark brown skin, dark hair and piercing blue eyes, gazing off into the middle distance with a small, crooked smile that suggests they know something we don't. And in fact, such is the case. Look at all the previous models and reconstructions of Cheddar Man over the course of the twentieth century. While the styles of illustration and facial hair change over the years in line with changing fashions, the consensus had always been that Cheddar Man was white. Now, between the latest model and the DNA evidence, a new consciousness had exploded in the minds of the British public – their history and their own sense of self was not as they had thought it was all this time.

When Krishnan Guru-Murthy asked me where I get the sense that I am British, I made it very clear that my nationality was a matter of public record. Over a series of years, I had applied for the visas, taken the test, sworn the oath and got the teaspoon. If only it were that straightforward, though. The question, 'where are you from?' lands differently when you're not actually from anywhere. I could say I'm Indian, but most Indians find that laughable – anyway,

I've never lived in India for more than a couple of weeks at a time. I could say I was born in Abu Dhabi, but I'm not Emirati and I haven't been there for years (even though I could now easily go without a visa). Nowadays, the message that this is potentially a fraught question has filtered through, so usually people don't ask me and assume, on account of my accent, that I was born in the UK, which, I'm ashamed to admit, suits me just fine. Sure, I contain multitudes, but I can keep them all inside.

As the ripples of surprise spreading out from the news about Cheddar Man had shown, a key assumption about English identity is that it's predicated on whiteness. So, I can be British, no problem, because British suggests a broader, international identity on account of the Empire and then the Commonwealth. But can I be English? Well, that's tricky. One of the hallmarks of English identity is that it is the exclusive preserve of people that are white, and no amount of Shakespeare or Shelley, or forms filled in or passports issued, can change the fact that I am not racialised as white. When I first came to England, I felt as though I was coming home, but home was not as welcoming as it should have been. In the years that have followed, things have only got worse.

In 2022, as I was writing this book, the UK passed the Nationality and Borders Act. The powers of this hugely controversial piece of legislation are mostly directed towards refugees and asylum seekers, alongside a much decried policy that they be sent to Rwanda to process their claim (this policy was ruled unlawful by Court of Appeal judges just over a year later in June 2023, although the Act still remains in place and the government has been granted leave to appeal the decision to the Supreme Court of the United Kingdom). Aside from these horrors stands the fact that the Home Secretary now has the power to strip a person of their British citizenship without any prior warning.

While it's illegal for the Home Secretary to do this to someone who would then be deemed stateless, it's also the case that if someone is simply eligible for citizenship of another country this could be enough for them to be considered as safeguarded against statelessness. Let's stop for a minute and think about the kind of people this new Act could apply to. For me, this involves going and looking in the mirror. After all those forms, all those application fees, all that time spent in immigration queues, it turns out I'm still not safe after all.

For want of a better expression, the Windrush scandal brought the whole thing home to me in no uncertain terms. This was a series of shocking and often devastating revelations that hundreds of British subjects had been wrongly detained, deported and denied their legal rights. Many of them had come to Britain as children in the 1950s and 1960s, and their collective name – the Windrush generation – references the ship that the panicked Clement Attlee desperately tried to get re-routed in 1948. A creeping series of legislation collectively designed to create a 'hostile environment' for illegal immigrants combined with the fact that the Home Office failed to properly archive records of their arrival all those decades ago meant that people were unable to prove when they had come to live here and with no recourse to their own government in their own country.

You might think it's just how things go. You pick a country, you take your chances. From where I'm sitting, however, that's far from civilised. And besides, when it comes to nationality, there is another major factor to consider. If our idea of what a 'nation' is depends on shared conceptions of culture and identity – ideas mostly used to keep other people out – then it's worth remembering there is another common value at play here in the West. As we've seen time and time again in this book, rules are made to be broken if there's a good enough reason. And the best reason of all is money.

*

The Second World War was over in Europe by July 1945, but King Peter II and Queen Alexandra of Yugoslavia had other problems. Four years earlier, the King had fled the German invasion of his homeland and eventually ended up at Claridge's, London's foremost hotel for émigré royalty in exile. While Germany's nationalistic fervour had been stayed by the Allied forces, it now looked as though communism, rather than the old monarchy, was going to govern Yugoslavia. Unable to go home, but still definitely royalty, how could the King and Queen ensure the safety and legitimacy of their soon-to-be-born child, heir apparent and claimant to the Yugoslav throne? True to what was a well-established brand, British Prime Minister Winston Churchill stepped in to save the day. Through an arcane act of diplomacy, Churchill decreed that, for single day, Suite 212 at Claridge's would be deemed Yugoslavian sovereign territory. He even arranged for Yugoslavian earth to be shipped to London and placed under the bed where the Queen would give birth. As a result, on 17 July 1945, Crown Prince Alexander could safely claim to have been born on his own native soil.

It's part of the job description for historians that we have to ruin everyone's fun with facts, so I'm sorry to have to tell you that, to date, there is no documentation to prove that a suite in Claridge's became Yugoslavia for a day. To me, the story seems little more than an outlandish fairy tale, with its stock characters of royal parents in distress, saved by the generous whim of a national hero-slash-fairy godfather, through the magic of diplomacy. As far as Balkan nobility goes, the bit about the soil is clearly more Count Dracula than it is Franz Ferdinand, but still, it makes for a better story, doesn't it? On top of all this, though, there is something else about the story of Suite 212 at Claridge's that is of interest to us and our current topic of discussion: the nation. This is not the myth of his birth, but the lived reality of Crown Prince Alexander's life. Despite being born a foreigner, Crown Prince Alexander was arguably more British than he was anything else. His godfather was King George VI and his godmother was Princess Elizabeth, later Queen Elizabeth II. He was born in a London hotel room, went to the same Scottish secondary school as the Prince of Wales, now King Charles III, and went on to train at Sandhurst and to serve as an officer in the British Army. Add to that the fact that in 1947 all but one member of the Yugoslav royal family had had their Yugoslavian citizenship revoked, and really, what was left but a Brit?

The Prince was naturalised, that is, legally made a British citizen as if he were born here (even though he actually was born here) when he was a teenager, in accordance with a law made in the eighteenth century. Called the Sophia Naturalisation Act, in 1705 it allowed for Sophia of Hanover, granddaughter of King James I and VI to be made an English subject. The Act applied to all of Sophia's descendants, most crucially to her son George Louis of Brunswick-Lüneburg, who is better known to us as King George I. Luckily for him, it also happened to apply to her eight times great grandson, who happened to be the Crown Prince of Yugoslavia, born in exile at the end of the Second World War. Fate smiled once more on Prince Alexander when his Yugoslavian citizenship was eventually reinstated in 2011 by the governments of what was left of that nation: Serbia and

Montenegro. The citizenship ceremony took place, quaintly and completely counter-intuitively, at Suite 212 at Claridge's. When the Prince and his family moved into the Royal Palace in Belgrade on his fifty-sixth birthday, he told reporters, 'I started my life as an émigré, I'm very happy that as a family we can return home as citizens.'

It's not often that I find myself sympathising with princes, from fairy tales or otherwise, but there is something in the story of Crown Prince Alexander of Yugoslavia that speaks to me quite viscerally. That is to say, it bypasses my brain and speaks straight to my gut. It speaks to the hopes and dreams I have for my life and, particularly, where I want to live it.

With every new step on my journey to becoming British, from student visa to unmarried partner's visa, to indefinite leave to remain, to the Life in the UK citizenship test, to naturalisation, there was another day spent travelling to Croydon to stand in a queue that snaked out of the building at the Visa and Immigration Centre at Lunar House. If you have never stood in a queue applying for a visa that will allow to you stay in the place you consider to be home, let me tell you, it is unremittingly, uniformly and consistently awful. There is no escaping the fact that a group of strangers has the power to determine where you can or cannot go and where you can or cannot make your life, even if you've already made that life without asking them first, because that is how life works. These applications do not have a guaranteed outcome. At the end of them, seemingly on a coin toss of bureaucracy, lies your fate. You can do everything: meet the conditions, fill in the forms, pay the fees, take the tests and you can still feel that at any moment the whole thing could go west. All the while, though, I had a serious advantage up my sleeve. Apart from our longing to belong somewhere we weren't born, Crown Prince Alexander and I had one other thing in common that helped us on our immigration journey: we were both rich.

Before you get the wrong idea, I should say I am not royalty-level rich or super rich. I once thought about going to Claridge's for afternoon tea as a fun, tourist-in-your-own-city type caper, but decided against it purely on the grounds of cost (so, perhaps I am more South Asian than I give myself credit for). Still, I can't pretend that money was a barrier on my particular path to Britishness and, as such, the whole business was much easier for me than it is for other people who don't have the privilege of inherited wealth. Was I concerned that I could end up paying thousands of pounds on what amounted to little more than a bet on an immigration system that was infamously weighted against people who came from where I came from? Of course. But, thanks to supportive and generous parents who had made a good living as immigrants in a foreign state, I could afford the stake. For the super rich, these are matters below their consideration. They have enough money – along with the power and influence money buys – to buy what the rest of us dream of: freedom. A heady assortment of private jets, private yachts and now even private spaceships allows them to come and go, within the stratosphere or beyond it, as they please.

Researchers who look into the lives of the super rich have discovered that really rich people are so different from the rest of us as to almost – and I do not use this metaphor lightly – be a separate species. For the super rich, national borders, visas and international law are all very much things that happen to other people. In her book, *Capital without Borders*, Brooke Harrington gained access to the super rich by talking to the people they trust most: their wealth managers. These are the people that move the money around, that keep it safe from the threat of tax collectors and who are often the only people the super rich can trust. They also have an insight into super rich lives without necessarily falling prey to the disease themselves, and there is a lot they can tell us about how nation-states work at their extremes. Harrington tells the story of a wealth manager who arrived at the airport ahead of flying to a meeting in another country, only to realise she'd left her passport at home. When she mentioned this to her client, he told her not to worry about it. As is the case in general with wealth managers, she was happy for this to be her client's problem, so she made no further complaint. And, it turned out, none was needed. Travelling by private jet, she went to a different country, attended the relevant meeting and then was flown home again, all without once being bothered by someone asking to see her passport.

This one little anecdote is a parable for how money, and having lots of it, works in our world. For all that we would like to think every person on the planet is subject to the same laws and national boundaries, the super rich, in fact, live in a completely different place where the rules don't apply. Along with their money, they live offshore. It's a place the writer and journalist Oliver Bullough calls Moneyland. Bullough argues that, by operating beyond the law, the super rich are free riding on our society. In his book, *Butler to the World*, Bullough describes how social elites, often government officials, can easily travel to Western nations like the UK to access cutting edge healthcare in Harley Street clinics. They can similarly buy up houses in exclusive neighbourhoods like London's Belgravia in order to enjoy all the luxurious advantages and advances this Western nation has to offer. Bullough makes the point that while the super rich keep resources like healthcare and foreign properties, along with vast quantities of unadulterated wealth, to themselves, they deny their fellow country-people the same benefits. They also, of course, deny the same to UK citizens, keeping in place a two-tier health system that is the diametric opposite of what the welfare state is supposed to provide for all of us. Incidentally, going back to a previous topic, one way to safeguard what passes for democracy in the UK is to not let Russian or, indeed, any oligarchs have free run of the country.

Part of the thinking behind the increasingly exclusive and racist immigration legislation in Britain was the idea that Black and Brown immigrants were somehow scroungers, that they were coming to Britain from their savage homelands to take advantage of the civilised generosity of the welfare state. Inherent in this appears to be the idea of a scarcity threat – times are hard, resources are limited, there's just not enough to go around, Britain is full. In reality, this is a value judgement, and its message is plain: you don't deserve any of these things. You don't deserve to belong here. This is completely contrary to what immigrants from African, Asian and Caribbean nations had said they were coming here for: to work, to earn a decent living and also, importantly, to contribute to the joint project of the British nation. They may have been leaving their homes and families behind, but they were also coming back to the Motherland to play an active and valuable role here. Although the Sophia Naturalisation Act had been replaced by the British Nationality Act of 1948, it was still used to naturalise Crown Prince Alexander of Yugoslavia. How was this possible? It's a stark example of what laws apply to which people, and how, depending on your royal status and if your godmother happens to be the Queen – in other words, if you are hugely privileged – your journey across international waters is pretty smooth sailing.

When we look at how the super rich jet in and out of Britain, how they use British expertise to keep their money safely tax-free in offshore accounts and how they use their money to buy healthcare and housing, it's easy enough to see who the real scroungers are. Here in the West, we don't really care who you are, where you come from or what you can do, provided you can pay for it. Given that historical events mean the money was never shared out equally in the first place, really it's hard to see our current situation as anything hugely different or advanced from the Middle Ages and the days of Magna Carta, King John and his barons – there is still the one rule for the barons, another for the rest of us. Or, perhaps more accurately, there are no rules for the barons at all.

At the Conservative Party conference in 2016, in the wake of the referendum where, by a slim majority, British voters supported the decision to leave the post-national dream that was the European Union, the newly minted prime minister caused an uproar with a single phrase from her speech. 'If you believe you are a citizen of the world,' said Theresa May, 'you are a citizen of nowhere.' It was a sentiment that was much discussed, and, by many people, much vilified. May had meant to chastise the moneyed liberal establishment, people who, she claimed, 'behave as though they have more in common with international elites than with the people down the road'. For many of us, though, this was not a phrase that stood by itself. What we heard was framed by the knowledge that these were the sentiments of a recent Home Secretary who'd prided herself on making our nation a 'hostile environment' for illegal immigrants. As any immigrant, legal or illegal, sanctioned or unsanctioned, will tell you, the nation wasn't exactly unhostile to start with.

'Empires come and go,' wrote Stuart Hall, 'But the imagery of the British Empire seems destined to go on forever. The imperial flag has been hauled down in a hundred different corners of the globe. But it is still flying in the collective unconscious.' The result, according to Hall, was a populism that connected the white elite, middle and working classes together in a 'gut patriotism laced with gut moralism'. It was this populism that ran through the sentiments of some Brits in the aftermath of the Brexit referendum in 2016: *we* voted 'leave', so why are *you* still here?

For nationalists everywhere, the great threat is the rootless cosmopolitan, a person nationalists envisage as knowing no loyalty. They have no respect for the sanctity of national boundaries, national laws or national visions, however racist those visions may be. The rootless cosmopolitan, we are told, is only ever on the lookout for what they can get for themselves. This question of national loyalty is a poignant one and one that regularly resurfaces in different, generally spurious forms. In April 1990, Norman (later Lord) Tebbit suggested that immigrants and the children of immigrants could not be considered fully British unless they supported England at cricket. My position on cricket is that I would rather eat my own teeth than watch team sports, so, really, this would be a bit extreme.

The conception of what it means to be British is very clear. Those of us who were not born here or, by extension, look as though we weren't born here, have to demonstrate our nationalism, our fervour for the British nation and its endeavours in ways that people who were born here don't have to. The accompanying demand that that expression of nationalism should be generally positive, in the light of Britain's imperial past and the concomitant nationalistic disaster we have seen in this chapter, is something of a sticking point. We are asked to say that we support our country, right or wrong, having borne the brunt of all the times it has been wrong. This is where I draw the line. If I think what my country is doing is wrong, I'm not going to support it. I don't support the actions of a government whose determination to create a hostile environment as a racist reaction to a foreign threat, ruined the lives of so many of my fellow British citizens: the children of those early waves of Caribbean migration to Britain known as the Windrush Generation. My nationalism, or my patriotism, if you prefer, knows moral boundaries really more than it knows national boundaries, simply because for me the former are more meaningful.

If you see my questioning my nation as a threat, that may stem from a place where you think I don't actually belong here. Or, perhaps, more accurately that I belong elsewhere. This is the experience of many immigrants to Western nations. Provided we toe the line, everything's fine. Demonstrate, through a combination of historical research and lived experience, that all might not be rosy in the garden of the nation, and – suddenly – it's time for us to go back where we came from. This, of course, is tricky for me. For all that I was born and grew up on a desert island that, at the time, was in the middle of nowhere, from almost as far back as I can remember, I've always really been English. I am, I propose, a rooted cosmopolitan. I feel a connection to this place that comes from being brought up with a set of ideas, a vision, in fact, and imagined community. It also comes from having built a life here over more than twenty years. It just so happens that, by an accident of history and of civilisation, people I don't know get to tell me where I belong.

Chapter Eight

ART FOR ART'S SAKE

The making of art – be it painting, sculpture, music, dance, opera, theatre or some other kind of performance – sits at the pinnacle of Western civilisation. It is the climax, the apex, the acme – pick whichever Greek-rooted word you like, it doesn't get any bigger or better than this. Accordingly, the history of Western art is well-documented, and its story arc is much the same as the one we are already used to. It's the sixteenth-century Italian painter, writer and architect Giorgio Vasari from whom we usually get this story. Vasari wrote that after the momentary, archaic flowering of classical art in ancient Greece, things were a bit quiet until the rediscovery and rebirth – the Renaissance – of those ideas in Europe just over a millennium later. While people in Europe continued to make art in the form of religious paintings and illustrated manuscripts, by dint of its direct association with religion, this work is often, unfairly, considered 'bad art'.

The distinction between 'medieval bad' and 'Renaissance good' was an important one to make because the art of the Renaissance was seen as the fertile intellectual soil in which European thinkers could then sow and grow their Enlightenment ideals. In that sense, art was both the result of and a context for the growth of Western civilisation. So, the flat and simplistic religious paintings and icons of the Middle Ages made way for a more naturalistic style, harking back to the forms of classical

Greek sculpture. Suddenly people looked like real people, and gravity seemed to have a greater pull on their clothes. There were scintillating frescoes by Giotto and Raphael, innovative new styles of portraiture by Giovanni Bellini and Leonardo da Vinci, exquisite miniature sculptures in silver by Benvenuto Cellini, incomparable plays on light and shadow by Caravaggio, and, of course, anything by Michelangelo because he could do it all. Northern Europe had its own Renaissance, embodied by the drawings and engravings of Albrecht Dürer, the rich and symbolic portraiture of Jan van Eyck and the Bruegels, along with the intricate, surreal whimsy of Hieronymus Bosch. All of a sudden, as if by magic, art was more advanced.

Vasari also made the link that through all of its various incarnations, as true in his day in the Renaissance as it was through to modern art in the eighteenth and nineteenth centuries, that an artist's labour and the product of that labour had been funded by a class of rich patrons, for whom the buying and selling of art was a means of conspicuous consumption. This used to be the Catholic Church, or members of the European nobility. Powerful and influential families like the Medici and the Borgias bought and commissioned art not simply for its own sake, but as a means of consolidating their wealth, power and status, and as a means of influencing the culture around them. Patrons commissioned portraits and other works where their own faces could be painted into an image, thus conveying whatever message they wanted to project about themselves. They were, as such, part demagogues, part Renaissance-style Instagram influencers. Today it's the inhabitants of Moneyland who, having bought their fill of houses, cars and yachts can now afford to invest in ideas. Historically an artist's success depended on finding a decent patron. Today, whether they are a realist, an impressionist, a cubist, a surrealist or an abstract expressionist, that success is predominantly based on being seen as a safe purchase and a solid investment.

Even with the advent of conceptual art – the kind of art where anything can stand as art – the story remains much the same. In fact, if anything, it has ended up at its most extreme and logical endpoint. Conceptual art is said to have been born when the French artist Marcel Duchamp submitted a porcelain urinal to a show of independent artists in New York in 1917. The urinal was turned on its side, daubed with a signature in dribbly black paint and christened *Fountain*. Historically speaking *Fountain* was a non-event. The original artwork hasn't survived (anything you've seen on display is a cast based on photographs of the original) and it was rejected by the Society of Independent Artists for their exhibition because they found it so outrageous (despite having expressly stated no artwork would be turned away on this account), and its creator has been contested. Some theories suggest it was made by one of two women who were friends of Duchamp, including the avant-garde performance artist Baroness Elsa von Freytag-Loringhoven. Despite this, Duchamp's 'readymades' – the pre-existing, often prefabricated or mass-produced everyday objects he turned into art – gained popularity in the art world during the 1950s and 1960s. By 2004, five hundred artists and historians voted *Fountain* 'the most influential artwork of the 20th century', cementing the status of conceptual art, along with decades' worth of '*modern art is taking the piss*'-based jokes. *Fountain* is as good an example as any to show that the definition of what art is – or if an artwork is any good, ground-breaking or shocking – really doesn't matter. It's about what certain people say and what they believe to be true.

For many art collectors in the late nineteenth and early twentieth centuries – who were building their collections at the same time as anthropologists and archaeologists were developing their ideas about what it means to be civilised – art also served a wider purpose: it was all about the greater social good. One notable art collector who clearly laid out his social mission was Samuel Courtauld, the English industrialist whose fortune grew after his family's company acquired the patent for the synthetic fibre rayon. Courtauld was an unusual capitalist in that he showed the makings of a conscience. Industrial capitalism, he believed, was ruining the world by diminishing working people. The system, as he saw it, was turning them into drones, mere cogs in a capitalist machine. Rather than do anything to change the system that guaranteed his own considerable income or to redistribute that wealth, Courtauld pulled on the mantle of cultural responsibility, commenting:

> Those whom fortune favours should use their money not only for their own natural enjoyment, but to advance the course of civilisation, and art is the most uniformly civilising influence which mankind has ever known. It is universal and eternal. It ties race to race, and epoch to epoch, and unites men in one all-embracing, disinterested pursuit.

This is a definition of art that seems familiar. It holds that, to varying degrees, art addresses people's inner lives. Art speaks to our souls. It speaks to what makes us human, not simply consumers of material culture but living, breathing, thinking and feeling beings. The point of painting is for painting itself. Art is for art's sake alone.

Courtauld was good to his word. Even today, anyone who can afford the price of entry and travel to London can go and look at the substantial and impressive collection of Impressionist and other artworks that he amassed at the Courtauld Gallery. The fact that the gallery reopened in 2021 following a multimillion pound makeover, including money from the National Lottery, goes to show that Courtauld's idea about the value of art maintains its social value in our society today. In this chapter, I want to take a closer look at this idea of art being the height of civilisation, of art having a civilising influence and, above all, about art being for art's sake. It's Courtauld's ideas about art as 'all-embracing' and 'disinterested' that I'm particularly struck by, mostly because they are so wrong as to appear naive. Art in the West has never been disinterested, far from it. And as for being 'all-encompassing', well, by now we should know better than to trust in a Western conception of universalism. It doesn't take much to look at the art world – that strange and, for most of us, arcane and far-off land where artists, curators, art dealers and, most importantly, their patrons live – for us to see that art as an idea is inherently both material and divisive. The question we need to look at is not so much about what constitutes the meaning of art, but, as with so many of the ideas in this book, who gets to decide?

*

The best time to look at the art world to try to understand it is when it wobbles. Luckily for us, it wobbles fairly frequently. Have a look on your viewing platform of choice, and odds are you will find at least one if not several documentaries about 'a huge scandal that shook the art world'. This is because the art world is easily shaken. One reason for this is it is a relatively small place, made up of only a few tens of thousands of people who have come to seek their fortune. For those of us who don't inhabit it (and statistically speaking that's a lot of us), the world of art and of art history may seem insular and self-referential, and, perhaps, with good reason. It is, by definition, exclusive. If you are an artist, you have to demonstrate your saleability, and if you are a dealer or a buyer, you have to demonstrate your class. Unlike other luxury, high-status objects that can be bought anonymously, the wealth of art dealers and art buyers rests on their reputation. Before any money can be exchanged, trust must be established. In a world where a fake could lose you your fortune, this makes perfect sense. It is also the case, however, that this heady combination of money, reputation and worshipping at the altar of authenticity makes the art world vulnerable. One of the best examples of this is also one of the most expensive.

In 2017, a painting that had recently been attributed to the genius artist and all-round Renaissance superstar Leonardo da Vinci was sold at auction for four hundred and fifty million dollars, making it the most expensive painting ever sold. This was an amount so astronomical that even some art critics seemed to find it offensive. Peter Schjeldahl at the *New Yorker* wrote, 'Four hundred and fifty million dollars spent for anything short of a next-generation strategic bomber, let alone a beat-up old painting, not only makes no sense relative to current markets in worldly goods; it suggests that money has become worthless.' This is quite a statement to make in the context of the art market, one billed as 'unlike any other' but which, nonetheless, works in much the same way as the market in other luxury goods, be it the latest in smartphones, televisions, furniture or cars. It only seems extraordinary when we are reminded of the astonishing amounts some people are willing to spend on what, at the end of the day, is a 'beat-up' old painting.

The painting in question was called *Salvator Mundi*, which means 'Saviour of the World'. It's a conventional front-on portrait of Jesus Christ, whose contrasting combo of sombre eyes and half-smiling mouth evoke the *Mona Lisa*, Leonardo's most famous work, generally acknowledged to be the most famous painting in the world. *Salvator Mundi* is a portrayal of Jesus strongly in the European mould, with wavy brown hair and light-coloured eyes. He holds a crystal ball in his left hand and holds up the first two fingers of his right hand in a benediction. His gaze is, admittedly, a bit bovine, but the overall serenity of his expression is highly soothing. Here is Christ in laid-back surfer mode. He looks as though he could save all of the world's souls and still be able to make you a decent flat white.

Salvator Mundi had not always been an earth-shatteringly expensive painting. When it was bought by a consortium of art dealers at an auction in New Orleans in 2005, they paid a mere $1,175 for it. It was only when the painting was being restored – an extremely involved process of removing previous conservation work, scraping off overpainting, removing a wormwood-infested panel and repairing the breaks in the wood – that the art restorer Dianne Dwyer Modestini started to think there was more to this painting than first met the untrained eye. For a start, she uncovered an original sketch underneath the layers of paint, suggesting this was an original work, not a copy. Modestini has also talked about how, as she continued to work on the piece, the perfection of the painting of Christ's smile in *Salvator Mundi* strongly brought to mind *Mona Lisa*. This was enough to convince her that not only was this an original painting, but also was by the hand of Leonardo. A group of five experts, including some acknowledged to be leading scholars on the work of Leonardo, agreed with this assessment after meeting in a closed room at the National Gallery in London. This was where, from November 2011 to February 2012, the painting was displayed in an exhibition called 'Leonardo da Vinci: Painter at the Court of Milan', labelled as the work of the master. The exhibition cemented the painting's reputation as a genuine Leonardo and was the key marker of its rising value in the run-up to the groundbreaking Christie's sale in 2017. Here it was billed as 'the male Mona Lisa', presumably to soften the Christian connotations of the painting for the international markets, particularly the potential Chinese and Arabic ones.

The tactic seemed to work, as the eventual buyer of the painting was soon reported to be Badr bin Abdullah bin Mohammed bin Farhan al-Saud, a Saudi Arabian prince variously alleged to be working on behalf of Abu Dhabi's Department of Culture and Tourism or Crown Prince Mohammed of Saudi Arabia. A few weeks after the sale, the Louvre Abu Dhabi tweeted its plans to have the painting on display. Then came the four hundred-and-fifty-million-dollar wobble. The art world wobbles when the arbitrary nature of authenticity is exposed to the cold light of day. How do we know anything is real? Because we trust the experts who tell us so. Sometimes, though, those experts can make mistakes that can have serious repercussions as to the value of the artworks in question. Like Wile E. Coyote, the *Looney Tunes* character running off the edge of a cliff, the trick in avoiding falling is to not look down. What happened in the aftermath of the Christie's sale of *Salvator Mundi* was that the art world looked down and was nearly knocked off balance by what it saw.

Despite the authentication by the five experts, and the stamp of approval from the National Gallery, the authorship of the painting was called into doubt. Experts in the field agreed it was likely the work of assistants in Leonardo's workshop, but not

– crucially for its now monumentally high price – the sole work of the hand of the master himself. The Louvre Abu Dhabi tweeted that its plans had changed, that the exhibition was being postponed and, to all intents and purposes, the painting disappeared. While rumours circulated that it was on a luxury yacht belonging to the Crown Prince of Saudi Arabia, sailing on the Red Sea, the odds are that it is most likely in an art storage warehouse, probably in Switzerland.

It's important to point out that in the general order of things, this is not unusual. Much of the art bought and sold in the world today ends up in storage, often in purpose-built warehouses in duty-free zones where they continue to be an asset to their owners without having to lose money through tax. Canny art buyers may consolidate their purchases by lending their artworks to museums. This has the double advantage of saving money on storage and insurance, and at the same time, as was the case with *Salvator Mundi*, gaining the sheen of authenticity on account of having been in a museum. Museums, in fact, are key players in the art world. As was the case with the National Gallery, being on display can be seen as a mark of authentication and affirmation. Being painted by Leonardo da Vinci elevated *Salvator Mundi* from that beat-up old painting to something on a whole other level. The name Leonardo, just as with Michelangelo and the other Ninja Turtles, carries a certain cachet. It is not a coincidence that the artists we have all heard of, from school or TV documentaries, from Vincent van Gogh to Pablo Picasso and Andy Warhol are also the artists whose work sells the most reliably in the art market today.

It may well be that the five people who authenticated *Salvator Mundi* as the sole work of Leonardo (as opposed to a studio work under his supervision, which is also an acknowledged category) were sincere in their judgement – in fact, I have no reason to doubt they were. It's not their fault the system of the art world rests entirely on our belief of experts, and the fact that the only way any of us can know if an artwork is 'real' is to take on trust what we are told. While it was socially transgressive to laugh at the fairy tale emperor swindled into buying non-existent new clothes, nobody would think twice if they heard the emperor had new art.

As for a Louvre in Abu Dhabi, you could have knocked me over with a feather when I heard the news that there was going to be one. When I first came to London, hardly anyone had even heard of Abu Dhabi. When I told them it was the capital of the United Arab Emirates, all I got was blank stares. I took to saying, 'It's in the Middle East – go to Iraq and turn left.' Even when the neighbouring Emirate of Dubai made a name for itself as an international holiday destination, there remained an assumption that, altogether, the country was a cultural desert as well as a literal one. But in the same way that the UAE's first President, Sheikh Zayed Bin Sultan Al Nahyan, built the infrastructure to ensure his desert capital bloomed, so his descendants, by the sheer dint of their wealth and ambition, were able to court and win the attention of the world's most illustrious art museums. It's never really been art for art's sake so much as it has been art for money's sake.

For the moment, *Salvator Mundi* remains disappeared. Whether or not it is, in fact, the sole work of a Renaissance genius, or something said Renaissance genius occasionally checked over while his assistants painted it, remains a question unanswered. What is more interesting to me, though, is how the situation is now spoken about. You don't have to look very far to see the lingering colonialism of the art world. Take, for example, what the art critic and historian

Ben Lewis said, unchallenged, on the BBC Radio 4 arts and culture review programme *Front Row*. Lewis is the author of *The Last Leonardo*, a meticulously researched account of the story of *Salvator Mundi* from Leonardo's studio, its loss and recovery and its journey up the price scale through a series of auctions to becoming the most expensive painting ever sold. When asked about the whereabouts of the painting after its last, record-breaking sale, Lewis replied that it was likely in Switzerland. He then went on to say, 'People generally think it's owned by the Saudis, and, I mean, I'm tempted to say that it's the Saudis' latest political prisoner – let's hope they don't behead it.' I don't know why I continue to be surprised at how blatant anti-Arab sentiment can be, but in a way I'm grateful that Lewis' message in that particular interview is so clear as to so easily make my point. For Lewis, and others, it appears the situation is simple: Louvre or no Louvre, when it comes down to it, the Saudis are still the barbarians at the gate of the civilised art world. They can't be trusted to take proper care of important art, even if, increasingly, they are the only ones who can afford to buy it.

For me, an earlier lesson about the persistent threat of the non-West came in March 2001, when, having previously tried to do the job with artillery and tank fire, the Taliban resorted to using dynamite to blow up two monumental statues of the Buddha in Afghanistan's Bamiyan Valley. I was in the second year of my archaeology degree at the time, and that week it felt as though hardly anyone in the whole department wanted to talk about anything else. There was much wringing of hands and much clutching of Birkenstocks. By the time our Public Archaeology seminar had rolled around, I was reaching the end of my rope. A mandatory course in the degree, Public Archaeology was designed to provide an important grounding in both the history and the practice of the public understanding of archaeology. It was a popular course, given that most of my classmates had chosen to study archaeology because they were massive fans of *Time Team* or Indiana Jones or both. (I very nearly chose to study Egyptian Archaeology on the strength of the 1999 version of *The Mummy* alone.) We also learned about the political aspects of archaeology, and how the discipline was often co-opted in the interests of nation building. From the German philologist Gustaf Kossinna, whose ideas about the Indo-European origins of German culture were a direct influence on the Nazis, to the destruction of the Babri Masjid by Hindu nationalists, we learned about the many ways in which an imagined past had been used to justify the present, often with pretty disastrous results.

That week, as we traipsed into class, we all knew exactly what the topic of discussion was going to be without having to be told. I also knew that I couldn't face it. For that whole week, the relentless obsession, despair and outrage about the Bamiyan Buddhas had brought home a sad truth. When I had first come to London, it was clear that news on an international scale was not something that happened here. Unlike in Abu Dhabi where UK and US news featured regularly in the headlines, in the UK a military coup in Pakistan the previous summer had gone almost completely unmentioned. The same was true about much of what had been happening in neighbouring Afghanistan for the previous three years. The news about the Bamiyan Buddhas, though, made the headlines quite spectacularly. Footage of the blast, filmed by Western journalists specially invited for the occasion, was played over and over again in the news for what I assume was emphasis. The same thing would happen a hundredfold six months later, with footage of the Al Qaeda attacks on New York's Twin Towers. All eyes are on civilisation when it's seen to be under attack. So, I realised, it wasn't that people in the UK were unaware of what was going on in Afghanistan, it was just that, for the most part, they didn't care. They didn't care about the lives of everyday Afghan people thrown into chaos and disorder, about people forced to flee their homes or live under an oppressive new regime. Afghan women, if their husbands had died, were forbidden from going out to work in order to be able to feed their children. It was altogether a completely barbaric situation.

Once they had blown up the Buddhas, though, the Taliban had everyone's attention. I just could not face it. So, before our lecturer had a chance to draw breath, I said that if we were going to be talking about the Bamiyan Buddhas, I was going to leave. My seminar group might not think the oppression of the Afghan people was as important as the destruction of some thousand-year-old dead and gone statues, but I was not going to be a party to it. While he clearly had not seen this coming, to his credit, our lecturer took me seriously. 'All right,' he said, 'in that case, let's talk about the Parthenon Marbles.' This had the benefit of being a much more local problem. The British Museum, where the Marbles are on display, was spitting distance from where we were sitting in Bloomsbury. A well-placed trebuchet on the roof the archaeology building, and we could probably have broken one of its windows. In retrospect, given everything I now know about the history of Greek sculpture and white supremacy, this wasn't necessarily the step change it could have been, but I appreciate the general sentiment, nonetheless.

Whatever happens in the art world, be it a scandal on the inside or dynamite from the outside, one thing is clear. Art in the West is what the West says it is, and it's only in the West that art can be properly taken care of. There is a violence inherent in this idea of care, one that plays out within the walls of another bastion of Western civilisation – the museum. As *Salvator Mundi* and other art scandals have shown, in a cult of authenticity, the authenticator is king. Museums have been in the business of dividing fake from fortune, right from wrong, civilised from uncivilised for a very long time.

*

Museums are nothing new. Some of the earliest known museums were in ancient Egypt, such as the Pharaoh Amenophis III's collection of flora and fauna. There are records of early collections from Shang Dynasty China, the classical Greek and Roman world, the early Islamic states and through to medieval and Renaissance Europe. Renaissance collections are often called 'princely collections', and they closely resemble how art is consumed today, with specially designated rooms in royal palaces, their walls crammed full of paintings or galleries full to the brim with classical sculptures. They are the kind of places a culturally-minded tourist drags themselves around for a bit of spiritual self-improvement while on holiday. Somewhere like, say, the Villa Borghese in Rome. As their name suggests, princely collections were the sole purview of rich noble families, who, through their conspicuous consumption of these decorative and inspiring objects, demonstrated their wealth, good taste and all-round cultural superiority.

It was during the sixteenth century that museums started to change from collections of objects displayed for pleasure and mostly aesthetic purposes to more scientific motives. These 'one of everything'-type encyclopaedic museums are the kind most of us are now familiar with, whether they are scientific collections of specimens like London's Natural History Museum, or national collections of art, archaeology and anthropological objects as seen at the nearby British Museum.

Encyclopaedic collections were based on taxonomy. They were a way of trying to work out the order of all living things in creation by placing them in a single room and organising them by time and space. One of the earliest taxonomic museums was the Museum Wormianum in Copenhagen, named for its founder Ole Worm. At first sight, illustrations of the Wormianum can be disappointing on account of the fact that it was not, as any reasonable person might assume, full of worms. Instead, it was a relatively small square room, with a black and white diamond patterned floor and an extensive system of bespoke shelves loaded with zoology specimens, both skeletal and taxidermy. The ceiling was hung with enormous preserved fish, and in one corner loomed a stuffed polar bear. What's interesting about the Wormianum, which is ostensibly a natural history collection, is that Worm also collected ethnographic objects. The Wormianum was one of the earliest iterations of anthropology as a specific discipline. At the same time, it was an iteration of objectifying non-Western cultures as 'other', as somehow naturally and fundamentally different from – and inferior to – the West.

By the nineteenth century, encyclopaedic museums became aligned with national projects. The British Museum, originally founded on the private collection of physician, enslaver and botanist Sir Hans Sloane, was the first ever national museum. Its neoclassical design, a rip-off of an ancient Greek temple, harks back to and appropriates the power of the classical world. National collections like those at the British Museum and the Victoria and Albert Museum in London were archives of the

British Empire, with its power rendered in three dimensions. One of the ways in which this was achieved, of course, was through the science of race.

While nowadays they are mostly safely tucked away behind the scenes, in their heyday Western museums were chock-full of human skulls. Many of these were 'gifted' to the museum by colonists at the outer edges of empires, some of whom picked through battlefield burials, looking for specimens. The remains of people from all over the world were collected, just as entomologists caught butterflies in their nets before pinning them into displays. The skulls were sent back to the metropole – the civilised, urban centres of the empires – where they were stored in museums. Shelves upon shelves, at the Smithsonian in Washington, the Natural History Museum in London and the Musée de l'Homme in Paris, were filled to overflowing with human skulls – washed, labelled and lined up by their toothy grimaces, ready to be studied.

The museum is a powerful and extraordinarily malleable cultural sorting house. They are places for demonstrating that the West is best, regardless of what the West has actually been up to. For example, when we hear the story of how Napoleon's troops in Egypt at the turn of the nineteenth century resorted to using dynamite to blow up a large, basalt statue of Rameses II, we needn't worry in the way we do about the Taliban. Even if they did blow up the Egyptian sculptures, Napoleon's motive was to get them into the French national collection. They would be safe there. When this attempt failed, the British consul general in Egypt, Sir Henry Salt, stepped in to do the job for the honour of Britain. Salt hired Giovanni Belzoni, a former strongman who had run away from the circus and eventually became an archaeologist in his own right. Belzoni managed to move the enormous Rameses using a system of levers and pulleys similar to the one the ancient Egyptians had used to put the statue in place millennia earlier.

If you walk through the Egyptian Gallery of the British Museum today (and you have to in order to get to the Parthenon Marbles), the monumentality of the objects is striking. Everything is enormous, as if ripped off the face of even more enormous palaces and temples, because, of course, that is exactly where they came from and exactly how they got here. In the middle stands the bust of Rameses II, cut off at the waist and with a hole blown out of the right side of his chest. The fact that Egyptian objects were now in European museums not only spoke to the power of Europe over Egypt, but served a narrative that the real cultural descendants of the ancient Egyptians and ancient Greeks were not, as could easily be assumed, modern-day Egyptians and Greeks, but the French, British and Germans who made the museums that now housed these objects.

Between them, European archaeologists and museum curators were instrumental in building up a harmful stereotype about Egyptian people. First, by having to 'rescue' Egyptian archaeology, they created the impression that Egyptians were incapable of taking care of their own heritage. In his autobiography published in 1931, the British archaeologist Flinders Petrie (who also happened to be a eugenicist and Francis Galton's protégé) described how: 'A year's work in Egypt makes me feel as if it were a house on fire, so rapid was the destruction going on. My duty was that of a salvage man, to get all I could, quickly gathered in.'

In her book *The Archaeology of Race,* the historian Debbie Challis outlines how new racial theories of the late nineteenth and early twentieth century, including some of Petrie's ideas, posited that modern-day Egyptians were, in fact, so racially different from the people who lived in the same land centuries ago, as to not actually count as their descendants. Petrie's ideas were tangled up with biblical history. He used the evidence of stylised portraiture in wall carvings and other artwork at the site of Amarna to argue that the Pharaoh Akhenaten, his mother, Queen Tiye, and possibly his wife, Nefertiti, were, in fact, of Syrian descent. Akhenaten is famous for having rejected the polytheistic religion of ancient Egypt in favour of his own, new monotheistic religion. By tying the rogue pharaoh to the Holy Land, Petrie made direct historical connections between ancient Egypt and the contemporary West. In short, Petrie argued that one of the most famous pharaohs in history was not of African descent, establishing the exceptional status of Egypt, along with all of the casting decisions for Hollywood biblical epics ever since. The Egyptian archaeologist Heba Abd El Gawad has described how these ideas were extended to imply that modern Egyptians were not the rightful inheritors of ancient Egyptian culture, and argues we need to reject these racist Victorians ideas that Egypt's heritage needed to be saved from Egyptians themselves.

Modern museums go well beyond dividing nature and culture. They also divide people into Western and non-Western in ways that make that division appear completely natural. The stories museums tell us go well beyond what we can see on display. They are not simply displays of things but displays of power. At the British Museum, the places and ways in which objects are displayed speak volumes. On the main level are the airy and spacious galleries of classical sculpture, from Greece, Rome and Egypt. If you are interested in looking at African art (notably, art from the whole of the rest of the continent not including Egypt), you have to make your way down to the basement. That is where we are headed for the final leg of our art appreciation journey. It's a place that illustrates another, perhaps more obvious function of a national art museum: as a storehouse of the spoils of war.

*

The word 'loot', the verb form of which means 'to violently rob, plunder or otherwise steal', and which as a noun refers to what is stolen, is the English version of the Hindi word *lut*, which means the exact same thing. It is a painful irony, given all the Greek we've had to deal with, that when we come to finding a word to describe colonial plunder, the British took one from their South Asian colonies. It is safe to say, though, that they made it their own. In fact, they virtually raised it to an art form.

In his book, *Small Wars*, Major-General Sir Charles Callwell quotes Field Marshal Garnet Wolseley as saying: 'In planning a war against an uncivilised nation ... your first object should be the capture of whatever they prize the most, and the destruction and deprivation of which will probably bring the war most rapidly to a conclusion.' By way of his military career, Wolseley is the Empire personified – he served in the Crimean War, the Indian Uprising of 1857, in China, Canada and in the Nile Expedition fighting against the Mahdis in Sudan. In 1895, he was made Commander-in-Chief of the Forces, the head of the British Army and it is a sad fact that, while carrying out Wolseley's instructions to the letter, the British military did not simply steal material goods from the colonies, they ripped the heart out of them too.

In 1897, the British launched what they called a punitive expedition against the Kingdom of Benin. Before the attack, it was an independent nation and a major West African power. As a direct result of the attack, it was absorbed into colonial British-run Nigeria (Benin City is now the capital of Edo State, in modern day Nigeria). The run-up to the punitive expedition is an object lesson in British colonial relations. It includes ambiguous wording in the written document of a treaty with a powerful local political leader – Oba Ovonramwen, the Oba of Benin – and the British reneging on that agreement in the interests of acquiring a greater wealth of natural resources, particularly rubber and palm oil. (Did you ever wonder why geography lessons at school were not just about the countries of the world and where they are, but their natural resources and economies too? Colonialism, that's why.) Then came the slaughter of a British expeditionary force whom the Oba had told to postpone their visit so as to leave Benin City in peace during a set period of annual ceremonial isolation. When the British consul James Phillips violated this request, he and most of his party were killed. In retaliation came the punitive expedition of five thousand British and African soldiers, one contingent on foot marching through the jungle, along with two flotillas of gunboats and warships that made their way along the coast.

The Kingdom of Benin was razed to the ground. All of its towns and its capital city were destroyed in a hail of three million bullets, fired from bolt-action rifles and a cohort of thirty Maxim machine guns – the most advanced and efficient killing machines (the 'next-generation stealth bomber') of their day. Then followed extensive looting of the capital city by the British forces, before the inner sanctuaries of the royal palaces, including the Queen Mother's residence, administrative and ceremonial buildings, along with the hundreds of houses of everyday citizens, were all set alight. Records show that eight British troops were killed in the attack. There is no British record of how many casualties there were on the Benin side. This was likely a deliberate tactic, as the British public back home had shown a clear dislike for the indiscriminate killing of Africans in similar earlier conflicts, including the famous Anglo-Zulu War of 1879. It's also worth noting the count of the dead in Benin included several hundred people killed on the orders of the Oba as a ritual sacrifice, in the hopes this would stave off the British attack.

We know there was looting in the Kingdom of Benin before its destruction because that is how some of the British soldiers described the amassed spoils of war in their letters and personal diaries. Then, of course, there are the many thousands of objects in museums all over Europe, and the word also appears on various archival museum labels and photographs. The British forces seem to have picked up everything they could carry, from large carved ornamental elephant ivory tusks to jewellery and ceremonial objects. Chief among these were the approximately one thousand brass plaques that were distributed to and displayed in museums all over Europe. Collectively, they are known as the Benin Bronzes. In London alone in 1897, loot from Benin was put on display at the Royal Colonial Institute, the Royal Geographical Society, the Horniman Museum in Forest Hill and, of course, at the British Museum in Great Russell Street, Bloomsbury, where a hundred or so remain on display today. They form part of the Africa Gallery in the basement of the museum. They are mounted in a grid display of eight columns across and seven rows down in such a way as they appear to be floating freeform in space. This display of the spoils of war, or colonial loot and plunder, made to look as though they are not meaningfully connected to the Earth is as powerful a statement about how these objects are seen in the West, as it is to their loss to Benin.

'It's like seeing your grandmother that you have heard so much about,' said the Nigerian artist and writer Victor Ehikhamenor. '[A]nd you eventually meet that grandmother and you find that grandmother is in chains, behind a cage.' Ehikhamenor is a world-renowned artist whose work uses the same traditional techniques that were used to make the Benin Bronzes. I met him in November of 2020 when he was part of the panel of speakers for the launch of Dan Hicks's book, *The Brutish Museums*, for which I was the host. Hicks is Professor of Contemporary Archeology at the Pitt Rivers Museum. His book, the source of much of the information in this story, was an important cultural landmark. It was the first time the curator of a European museum argued for the repatriation of looted objects, based on the detailed study of their own museum archives. Hicks's research demonstrated the crime of the theft of the Bronzes. It also addressed a point made by the activist collective Rhodes Must Fall Oxford, which works to address the legacies of colonialism at the university. As part of its campaigns, in 2015, they called the Pitt Rivers Museum 'one of the most violent spaces in Oxford'. The point of the museum, they argued, was both to house the loot and hide the truth.

It was during that book launch that Ehikhamenor said something that made me prick up my ears. 'Art for art's sake,' he said, 'is a Western concept.' There is no doubt the Benin Bronzes are art objects, in fact, their inherent technical and aesthetic power astounded the Western nations that so eagerly grabbed at the loot and put them on display in their museums. How was it possible, they wondered, that such a primitive and savage people as the inhabitants of the Kingdom of Benin, could have produced such complex and beautiful objects? The answer, of course, is that Western notions of beauty, sophistication and intellectual superiority – in short, Western notions of civilisation and white supremacy – led to a kind of wilful ignorance about Benin, about Africans more broadly, about all non-Westerners, in fact, that they all were simply incapable of such advanced cultural behaviour, no matter what the museum exhibits showed. (In the early decades of the twentieth century, the German ethnologist Leo Frobenius would insist the Benin Bronzes were the work of survivors from – wait for it – the lost civilisation of Atlantis.)

The idea is that art is for art's sake alone justifies the Benin Bronzes being on display in a national art museum. It does not account for how the descendants of the Kingdom of Benin see these objects as the embodied soul of their ancestors and relatives. Just like the khipu in Peru and the song lines of the Dreaming in Australia, the Benin Bronzes were sa-e-y-ama – 'cast in metal' as a method of remembering, history and commemoration. They are accounts of the long history of the Kingdom of Benin, its rulers, the laws they made and things they did. The Bronzes are not dead objects. It's true they are in limbo now, either in a museum's displays or, as with *Salvator Mundi*, hidden away in its storerooms, but their absence and the memory of their theft remains a gaping wound. They are people, and their people continue to feel their loss. The descendants of the Kingdom of Benin have asked for their relatives and history to be returned to them (the first official request dates to 1936). Save for a handful of notable exceptions that have made the headlines recently, their requests continue to go ignored.

The case of African objects in Western museums came into the international spotlight when a report commissioned by the French Prime Minister Emmanuel Macron was published in 2018. Compiled and written by Senegalese scholar Felwine Sarr and French art historian Bénédicte Savoy, the report revealed that ninety per cent of all of the heritage of Sub-Saharan African nations was in the possession of Western museums. Take a moment to imagine what that would mean in reverse. Imagine nine-tenths of the whole heritage and patrimony of the West held in storage in African museums. That's not only nine out of ten of all of the hundreds of thousands of paintings and sculptures in European and North American museums picked off the walls and shipped elsewhere, it's the literature of Shakespeare, Whitman, Voltaire, the music of Mozart, Beethoven and Bach, the history and philosophy of Hume and Kant – all of the figureheads of Western civilisation, blown apart, wrenched out of context and, most likely, packed away in storage. This is cultural imperialism on a monumental scale, and the continuing outrage of people from African countries in demanding their things back is understandable, because it is not just individual works of art that they have lost, it is their whole culture and family too.

*

When he returned two looted Bronzes to the Oba of Benin in 2014, Mark Walker – a retired microbiologist – found himself in receipt of an unexpected gift. Walker had brought back two of the Bronzes looted from Benin City that his grandfather Captain Herbert Sutherland Walker had taken to the UK. For decades, one of them had been used in the family home as a doorstop. In return, Walker was presented with a large metal sculpture, a stylised leopard's head (the leopard is the symbol of the rulers of the Kingdom of Benin). Speaking in an interview with the journalist Marc Fennell on Fennell's podcast *Stuff The British Stole*, Walker said, 'I was thoroughly embarrassed ... I didn't deserve all of this. I was only doing something I felt which might help with the wider problem of how we're going to reconcile our different histories.' This is a similar reaction I've seen from colleagues in European museums who have arranged for the repatriation of human remains. They are happy to host ceremonies in their museums, to take part in the processions and chanting involved in welcoming a lost relative home, but they often balk at the point when gifts (usually cultural objects) are given in return. Like Walker, these museum curators see their role as righting a historical wrong. They don't want thanks and they certainly don't want to be lumbered with more stuff.

But again, these gifts are not simply objects, they are gestures of gratitude and, perhaps more importantly, of reciprocity. The giving and receiving of things creates a connection between different groups of people. Historically, what was taken can be returned relatively easily. But what was lost between people is not so easily regained. The Cameroonian historian and philosopher Achille Mbembe has said that the 1897 Expedition and other European colonial disasters in African nations are so inescapably traumatic that, to a degree, Africans will have to learn to live with the loss. He also says that, by the same measure, Europeans will have to own up to the role they played in that trauma. Acknowledgement is the first step on the long road to reconciliation. The trouble is that in the West, we continue to hold on to our civilised ideals to the detriment of everyone else. The inescapably political position of Western museums is that the Bronzes have to stay where they are because that is where art objects belong and can best be taken care of, even if the museum continues to undermine their value as art altogether. The West continues to hold sway over deciding the value of art as well as the value of the people it has taken that art from. It continues to block the path that would allow for the cultural heritage of non-Western places to be passed down and feed the history and identity of future generations. To heal the rift means making an end to the division between civilised and *un*civilised, making a meaningful cultural exchange and connection. It's the kind of relationship building that requires everyone to come to the table with a level of parity. It's the kind of social interaction that is, in fact, an art in itself.

Chapter Nine

DEATH IS THE GREAT EQUALISER

The ninth of June 1832 was a dark and stormy day in London. At the anatomical school in Webb Street, in the borough of Southwark, the weather rattled the glass in the windowpanes. Inside, the prospect was no less grim. There, at centre stage in the crowded operating theatre, stood Dr Thomas Southwood Smith, looming over a body three days dead. The body had belonged to Smith's friend, Jeremy Bentham. First in life and now in death, Bentham was a famous philosopher, upheld as one of the greatest and most original minds of the Western canon. The attending crowd listened while Smith delivered a funerary oration over Bentham's body, commending his friend's bravery and dedication to their common cause. He then informed the audience that at the next lecture, in two days' time, 'there would be a demonstration performed on that body, of the anatomy of the lungs and of the heart'. Accordingly, on the eleventh of June, the anatomist Richard Dugard Grainger performed a dissection of Bentham's body. Despite being at Bentham's direct request, this was an epically controversial and illegal scene. And they were only getting started.

Smith's next move was to have Bentham's head severed from the rest of the body. He arranged for the skeleton to be defleshed and then reassembled around a metal strut that functioned as a new spine, holding the 'body' upright. The bones, even down to the tiny finger and toe bones, were articulated with wire to render the whole thing a sort of skeleton marionette, which could be posed as its puppeteer wished. This was then dressed in Bentham's clothes and padded with cotton wool, wood wool, hay, straw and paper ribbon, in order to render the most lifelike effect. Things did not proceed so smoothly in this regard when it came to preserving Bentham's head. Bentham had been 'full of the notion of having his head preserved in the style of the New Zealanders', a practice known as *mokomokai*. Unfortunately for Bentham, New Zealanders were thin on the ground in Georgian London, and the job to preserve his head had been botched. Smith and Bentham's other friends joined forces to commission a French sculptor called Jacques Talrich to model a new head in wax, and this topped off the whole affair. Posed in the attitude he took when he was thinking – seated, hands in his lap, gazing pensively into the middle distance – the work was now complete. The liberal politician and Benthamite Henry Brougham thought Talrich had done such a good job that the thing was 'so perfect that it seems as if alive'.

In the years that followed, Smith kept Bentham's 'auto-icon' – Bentham's fresh-minted word for a post-mortem self-portrait made from the subject's own body – in his consulting rooms, first at 36 New Broad Street and then at 38 Finsbury Square. When he retired in 1850, Smith gifted the auto-icon to University College in London, a venture in part inspired by Bentham's philosophy that higher education should be open to all, regardless of their religion. It is still there today. Should you so desire, you can go and see it in its bespoke display case at the Student Centre on Gordon Street, just down the road from Euston Station.

If you had visited a few years ago, you might have bumped into me. Back in the day, I worked with the dead. It was while I was curator of the Science Collections at UCL, which includes a pathology museum. This was a conglomeration of some eight thousand specimens of human remains, gathered together from the different teaching hospitals that now make up the UCL Medical School. My job was to make the specimens physically and intellectually accessible for teaching, research and public engagement at the university. That's what it said on paper. In real life what it meant was spending my working day – lunchtime and tea breaks included – surrounded by a varying assortment of human organs, preserved in fluid. There were cancerous tumours, skin samples ripped by bullet wounds, broken bones, kidney stones, brain haemorrhages, cirrhotic livers and miscarried pregnancies, all – by the time I was done with them – neatly lined up along the museum and storeroom shelves like diseased gems in a jeweller's window, waiting out their portion of eternity.

I absolutely loved it. Whatever careless assumptions and stereotypes I had about the job before I started doing it were soon dispelled. Saint-Saëns' 'Danse macabre' did not play on a constant loop in the background (although it was on my personal playlist for days working alone). The museum did not reek of formaldehyde, instead the preservative was a slightly viscous, slightly sour-and-sweet-smelling, mostly water-based solution. Rather than ancient-looking glass jars filled with alcohol, the specimens were mounted in perspex 'pots'. This made them lighter and, nominally, less breakable, and thus much more useful for teaching. The remnants of sometimes grim, violent and untimely deaths were not gruesome; they were abstract and quiet. In fact, the whole place was calm and also strangely mundane, tucked away in a forgotten corner of the Royal Free Hospital, off a dimly lit corridor. There were offices and laboratories next door, and the occasional lost patient wandering about the place. The ceiling leaked constantly and I was ankle-deep in emails. But all told, there was something rather comforting about working with the dead.

The eight thousand specimens in the UCL Pathology Collections were, by and large, unremarkable. They had been made that way. The whole point was that these were supposed to be standard representatives of different diseases. As such, the names of the people those specimens had been or had come from had been removed or anonymised, so all that was left was like an illustration in a medical textbook, only in three dimensions. Then, of course, there was our local hero.

The auto-icon of Jeremy Bentham was easily the most famous and the most misunderstood of all the bodies I worked with in my time as a museum curator at UCL. The thing is shrouded in myths, half-truths and ignorance about Bentham's relationship with the university (he was not a founder) and the auto-icon's supposed wide-ranging career (it does not attend or vote in university council meetings, and no one – I still can't believe I have to tell you this – has ever played football with either of its heads).

The auto-icon is an eccentric object, the product of such an eccentric mind, that it's understandable most people usually don't want to engage with it beyond momentary, bewildered awe. Gawp at the preserved corpse for a minute or two, and then it's time to get on with your life. Which is a pity, because the auto-icon is both an emblem of and a memento from a key moment in the social history of death and dying in the Western world. Bentham may have been an extreme character and notoriously cranky, but he also forever changed the way we think about death in the West.

★

Bentham's auto-icon quite literally embodies a rational approach to the dead body. I've mentioned that when Grainger dissected Bentham's body, he did so illegally. At the time, the only legal source of cadavers for anatomists and medical men like Grainger and Smith were the bodies of executed murderers, a form of social punishment that had been codified in the Murder Act of 1752. This meant that the scientist depended on the coroner to supply his work, and the problem was that there weren't nearly enough legal cadavers to meet the rising demand of the growing number of medical schools. The practicalities of the Murder Act meant there was a double social stigma relating to a body being dissected. First, there was disgust at the desecration of the body itself. Then there was the humiliation at the fact that it was quite unambiguously a punishment for criminal activity. For the medical men in their ivory towers, the solution was simple: bypass the irrational fears and concerns of the common herd and pay someone to rob newly dug graves, guaranteeing a steady supply of cadavers. These so-called resurrectionists were at the spade end of both the graverobbing trade and the law. If caught, they were the ones who would suffer the consequences. The growth of this new profession added yet another social fear of anatomy – the fear that you were not safe in your own grave. The situation became graver still when some people, most notoriously the Edinburgh-based murderers Burke and Hare, realised they could cut out the middleman and simply kill people directly, saving the effort and risk involved in digging up graves by candlelight. The Burke and Hare case was one of many causing a sensation as well as a public outcry in the early nineteenth century. Was there nothing to be done to keep people safe from the anatomist's table?

For Jeremy Bentham, a scholar and philosopher with a critical legal mind, the solution was equally simple. What was required was a change in the law. Bentham also turned his considerable intellectual energies towards the question of what it meant to be dead. Towards the end of his life, Bentham gathered together his thoughts on the subject, and these were eventually published posthumously in a short pamphlet called 'Auto-icon; or, farther uses of the dead to the living'. In this satirical work, Bentham suggested that preserving and transforming dead bodies into auto-icons would take both the sting and the stigma out of death. Those nearest and dearest to the dead person would benefit from having their preserved bodies close at hand. They could be wheeled out for special occasions or used to decorate the house and grounds, and the poor could keep hold of their money instead of giving it to the Church, safe in the knowledge there was no God or an afterlife to worry about. To his credit, Bentham was true to his word, as anyone can see today.

The historian Ruth Richardson has argued that another document that Bentham had drafted to address this question – his 'body providing bill', 'almost certainly provided the basis of the first Anatomy Bill', which was enacted into law as the Anatomy Act of 1832. The Act was passed two months after Bentham died. It provided for the licensing of anatomists (the first ever British legal Act to establish a national licensing body) and otherwise reproduced almost entirely Bentham's ideas about the unclaimed bodies of people who had died in hospital. Richardson argued that as far as the realities of this new supply of bodies for the anatomist's table was concerned, Bentham's ideas were markedly short of a social revolution. In fact, they actively reiterated existing social inequalities. While we in the West hold death to be the great equaliser, the reality here was that, as with so many things, poor and working people always have to pay a greater price.

Much of what was thought about death and dying in Bentham's England was about class. When the legal supply of cadavers was running low, anatomists paid graverobbers to commit the crime of acquiring bodies for them. It was only when the law changed in the late 1820s, making anatomists as equally culpable as the people they sent out to rob graves, that the men of the medical profession began to petition for a change in the law to supply them with bodies. It was also clearly the case that the fear of humiliation by graverobbing and dissection was not limited to the poor. It was simply that rich people could afford to protect their corpses by investing in break-proof coffins and the digging of deeper graves. Its supporters claimed the new Anatomy Act would be 'a step in civilisation, useful to all, but most particularly to the working people who would show their good sense and the decrease of absurd notions and superstitions by signing the petition in its favour'. They dismissed opponents to the bill, saying they had let 'passion and prejudice' override their rational good judgement. In this they did their opponents a disservice. The famous resistance to the Anatomy Act was not, as has been commonly assumed, the resistance of irrational, superstitious, petty minds. Instead, it stemmed from an understanding that the people who would suffer from it the most would be the urban poor. While the Act conceptually cut the cord between anatomisation and punishment, the reality was very different. 'What had for generations been a feared and hated punishment for murder,' Richardson wrote, 'became one for poverty.'

Between them, Bentham, the medical men and the legislators who brought about the 1832 Anatomy Act took it that some people were less dead than others. The idea of the 'less dead' was conceived by the criminologist Steven Egger, a term he came up with to define the victims of serial killers. These are often the most ignored – and as a result the most vulnerable – people in our society, be they sex workers, illegal immigrants or unhoused people. There's a general, unspoken consensus that the lives of these people count for less than the lives of others, a value that is set in stone by their deaths, which often go unnoticed and unavenged. For Bentham, sending the bodies of the urban poor who died in hospital to the anatomist's table was a price worth paying in the interests of the greater social good in that it would expand the body of medical knowledge. This was in accordance with Bentham's famous 'Greatest Happiness Principle'. The increase in medical knowledge, he argued, would be of greater benefit to everyone, the poor included, even at the expense of their own dignity.

Bentham's pragmatic approach to the law relating to death and dying was something that continued into the following centuries. Over time, the results were ever more rational approaches to death in every aspect, from medical treatment to bereavement and grief. So rational and so unemotional that it seems as though the West ruined death for everyone. A significant catalyst for this was the First World War, when the loss of life was so monumental it changed the ways in which people thought about and tried to cope with death. Soldiers were buried in makeshift graves, many of them unidentified because their injuries were so severe, and many of them never properly accounted for. As a focus for the grief of a nation unable to properly mourn its dead, monuments were set up as a way for people to channel their grief. At the Tomb of the Unknown Warrior in London, the burial of a single, unidentified soldier was made the focus for people whose loved ones had not made it home. The same was true of the Cenotaph, this time with a monument composed of an empty tomb.

The changes in Western death culture during and after the First World War were in stark contrast to the rich death cultures of the Victorians and the Georgians that had preceded it. The Victorians, in particular, are renowned as having been indulgently death-obsessed, with Queen Victoria, for whom the epoch is named, something of an icon for dedicated widowhood (even though many of her contemporaries felt she had fallen too far into her grief). The Victorians also, as they did with most things, combined death with capitalism. Widows mourned their dead husbands for a year demarcated by a complex fashion schedule, starting with wearing black dresses when the loss was fresh, then their colours getting lighter over the coming months until such a time as their grief was, for example, merely purple. This was also the peak of the fashion for mourning jewellery, particularly elaborate hair work plaited or woven out of the dead person's hair. They took photographs of and with their dead, dressed and posed as if they were still alive. The general idea in our modern society is that the Victorians were morbid. Really, it is more the case that our post-war consciousnesses are actually unhealthily death averse.

Towards the end of the Victorian age and on into the twentieth century was when death moved out of the house. What had been domestic, family or community-based affairs, often run by the women of the household, became displaced to hospitals and other more professional dying spaces, such as funerary homes. Alongside advances in the treatment of the body came advances in the treatment of the mind, and changes in the way people looked at grief. As was the case with so many of his other ideas, the work of the psychoanalyst Sigmund Freud shaped twentieth century ideas about bereavement and grief in highly unhelpful ways. We're going to look at Freud and his work in more detail in the next chapter, but for now it suffices to say that his 1917 essay, 'Mourning and Melancholia', influenced much of the way in which grief was seen in the twentieth century.

For Freud, the most important thing for a bereaved person to do was to emotionally process and 'get over' the death of their loved one so as to be better placed to build and benefit from new relationships. Freud framed this as happening in three stages: first, the freeing of the bereaved from their bond with the deceased, then, the readjusting to their new life, before, finally, going on to build new relationships.

It's worth pointing out that as a psychoanalyst, Freud did not take pains to help himself. When his father died, he was, unsurprisingly, devastated. In a letter to a close friend he said, 'My inner self, my whole past has been reawakened by this death. I now feel completely uprooted.' Thirty years after the fact, Freud also clearly still had strong feelings about the death of his daughter.

The well-known five stages of grief and dying as described by Elisabeth Kübler-Ross was a similar model to Freud's that has so permeated our collective subconscious that even Homer Simpson could run through them in less than twenty seconds (in the episode where he thinks his Japanese dinner has fatally poisoned him). The first of Kübler-Ross's phases of coping with death, either your own impending death, or that of a loved one, is shock and denial. The second stage includes anger, resentment and guilt. Then come stages three – bargaining – and four – depression, and finally acceptance.

There is something in both of these theories that makes them seem like a paint-by-numbers approach to death and dying. Again, there is an inevitable capitalism here – the idea that you can tick through your various different emotions in order to piece yourself back together and carry on with the business of being a productive citizen. Freud and Kübler-Ross no longer hold centre stage in the psychology of death and dying. Their once orthodox ways of how to handle bereavement are now thought of as potentially damaging and dangerous notions given that it seemed as if, for example, you didn't do them all properly, in the right order and all the way to the end, that somehow you were psychologically deficient. Nevertheless, death itself remains a problem to be surmounted in the West. In some ways, this seems to be a theme that goes a long way back, the ghost of an idea that has slipped through the rational revelations of the Enlightenment and continues to haunt us today.

In St Paul's first letter to the Corinthians, 'The last enemy that shall be destroyed is death.' The Corinthians hardly needed to be told this, as, since the third century before Christ, Greek medical men had been following that first great physician Hippocrates of Kos in swearing 'First do no harm.' The definition of 'harm', of course, is a movable feast, but it is generally taken to mean: 'kill as few patients as possible'.

Certainly, scientific advances have moved the counter along as to when death happens. It used to be when a person's heart stopped beating. Then it was when they stopped breathing. Now it is when their brain stops functioning. Western medicine, in terms of its theories, technologies and practices is so advanced that it can take a body submerged in a frozen lake for half an hour and, slowly but surely, bring them back to life. Here in the West, we have rationalised ourselves to death. Or perhaps more accurately, to one step short of death. In the West, we keep death at arm's length. Elsewhere in the world, the dead are closer to hand.

*

In Tibet, dead bodies are dissected as a matter of course in funerary rituals before being laid out for the vultures to eat. On the Día de las Ñatitas, the Aymara people of Bolivia pray to human skulls that have been decorated with flowers, adorned with sunglasses, or have offerings of cigarettes smouldering from their fleshless jaws. The Toraja people, who live on the island of Sulawesi in Indonesia, preserve the bodies of their dead in the family home for a year, to allow enough time for mourners to work through their grief and to say their goodbyes. It seems as though death brings out the creative spirit in us. Stick a pin in a map and the odds are – outside of the civilised West – you will find unique and elaborate death cultures and practices.

In Haiti, for example, the dead walk. Or they did, at least, in 1997. That was the year of a small, definitive and, to my mind, strangely ignored study that demonstrated the existence of zombies. The paper was written by Roland Littlewood, a psychiatrist and anthropologist based at UCL, and Chavannes Douyon, a doctor at the Polyclinique Medica in the Haitian capital Port-au-Prince. It was published in the British medical journal the *Lancet*, and runs to a mere three pages, but the whole of human life, along with some of the more interesting aspects of human life after death, is there. Now, I need to be clear here that nobody, least of all me, is arguing that zombies are real. Nonetheless, it turns out they do exist. Understanding how both of these things can be true is a challenge both helped and hindered by science, along with the ways in which Haitian zombies have been studied by Western scholars for nearly a century.

One of the first researchers to look into and try to understand the phenomenon of zombies was the renowned African American writer Zora Neale Hurston. Before she made her name as a novelist, Hurston had been an anthropologist. She studied under one of the most famous and influential minds in the field, Franz Boas. A German Jewish immigrant to the US, Boas was a founding professor of anthropology at Columbia University. Like most anthropologists of his day – crossing over from the nineteenth into the twentieth century – Boas believed in the concept of race, that is, of heritable biological differences between physically similar-looking groups of people. Unlike many anthropologists of his day, though, Boas was not a white supremacist. If anything, contrarily, he believed in the cultural sophistication of people supposedly lower down the racial ladder. These savages, Boas argued, were civilised too. In 1936, Hurston travelled to the Caribbean on a Guggenheim grant to carry out a study of Vodou (the Haitian religion more commonly known as voodoo).

Vodou was reclaimed as an official religion in Benin in 1996. It is a complex system of religious beliefs and ritual practices that were spread by slavery and that are found today in modern nations like the Dominican Republic and embedded in the cultural practices of the American Deep South. In Haiti, Vodou is one of the main religions and zombies are one manifestation of this system of belief. According to the precepts of Vodou, a zombie is created when a person's physical body, their *corps cadavre*, and spiritual self (a combination of their agency, memory and self-awareness), the *ti-bon-anj*, are separated by sorcery. The maker of evil magic, or bokor, is supposed to keep their victim's *ti-bon-anj* in an earthenware pot, where it is known as the zombie astral. The bokor can then keep the zombified person either as a personal servant, or share them with their friends. As a philosophy of self, the ideas inherent in conceptualising zombies are complex. John Locke conceived of the body–soul divide in the much the same way and he was a great Enlightenment philosopher.

Hurston's study of Vodou quickly zeroed in on zombies, and her 1938 book, *Tell My Horse*, included the story of a woman supposedly called Felicia Felix-Mentor: a woman who had died in 1907 and who had not been seen again until 1936 when, as Hurston describes it, she was found wandering naked in the middle of a road. The woman's identity was confirmed by her brother, her ex-husband and her son, who had been two or three years old at the time of her death. Hurston took Felix-Mentor's photograph and this was published in *Life* magazine in December 1937. It shows a woman with a broad and otherwise unlined face, glowering into the camera. Speaking in 1943 to the radio host Mary Margaret McBride, Hurston was clearly in no doubt whatsoever as to the existence of zombies.

'I do know that people have been resurrected in Haiti,' she said. '. . . There have been cases proven, where folks have been dead and folks thought they were done for and months later somebody finds them somewhere in some hidden place actually alive, but without their minds.'

It's equally clear that the idea of zombies and zombification, whether as the resurrection of a dead person or simply a reanimation of their corpse, is a metaphor for slavery. In its colonial heyday, during the second half of the eighteenth century, Haiti was the most productive and profitable colony in the world, with French colonisers reaping the benefit of coffee and sugar grown and harvested using enslaved labour. Hurston's own description, again from the interview with McBride, attests to the validity of this symbolism. 'A zombie,' she said, 'is supposed to be the living dead: people who die are resurrected, but without their souls. They can take orders, and they're supposed to never be tired, and to do what the master says.'

A zombie, then, is like a person enslaved.

Cultural historian Roger Luckhurst has likened the way movie and TV zombies walk to the shuffling gait of people in chains. Journalist Amy Wilentz has described how Haitian cosmology configured the zombie as a cautionary tale to keep enslaved people in their place. A zombie, missing its stolen soul, is stuck in limbo, unable to make the journey to heaven. The idea and associated fear of becoming a zombie was a way of keeping people from killing themselves in order to escape the living hell of slavery. Perhaps it's unsurprising that an obsession with people enslaved through sorcery or, indeed, through other more mundane means, plays out so plainly in Haiti. This was, of course, historically the first nation to outlaw slavery in an article of its founding constitution in 1801.

People have looked for scientific explanations for the creation of zombies. In the 1980s, a Harvard anthropologist and ethnobotanist called Wade Davis carried out a study of different 'sorcerer powders'. He discovered first a potent cocktail of frog and pufferfish toxins that could throw a person into a death-like paralysis, a nightmare state in which they were fully conscious but not able to move. Davis also analysed another powder that turned out to be made from various plant and hallucinogenic compounds, which could potentially be used to keep a person in a 'zombified' dissociative state. Along with the recipes for making a zombie, Davis considered the social aspects of the practice, too. Just as in the days of slavery, the idea of the zombie was a means of social control, a threatened punishment within secret societies made up of the descendants of people who escaped enslavement during colonial times. Regardless of whether you were or were not enslaved, the threat of enslavement, in this world or the next, was a constant source of fear and so by extension a way of keeping people in check. Davis considered that he had solved the mystery of the zombie, but there is another aspect to the story that's of interest to us here. Which brings us back to Littlewood and Douyon.

The 1997 *Lancet* article Littlewood and Douyon published recounts their research in Haiti. Rather than focus on the bokor and their intoxicating agents as Davis had done, Littlewood and Douyon followed Hurston's example and conducted interviews with the zombies themselves. For all that it is a serious scientific article published in a serious scientific journal, it's hard not to read Littlewood and Douyon's work as you would read an Agatha Christie novel. With each interviewee, they set the scene with a physical description and go on to tell the story of how the person became a zombie. As you read through, it's impossible not to try to work out – given that zombies are not real but they apparently exist – the true solution to the mystery.

First on the books was Wilfred D., the apparent twenty-six-year-old son of a Tonton Macoute (Haiti's notorious secret police), who claimed to have become ill and to have died years earlier at the age of eighteen. Just over a year and a half after this, Wilfred returned to his family. They claimed to recognise him, as did the people in his community, including the magistrate and the local Catholic priest. Apparently, Wilfred had been turned into a zombie by his uncle, as punishment for stealing coconuts. The uncle was tracked down and confessed to doing this, although the confession was obtained under torture by the police. Wilfred returned to the bosom of his family, but it was clear he wasn't the same as he had been before. His body was stuck in a twist, the lower limbs pointed to the left and the upper limbs to the right. He barely spoke and, when he did, it was in single words. His family kept him tied up to stop him from wandering off and they had to bathe him because he couldn't do it himself. Following a CT scan, Littlewood and Douyon diagnosed Wilfred with organic brain syndrome – a degenerative neural disease – along with epilepsy.

The second zombie was a woman called Marie M. The story of her zombification was similar to Wilfred's, in that she claimed it had happened after she died young, following an illness where her body had swollen up. It had taken Marie longer to come back. Thirteen years after her death, she had approached her brother in the market at Les Cayes, the public housing project where her family lived. She said she had been held captive by a bokor and had only now been able to free herself because he had died. Marie was much more lively than Wilfred in that she could speak and laugh easily and enjoyed physical contact. While Littlewood and Douyon found it relatively straightforward to diagnose Marie as having learning disabilities, her story did not end there. On a visit to Cabaret, where she said she had been held captive as a zombie, Marie was immediately recognised and claimed by another family. Another man was adamant that she was his sister and Marie recognised a little girl in the family as her daughter who, Marie said, had been fathered by another zombie.

Along with their medical and psychiatric knowledge, Littlewood and Douyon had one more diagnostic tool to deploy. In what was cutting-edge technology for the time, they conducted DNA tests on Wilfred, Marie and the people who claimed them as resurrected relatives. The results showed that neither Wilfred nor Marie were related to any of the people who insisted they were family. The only connection they were able to make was that Marie likely was the mother of the little girl in Cabaret.

So, there you have it. Zombies are not real.

A century's worth of scientific investigation, from ethnography to ethnobotany, psychiatry and DNA analysis has laid zombies to rest. And yet, they do exist. While they had proved comprehensively that Wilfred and Marie were not the living dead, Littlewood and Douyon found zombies to be endemic in Haiti, with reports of anything up to one thousand new cases of zombification a year. This, despite the fact that the act of zombification is clearly defined as murder by the Haitian penal code, even though the victim has not actually been killed. So what is actually going on here? According to Littlewood and Douyon, what was at play was a system of community adoption. 'The ready local recognition of zombies . . . and their generally considerate treatment,' they wrote, 'might be seen as an institutionalised restitution of the destitute mentally ill: recognition and incorporation of a zombie into a family provides public recognition and sometimes material advantage.'

While I can appreciate that two zombies do not make a summer, there are two things about this story that I just cannot move past. The first is the sheer open-heartedness of the whole situation. The idea that in Haiti, rather than being considered a burden on society, as is the case in the West, people with mental illnesses and learning disabilities are brought into families as long-lost, treasured relatives. The other thing is: how do we not talk about this more? Why is it that whenever we hear 'Haiti' we immediately think of earthquakes and the social disasters that make the aftermath of earthquakes worse – poverty, lack of infrastructure and investment? Why, when asked the question 'which was the first country to outlaw slavery?', do we look to Britain for the answer, when Haiti did so decades earlier? Why do we know so little about this place, not only as the beginning of an anti-slavery revolution, but also as the inspiration for a much more human way to treat each other? In Haiti, the seeming generosity of international aid and charity (used as a plaster to cover the gaping wound caused by colonialism) is nothing in comparison to the generosity of people who, we are told, have nothing. They are not out to catch the criminals, be they sorcerers or your more garden variety-type murderers. Instead, they argue and fight over who gets to care for the living dead.

Am I suggesting Haiti is perfect, some kind of utopian paradise? Not at all. It's highly likely that Wilfred's adoptive family accused his putative uncle of turning him into a zombie in order to get him out of the way and take over control of his land. Haitians have their problems, just like everyone else, and some of those problems are pretty spectacular. The Haitian demagogue 'Papa Doc' Duvalier used superstitions around zombies to cloud and obfuscate tens of thousands of political abductions and murders. To journey into zombieland is to wade into muddy waters. Nonetheless, I believe there is something for us, in the West, to learn from here.

In the West, the word 'zombie' conjures images of on-screen monsters. Like so many tropes of the horror genre, zombies are a vessel into which we can pour our contemporary concerns. They can symbolise the husks that are left of us as capitalism sucks us dry and leaves us as though sleepwalking into disaster. The zombie is a metaphor for social failure. When it comes to social care, the term zombie has been applied to people who need help, people with dementia or other neurodegenerative disorders. To us there is something about these illnesses that render people as somehow less than themselves. They seem to be some form of the living dead and, as such, are burdensome. We see the deficit as being with them, when really it is with us and the myriad ways in which we continue to fail each other. Death should be a place of communal care. The case of the Haitian zombies opens up what it means for us to keep the dead close at hand, and to care for each other in our society.

*

I have learned through bitter experience that there is nothing like a deadline to concentrate the mind. However, when it comes to the ultimate deadline – the one right at the end of our lives – it seems as though most of us in the West have barely given it even a moment's thought. After all, we are so busy. It is only on those rare occasions when our rapidly spinning world is slowed down by something like, say, a global pandemic, that we are forced to confront the reality – and the precariousness – of our lives and the lives of those around us, be they our friends, family or neighbours. The West has ruined death for everyone. From the Enlightenment on, the goal was to be rational about everything in this world, even, it turns out, the leaving of it. But, as you will know from your own experiences of loss and grief, death resists rationalisation. It also resists all of our attempts to do away with it. The doctor and writer Atul Gawande summed it up best when, in the course of his 2014 Reith Lectures, he said, 'We have no greater unfixables than ageing and death themselves.' Science is really no help to us here. The best definition of a thing that is dead, scientifically speaking, is that that thing is no longer alive. Death resists definition. For all of these advances, none can help us work out how to live with the reality of what it means to die. Or to work out what it means to live well in the first place.

While there have been significant strides forward when it comes to palliative or end of life care in the West, death predominantly remains a glitch in the matrix; a problem to be solved. The result is that more and more people die in hospital, sometimes in severe pain and discomfort, away from their families, all in the interests of eking out a few extra days of life. Gawande also said that, while he strongly believed that a terminally ill patient should be in charge of how to manage their own treatment, there was something disturbing built into this choice. 'In the Netherlands it's bothered me,' he said, 'that now the number of people who are taking the assisted death path has risen to about three to four per cent, and the number one reason is no longer unbearable suffering, it's become that people don't want to be a burden on the family and society any more.' Gawande made clear that the fact that people would rather kill themselves than let their illness be a weight for others to carry constituted a social failure. What we need to do, he said, is 'value people who are not suffering but in fact simply living, and by their living serve some worth in the world'.

In the West, the rational approach is to measure things. Over the course of this book, we've seen people try to quantify everything from hair colour to happiness. As Westerners, we measure our contribution to the world, to society at large, in terms of what we are able to produce, be it work, wealth or knowledge. In such a world, it is difficult, if not impossible, to take for granted that our simply being here is enough.

*

There were many days when I ended up working at the Pathology Museum on my own. The museum was at the Hampstead campus of the UCL Medical School in north London, and most of my colleagues were based further south, in Bloomsbury. Of course, our small team regularly got together to work on projects or sort out the museum specimens, but I particularly remember those days on my own, Saint-Saëns in the background, sifting through the archives or, more usually, moving specimens around from the museum displays to the lab and back again. I may have been alone, but I never felt lonely. How could I be when there were so many thousands of people all around me? The writer Hilary Mantel began her own brilliant series of Reith Lectures by reminding us, 'Saint Augustine says, "the dead are invisible, but not absent".' Maybe St Augustine had been a pathology curator too.

For me, working in a pathology museum was both a pleasure and a privilege. The human body, in all its wondrous forms, is one thing all of us have in common. Another thing we all have in common is that, inevitably, something is going to go wrong with that body to the point that it stops working altogether. Working with the dead brings a very particular insight into how we deal with death in Western society. For most people, death happens at a distance. Dead bodies are relegated and confined to very specific spaces: hospitals, mortuaries, funeral homes and, more rarely, museums. Of course, there is a practical reason for this, to do with hygiene and preventing the spread of disease. Another reason, though, seems to be that death is somehow better off out of sight and mind. Here in the West, we are not very good at talking about death.

I know this because it doesn't take long, when someone visits a medical museum, for the subject to turn to death. The museum wasn't open to the public because, to start with, we didn't have the appropriate licence. Nonetheless, we had lots of visitors: medical students, lecturers, consultants, visiting researchers, colleagues from around the university looking for information or inspiration. (Never mind *Salvator Mundi*. Leonardo would have loved a pathology museum, where he could have sat for hours, undisturbed, looking at all the intricacies of the human body he had only just started to uncover when he was alive.)

'Is it real?' is the question most people who work in museums hear most often. For me, though, the inevitable follow-up would be: 'Is it human?' It often happened that, in the course of what seemed like a regular conversation, the person I was talking to would pause, look thoughtfully at a specimen and say, 'yes, I had that'. Or 'yes, my mother had that'. Or maybe it was their aunty or grandmother or someone else close to them. It seems as though what people are looking for is a connection to some-thing bigger than themselves. Perhaps it's because the sight of death brings into unavoidably sharp focus who we are as indi-viduals and as a society: artless, stuck in time, and now such rational animals that we are not very good at living.

Sometimes whatever 'that' was got treated. Sometimes it didn't.

Whatever the outcome, there was always a story to tell, and a conversation to be had. Even when sometimes what I really wanted to say was 'Please can I sign that delivery note, I am ankle-deep in emails and I really need to get on with my day,' I would keep my mouth shut and listen. There was the delivery man whose nephew had been born looking just like that speci-men, all of the organs that should have been on the inside on the outside, but they did an operation and he's fine now. There were also my colleagues: the professor scheduled to have an operation for a peptic ulcer, in two minds as to whether to look at the relevant specimen before or after her surgery. And there was my friend, her back to me and her whole body shaking with grief at the sight of the skull of a child who had died of hydrocephalus (also known as water on the brain), just like her little baby daughter had.

I had my own specimen story, of course. There is a genetic heart defect that runs on my father's side of the family. It killed my paternal grandmother when I was about a year old and then, when I was in my teens, it got my aunty and one of my uncles, and the day after I turned nineteen, it got my dad too. The disease may, or may not, be a teeny, tiny, ticking time bomb, inescapably locked into my chromosomes. Just as I can't see if I have it, I also can't see its counter, ticking off the time I have left. I could have a genetic test done to work out the former, at least, but given there is no particular treatment for this condition short of keeping well or a full heart transplant, I find myself feeling I would rather not know. I am lucky, blessed, privileged enough to enjoy the life I've got and not feel like I want to do anything too much differently.

When Dad died there was a lot of comfort in having a house full of admittedly very sad visitors, who made sure we had enough to eat and were happy for me to wander off to my room and shut the door. In the event, rather than stare at the wall like I thought I wanted to do, I ended up emailing my friends at university to let them know what had happened. The other thing I remember is a series of hands at my elbow. There was my aunty, not a blood relative but someone who has been there all my life, who watched me grow up. As I came from seeing my dad's body in the hospital, she took a tight hold of my arm and quietly said to me, 'You have to be strong now.'

222

Then there was my uncle, an actual uncle, although I'd only met him once before. He so closely resembled my dad – his eldest brother – that for a moment I wondered if death was even real. 'Don't look back,' he told me, as he took me by the arm and walked with me down to the river where we submerged my father's ashes. These are things that make a life too. Little moments in a huge grief, shared with each other.

Chapter Ten

WE'RE ALL IN THIS TOGETHER

If you happen to find yourself – as we all do from time to time – wondering about what you have done with your life and feeling a little blue, it's probably best not to think about the time Sigmund Freud wrote a book while on holiday because he was bored and didn't have anything else to do. 'One cannot smoke and play cards all day . . .' he wrote. As with so many other things, Freud was wrong about this, but nonetheless his project is of interest to us because, Freud being Freud, he decided to take on the whole of the idea of civilisation.

Sigmund Freud is, of course, is one of the most influential and highly regarded minds of the Western canon, credited with inventing the field of psychology pretty much single-handedly. Psychology is the study of the human mind, its workings, development and motivations and it has both been shaped by and gone on to shape how we look at individuals in the Western world. The whole conception of society in the West, from how someone is educated and how justice is meted out to them, to the degree to which they contribute to democracy and visions of nationhood, rests almost entirely on who an individual is seen to be. In many ways, the individual is the working unit of Western civilisation.

This is most apparent when we look at the history of the West. All the way from political and religious rulers – popes, emperors, kings and queens – to artists and the great minds of the Enlightenment and the geniuses of the age of science, the history of the West is told through the lives of great men or, occasionally when it serves, through the story of someone who is not white or not a man, for balance. The great Western values – life, liberty, freedom and the pursuit of happiness – are all individual values. Alongside this sits something of a paradox. While in the West we clearly hold some people above others in a social hierarchy, we nonetheless insist that the notion of equality is paramount, and that it should govern how we all get along. At times of crisis our leaders implore us to remember: we are all in this together. Despite this, concerns about the decline of Western civilisation tend to arise in the space where individual freedoms and liberties rub up against each other. 'Your freedom to swing your arm,' so the saying goes, 'stops where my nose begins.' Psychologists like Freud and his colleagues in the first half of the twentieth century set about answering the question of what makes us individuals. How do we come to be the people we are? Why do we act the way we do? How is our behaviour shaped by the circumstances and the other individuals around us?

Freud was a big player here. He shaped our understanding of what it means to have an ego and, through his invention of psychoanalysis, he elevated every conversation that begins, 'And how is your mother?' to the level of a science. Given all of this, it may surprise you to learn that, as far as the father of modern psychology was concerned, civilisation was a total bummer. The book he started writing on a whim while on holiday was a short volume entitled *Das Unbehagen in der Kultur*. Published in German, in 1930, it has since been generally translated as *Civilisation and Its Discontents*. In it, Freud attempted to uncover the root of happiness in an individual's psychology, and it is possible that he dug up more than he was looking for.

'The development of civilisation,' Freud wrote, 'is a special process, comparable to the normal maturation of the individual.' Freud was interested in what it meant for an individual to function within and against the overarching dictates of their surrounding society. Was it possible, he wondered, for an individual to be happy, given that they had to think about other people, rather than simply pleasing themselves? He concluded that the news was not good.

In *Civilisation*, Freud took his existing, pioneering psychological principles – the id, the ego and the superego – and added two more. He called them Eros and Thanatos, the lust for life and the death wish. As Freud figured it, a person could only really ever be happy for a few moments at a time because of the constant, seemingly futile struggle between our love of life and our equally strong desire for death. His calculations were based on the simple equation that pleasure equals happiness, but this only worked sporadically and unpredictably. Our desire for permanent happiness is doomed from the start because our bodies decay and die, our physical environment can be treacherous and hostile and our fellow human beings impose on us all the limitations of society. In other words, happiness cannot possibly survive at the hectic and dangerous intersection of the individual psyche and the wider, outside world. East is East and West is West and never the twain shall meet.

Freud may have been something of a gloomy bunny, and he may have written his book on a whim and without much reference to outside material, but *Civilisation* is nonetheless a classic of the twentieth century. Look up 'Great Books of the Western World' and you will find it listed there (alongside the actual classics, and works by Shakespeare, Dante, Goethe, Kant, Voltaire and all the other authors cultured people claim to have read). Yet one of the most influential books in the field of psychology is not really scientific at all: *Civilisation* is based on a very limited number of cases, Freud's own intuition and highly personal interpretations.

It is something of a cliché to say that all the things Freud ever wrote tell us more about Freud than they do about our – individual and collective – selves. That being said, it is difficult to look at almost anything Freud wrote and not come to that conclusion. His idea that there is an inherent death wish buried in the centre of our unconsciousness was one that he played out in his own life. For fifteen years, Freud's jawbone was riddled with cancer, likely caused by his habit of chain-smoking cigars. The pain got so bad that the simple act of opening his mouth was excruciating. A lesser mortal may have taken the hint, but, seemingly, the Thanatos was strong in Freud. He wedged his mouth open with a clothes peg and kept right on smoking.

For Freud, humankind was little more than a collection of base animals, trapped by their base instincts. The savage, according to Freud, is baked into us, so really what can civilisation do? The best we can manage is to try to remain as rational as possible and, feet firm, try to hold back the flood rising within us. In other words, all there is really left for us is to do as he did. You may as well wedge your cancer-ridden jaw open and keep on smoking.

Abraham Maslow changed all this. When it came to the future of humanity, both as individuals and for our wider society, he took an altogether much more optimistic view. Through his research, Maslow argued that personal happiness and fulfilment are not only possible, they are the ultimate goal of human endeavour. He didn't stop there. The entire purpose of developing ourselves as individuals, Maslow came to believe, was to contribute to the communal good of our society. Maslow is another revolutionary figure in the history of psychology, made famous by his one big idea. How he came by that idea – and how we came to know it – is a yet another example of the narrow and limiting confines of Western civilisation. It serves to remind us that, however much we might like to think we are all in this together, we would do well to remember that this particular game was rigged from the start.

*

Abraham Maslow's 'Hierarchy of Needs' – a schema for personal development usually depicted in the form of a pyramid – is an icon of the twentieth century. Even if you didn't study psychology at school or university, you will likely have come across the idea, which continues to get considerable airplay in human relations management theory and social media memes. The pop quiz in your email newsletter that promises to tell you whether or not you are living your best life. All those romcoms where the female lead decides she wants to pursue her joy (and for some reason that joy is always cupcakes). This is the guy who came up with the idea that makes them all possible.

Maslow first outlined his ideas for the hierarchy in a 1943 paper in the *Psychological Review,* entitled 'A Theory of Human Motivation', and he went on to describe it in greater detail in his 1954 book, *Motivation and Personality*. Maslow's Hierarchy of Needs is not complicated. In fact, it is almost completely intuitive, which is one of the most notable things about it. It's based on the principle that we are all capable of reaching the ultimate goal of human development – of being the best we can be – provided a series of more basic needs are met first.

Imagine yourself as the itty-bitty baby you were at the very beginning of your life. Your eyes are just starting to focus, you cannot speak or fend for yourself, in fact, you are completely dependent on the help and support of the people around you. Those people could be your parents, your parents' siblings or their parents – they may not even be directly related to you, but their actions have a real and immediate impact on your life. It's up to them to provide you with the basic level of the Hierarchy of Needs, your 'physiological needs' for clean air to breathe, food and water. Then, as you grow up, they can also provide you with what Maslow called 'safety needs' – basic things like clothing and shelter and then later still, as you grow older, more abstract things like the means to make a living.

With all of these things in place (at least to some degree – Maslow did not take an all-or-nothing approach to this), the next level up is love and friendship, the acceptance and general feeling as though we belong in our society. This makes sense, doesn't it? These are the sorts of relationships we feel are important to cultivate, and without them we can feel lonely and socially isolated. If you are lucky enough to have these, you can take another step up to build your 'esteem' needs, things like status, recognition, social importance and respect. This lower level of esteem needs still depends on other people, but with them you can propel yourself up to the space in the hierarchy where you build esteem for yourself, through self-respect and gaining competence in or mastering different skills or arts. These, finally, help us step up to the summit of the hierarchy: 'self-actualisation'. From up here, you can take a breath to enjoy the view before you start to work on or do the things that make you uniquely, incredibly, unforgettably *you*.

The fact that we metaphorically climb up Maslow's hierarchy means that his conception of the world is usually depicted as a mountain or a pyramid – something triangular, anyhow – with the basic needs creating a broad foundation at the bottom, and the other levels of the hierarchy narrowing upwards to the pinnacle of self-actualisation at the top. According to Maslow, self-actualising individuals are the exception in Western society. In all the years he worked on the idea, Maslow could never name more than a handful of people that he considered to be self-actualised. There was Eleanor Roosevelt, Mahatma Gandhi, Albert Einstein, Mother Theresa – and there was him. Some habits, it seems, are harder to break than others.

It's easy to look at Abraham Maslow and to think of Albert Einstein. For one thing, the two men resembled each other. If you look up Maslow online, the photo that crops up the most is of a laughing middle-aged man, his creased and jovial face framed by neatly trimmed hair and a moustache. It's unusual for the portraits of great scientific minds of the West to show their subjects laughing or as otherwise frivolous, so when I look at this photo of Maslow, I almost inevitably end up thinking of Einstein, particularly that iconic black-and-white shot of him, with considerably messier hair, sticking his tongue out at the camera. Both men were Jewish, both found fame in middle age and both were responsible for revolutions in thinking in their respective fields. In fact, in many ways, Maslow was something of an Einstein in the world of psychology. His innovative and unique research tipped the existing body of knowledge in his field upside down and shook out its cobwebs, much in the same way that Einstein untethered our understanding of the universe from its limited Newtonian bounds.

Maslow developed his hierarchy out of his interest in the psychology of human motivation. What is it that drives us to do things? And how do the people who achieve greatness get themselves there? The answer Maslow came up with was that high achievers like Einstein and himself were motivated from within. Rather than being prey to outside influences, they were finely attuned to their personal and individual desire to contribute to the world and their wider society. Their work was intrinsically worthwhile to them. It was an achievement in itself, not the means to anything else. Maslow's groundbreaking theory was the makings of a Western icon. His Hierarchy of Needs is a standard feature across the board in psychology and management studies textbooks. Unlike Einstein, though, we're more used to seeing Maslow as if we're wearing sunglasses. The world looks pretty much the same, but the light is polarised and its rays are all lined up in the same direction. It's an almost complete picture, but not quite.

What almost none of these books will tell you is that, in a world where we divide savage from civilised, black from white and right from wrong, Maslow's ideas came from an unexpected source. They came from the brief, but life-changing six weeks that Maslow spent as a guest of the Blackfoot Nation at Siksiká, one of the reservations allocated to the Blackfoot Confederacy, about an hour's drive east of Calgary in Canada. The absence of the Blackfoot from Maslow's more widely known story, along with how we lost sight of them, is a lesson for us on the limiting, biased and outright racist trappings of civilisation. It also provides us with a different view of society, of a more collective, rather an individualised approach to living together.

Maslow started out his career as a behaviourist. Into the twentieth century, behaviourism was the main school of thought that sat alongside Freudian psychology, and behavioural psychologists went about investigating the effect of the environment on the behaviour of humans and other animals. As a field of study, behaviourism was strongly positivist, that is, it took as its sole focus of study those aspects of the world and human behaviour that could be directly observed and measured. In other words, it looks like a highly scientific and a highly rational approach to psychology, in stark contrast to Freudianism, which laid its focus on the interior world of the human psyche. Leading behaviourists include the Russian Ivan Pavlov, with his famous experiments with dogs, and American Harvard Professor B. F. Skinner, who worked with pigeons (among other things, he taught them to play ping pong).

Maslow's journey to his big idea started out as a journey to somewhere completely different. To start with, Maslow was just like his fellow behaviourists. He was all about the science and his work was exclusively experimental. His work on animal eating habits led him to one of his first big ideas, which he called the 'salient appetite'. This was an appetite that exists over and above the need to be fed. Maslow also noticed that, in groups, animals created and maintained hierarchies and pecking orders, which were kept in place through the application of sexual power. He figured that humans likely did the same and set up an experiment to establish what he called the Social Personality Index. This took the form of a two-part questionnaire that combined a personality test with a sex survey (so maybe he was a bit Freudian after all). In analysing the answers to the questionnaires, Maslow found that those people who were more self-assured – those with a high level of 'ego security' – tended to have more experimental and what were perceived to be more outlandish sex lives. Conversely, those people with lower ego security were more conventional between the sheets. Convinced he had found an overarching and universal trend in human behaviour, Maslow started to formulate a theory about political power and sexual dominance. He felt that his idea was a significant innovation in the field, and that it was going to be his big break, academically speaking.

It was at this decisive moment in Maslow's life and scientific career when, having moved back to New York City from the University of Wisconsin, he fell in with a bunch of anthropologists. These were, thankfully, not your garden variety anthropologists, but the next generation of scholars following on from Franz Boas, a towering figure in the history of anthropology, perhaps somewhat ironically given his desire to raze the whole discipline to the ground and start again. We saw from his work with Zora Neale Hurston in the previous chapter that Boas rejected the racist ideologies inherent in the practice at the start of the twentieth century, insisting that the ideas of non-white, non-Western people were worth knowing too. 'I often ask myself,' Boas wrote, 'what advantages our good society possesses over that of the savages and find, the more I see of their customs, that we have no right to look down on them.' Boas developed new techniques of anthropological investigation, mostly geared around observations and interviews, and not presupposing things about the cultural beings you are studying before you get to know them on their own terms.

One of Boas' star successors was an anthropologist called Ruth Benedict. She agreed with Boas about the need for a fresh start in anthropology, one that, while still being systematic and based on real-life observations, nonetheless questioned the big ideas that, for the last couple of centuries, had been taken for granted. At the time Maslow had returned to New York and settled into teaching at Brooklyn College, Benedict was an established academic at Columbia. There she hosted her famous colloquia – gatherings where researchers from different fields would come together to discuss the different social questions of the day. For Benedict, the big question about Western society was about the nature of competition. In an age where Darwinian approaches to human society – that the strong prey upon the weak, that only the 'fittest' survive, that some people are some-how naturally superior to others – were dominant, Benedict looked to question the systems of thinking that kept social inequality in place. She said:

Now, more than ever we need data on the consequences for human life of different human social inventions. We need to know how different inventions have worked – inventions like the absolute state, or inventions like wars for conquest, or inventions like money. We have no longer the normative faith that social problems can be solved by an appeal to the eternal values. Eternal values themselves are suspect.

In short, when it comes to sociology and anthropology and their core ideas like, for example, civilisation, nothing should be taken for granted. There simply is no such thing as normal. Maslow, fresh out of grad school and riding high on the strength of the consensus in his questionnaire results, straight up disagreed. Competition, as he believed his research proved, was both a natural and inescapable part of human behaviour. Try as we might, at the end of the day, it's our inner monkey sexpots that are in charge, and they like to fuck and fight and win.

Benedict, who had spent many years of her career living with various Indigenous peoples of the Americas, knew different. Judging by what happened next, she also clearly thought that Maslow would benefit from the exercise of taking his head out of his arse and finding this out for himself. Benedict set Maslow and his research a challenge. If his questionnaire could truly deliver a universal result, then he should go out and test it in a completely different, non-Western culture. She arranged for Maslow to tag along with Jane Richardson, one of her research students, on a six-week field trip to live with part of the Blackfoot Confederacy. Neither Maslow nor Benedict could have known it, but those six weeks were going to change the world.

I learned the story of Maslow's time at Siksiká by listening to a lecture by Ryan Heavy Head, who has what is called a portfolio career. A member of the Blackfoot Nation by marriage, he wrangles rattlesnakes and teaches Kainai Studies at Red Crow College. Heavy Head is scintillatingly charismatic, knows every aspect of his material inside and out, and – a rare feature in academia – he can really hold a room. In one of his many public lectures about the Blackfoot philosophy that inspired Abraham Maslow, he speaks for two and three-quarter hours uninterrupted, the whole time with the room in his thrall. His expertise comes from a combination of lived cultural experience, archival research (including Maslow's notebooks, letters and papers housed at the Archives of the History of American Psychology in Akron, Ohio) and interviews with tribal elders who were there at the time. Heavy Head also met and interviewed Jane Richardson, Benedict's student and Maslow's guide, before she died, in 2014, aged one hundred and six, so, at least to some degree, he is able to tell the story from both sides.

The way Heavy Head tells it, Jane was not thrilled to have been saddled with Maslow. He ignored all of her plans and advice and barrelled headlong into his own research, trying to get the Blackfoot elders to give him answers to his questionnaire. In this, they were uncooperative. In fact, they outright refused to talk about themselves, or to compare themselves with other people in their community. When Maslow persisted in asking, they looked straight through him as if he wasn't there. Desperate for data, he approached some of the younger members of the community for responses, leading the elders to threaten to kick him out of Siksiká if he didn't pack it in. So, in the end, Maslow was forced to give up psychology and, finally following Jane's advice, took to being an anthropologist instead. Whatever he observed, whatever the Blackfoot were willing to share with him, he wrote down. He took on, in fact, that very Boasian technique for documenting the complexity of a different culture in their own terms. While Jane Richardson and Lucien Hanks, the third member of the expedition, were carefully making notes about the techniques, symbolism and philosophy relating to tobacco farming, Maslow started to look at the way individual members of the community interacted with other.

One of the things he saw was a transfer ceremony. Transfer ceremonies happen at key times of the Blackfoot calendar when different families lay out the new things they have accumulated over the course of the year and share them out to those in need. To Maslow, this defied explanation. If he were to do the same thing back home in Brooklyn, it would lose him everything and gain him nothing. Here at Siksiká, though, personal gain had no cultural cachet for the Blackfoot. They seemed more interested in helping other people. The other big surprise for Maslow was that, despite their lack of material wealth and social dominance, almost every Blackfoot person he met seemed to have a high level of ego security.

Maslow was forced to conclude, as Benedict had likely known, that self-esteem did not depend on social dominance. So, he started to look into how this was achieved, and thought he found an explanation in the way the Blackfoot raised their children. Unlike Westerners, the Blackfoot did not look down on or pander to their children, instead investing them with respect from the outset. Children as young as ten were brought into Blackfoot ceremonial life, entrusted with treasured objects and expected to contribute to the community.

Another thing Maslow observed was what the Blackfoot called kimmapiiyipitssini. Maslow translated this as Blackfoot Altruism, although Heavy Head points out that there is no direct translation of altruism in the Blackfoot language. Instead, the word refers to the practice of habitual compassion and kindness towards each other. A great example of this came in the form of a man called Teddy Yellow Fly, a charismatic young leader of the tribe, who was just as at ease at Siksiká as he was leading negotiations with the Canadian government in Ottawa. Teddy Yellow Fly was the only person at Siksiká to own a car. This he shared with the whole community. If you needed to get somewhere, Yellow Fly would either drive you himself or hand over the car keys. Then, when he announced at a public event that he would be castrating and branding his cattle the following week, a group of young men turned up to help, working without payment until the job was done. This was kimmapiiyipitssini. Teddy Yellow Fly could be generous because he knew the help would come, and the help would come on account of his generosity. The community at Siksiká was held together by how its members prioritised their collective good, rather than by socially elevating and holding some people up to the detriment of others.

Maslow left Siksiká a changed man. That September, he set up a new course at Brooklyn College called Normative Human Behaviour where the norms, quite astonishingly, were the traditions, practices and beliefs he had seen in his time with the Blackfoot. He also began writing what became a ten-year-long series, the Good Human Being Notebooks. Maslow's message to the scientific community he was a part of was clear: his time with the scientific method and experimental approaches to human psychology were done. Instead, he was making the switch to more intuitive techniques, with the goal of working out just what it was that allowed the Blackfoot to be so confident and kind. Over the following years and decades, Maslow's research would culminate to form what is now his famed Hierarchy of Needs.

*

There is a notion in circulation that Maslow took the idea of the Hierarchy of Needs wholesale from the Blackfoot Nation who embedded it in the iconography of their teepees. In the frame of this hugely appealing notion, the shape of the pyramid is actually the shape of a teepee, and the banded designs of Blackfoot teepees mirror the levels of the hierarchy. This was one of the reasons that drew Heavy Head and his friend and colleague, Narcisse Blood, the founder of Kainai Studies, to look into the history of Maslow at Siksiká in the first place. It turns out there are several problems with this theory, not least of which is that the Blackfoot don't use the teepee to symbolise their world-view. Another, arguably the nail in the coffin of the idea, is that Maslow did not draw the pyramid in the first place. Instead, it was the invention of a psychologist called Charles McDermid, designed specially for his article, 'How Money Motivates Men' published in *Business Horizons* in 1960. It was in fact, management studies and not psychology that made Maslow an icon and, interestingly for us, it is the co-option of the co-option of the Blackfoot ideal. Rather than contributing to the collective good, the management version of Maslow's individual is predicated on the idea that people have to have some basic needs met before they can turn to the task of becoming the ideal worker.

Just as we saw in the chapter on time, your work persona is less about who you are, and almost entirely about what you can be relied on to produce. Where Frederick Winslow 'Speedy' Taylor shaved time into ever smaller increments, shuffling minutes and seconds around in the interests of greater efficiency, management studies used Maslow's hierarchy to ensure the greatest health and productivity of the cogs in the workplace machinery. The cogs, of course, being us.

When it made the jump to management studies textbooks, the Hierarchy of Needs took on a life of its own, one that compounded Western capitalist ideals in exactly the opposite way that Maslow was trying to confound them. In management studies, the view of the hierarchy is as a stepwise up approach, of human needs as some kind of computer game where you have to successfully complete one level before you move on to the next one. Those who put the Hierarchy of Needs to the test throughout the 1960s and 1970s greatly appreciated Maslow's creation of a new field of research with his theory that behaviour was not just the result of unconscious desires, as the psychoanalysts conceived, or shaped by rewards and reinforcement, as the behaviourists had imagined, but was also driven by the desire to fulfil internal needs. Over the 1970s and 1980s (that is, after Maslow's death in 1970) capitalism and the scientific study of human behaviour combined in the form of business sciences. The goal was not to encourage us to be a useful member of society; it was to make us do as much work as we could.

The individual in management studies is a proxy for their wider society. If a single individual is achieving self-actualisation, then society as a whole benefits by default, even if all of those individuals are not doing anything in the collective interests of their overall society. Blackfoot philosophy is bigger, wider and, it seems to me, better than this. It is not about increasing complexity, with people stuck in particular roles, but a society that pulls together to ensure that no one is left behind. Having a car is not about keeping up with the Joneses, spending all your time working away from your family and friends in order to be able to afford a bigger and better car next year. A car is for getting around. In the West, society has become an individualised isolating performance. For Westerners like Freud, other people are the problem. For the Blackfoot, other people are all there is.

The Blackfoot do not deny that individuals exist – it's more a case of how they are seen by their wider community. From a social philosophy point of view, they operate in a completely different paradigm. In the West, we operate on a deficit model. A person has to earn their social position through the accumulation of wealth or through some sort of social performance, like getting a university degree. So, they supposedly start with nothing and work their way up to a position in society. On the face of it, this sounds like the perfectly sound basis for a meritocratic society. All things being equal, if you work hard, you will achieve things and be rewarded accordingly. In the West, though, as we've seen happen through the development of ideas, step by step, chapter by chapter, all things are not equal. We are, very clearly, not all in this together. In the West, people who fail, refuse to conform or are unable to do so due to limiting socioeconomic reasons are seen as lesser, or to have failed at society outright. Whether you are unhoused, disabled or marginalised in some other way, or maybe you're just some damn hippie, you are deemed to be losing the game of civilisation. At Siksiká, Maslow saw a society in which a person's value did not have to be earned because it was assumed from the start. A person was born 'credentialled' and spent their lives living up to the standard.

'That top segment, that self-actualisation,' says Ryan Heavy Head, 'I think the model for that is almost assuredly coming from the Blackfoot community. [Maslow's] idea of what it is to be a healthy human being changed in the six weeks he was there, and he spent a good part of the rest of his life trying to figure out what was going on there, and how people came to develop that.'

Maslow held that we are at our happiest when we are trying to become the best we can be. At least, that's what he said if you read the management manuals. He actually said something else, something that for much of recent history did not make it into the management manuals. Embedded in Blackfoot society and cultural wisdom, Maslow understood that individual achievements meant nothing on their own and that our individual fulfilment should be embedded in contributing to our wider community. Rather than progress from one stage of hierarchy to the next to be free-floating, self-actualised individuals, we need to transcend our individual selves to the benefit of the people and the world around us. As Cindy Blackstock, member of the Gitxsan tribe and activist, explains: 'First Nations people often consider their actions in terms of the impacts of the "seven generations". This means that one's actions are informed by the experience of the past seven generations and by considering the consequences for the seven generations to follow.'

The real power of the individual in the Blackfoot world-view is to contribute to the collective power of the community.

*

One of the other things Maslow observed in his time at Siksiká was the flagrant racism of the white settlers who were the Blackfoot's neighbours. These were people who, over the course of previous decades, had been steadily encroaching on the already restricted Blackfoot land. They had benefited from new laws passed in both Canada and the US that allowed them to lease Blackfoot territory to graze their sheep at the direct expense of what had been thriving Blackfoot cattle herds. In Maslow's eyes, these people did not cover themselves in glory, and this presented an interesting problem. 'The more I got to know the whites in the village who were the worst bunch of creeps and bastards I'd ever run across in my life,' Maslow wrote, 'the more it got paradoxical.' How was it possible that the supposedly civilised white people were behaving in such a base manner, and the so-called savages were apparently so psychologically advanced?

It was a paradox not lost on Indigenous Americans themselves. Lakota Medicine Man John Fire Lame Deer, for example, was in no doubt as to what was going on.

Before our white brothers came to civilize us we had no jails. Therefore we had no criminals. You can't have criminals without a jail. We had no locks or keys, and so we had no thieves. If a man was so poor that he had no horse, tipi or blanket, someone gave him these things. We were too uncivilized to set much value on personal belongings. We wanted to have things only in order to give them away. We had no money, and therefore a man's worth couldn't be measured by it. We had no written law, no attorneys or politicians, therefore we couldn't cheat. We really were in a bad way before the white men came, and I don't know how we managed to get along without these basic things which, we are told, are absolutely necessary to make a civilized society.

Maslow's Blackfoot influences are barely mentioned in his published works beyond maybe the odd sentence in passing or, at best, as a footnote. Why did Maslow never publicly acknowledge the Blackfoot source of his ideas? Would you have done so in his shoes? For centuries, Indigenous people had been diminished in terms of their legal standing, their allocated land, their entire humanity. So tell people that his revolutionary idea in the serious civilised science of psychology was inspired by the Blackfoot Nation? Maslow might as well have said he got the idea from talking to his dog. In fact, it strikes me that he took pains to come up with an origin story that deliberately and completely removed his ideas about self-actualisation from any association with his time at Siksiká. The way he told it, his inspiration had come much later. Not from Siksiká in 1938, but towards the end of 1941, striking like lightning, a bolt out of the blue.

One day, just after Pearl Harbour, I was driving home and I had a vision of a peace table with people sitting around it talking about human nature and hatred, war and peace, and brotherhood. I was too old to go into the army. It was at that moment that I realised that the rest of my life must be devoted to discovering a psychology for the peace table. The moment changed my whole life. I wanted to prove that humans were capable of something grander than war, prejudice and hatred.

★

The story goes that when one of her students asked American cultural anthropologist Margaret Mead what they should look out for as the first sign of civilisation, she referred to an example from archaeology – a healed human femur, a thigh bone. Rather than focus on the technologies and supposed cultural advancements of civilisation – everything from writing through to art and democracy, for example – Mead focused on what the archaeological record can tell us about the way ancient people treated each other. For any animal, a broken leg is a big deal. If you can't walk, you can't hunt or gather your food or run away from danger. Therefore, if in the archaeological record you can find an example of an individual whose broken leg had had time to heal, you have evidence of a civilised society, where people take care of each other, even when they are not able to contribute directly to the work of that society.

There are a lot of apocryphal stories in this book. In fact, I'll admit that I didn't know a lot of them were apocryphal until I started to look into them further, to try to work out the truth of them. Some ideas, it turns out, have phenomenal staying power, whether they are true or not. Of all the apocryphal stories, this is the one I like best. Part of that has to do with how it is undeniably political. That's no shock when you place Mead in her academic and historical context as another of the new generation of anthropologists trying to rewrite the discipline in the twentieth century.

Mead was one of the cohort of researchers who learned at the feet of Franz Boas, she worked alongside and was romantically involved with Ruth Benedict, and she was also a figure in popular culture, advocating against poverty and racism and in support of women's rights. The story of the femur is firmly on brand for Mead, and it's a world-view I can totally get on board with.

What it lacks is the authoritative distance of the observant scientist. As I've hopefully been able to show you, the body of science Mead was reacting to – the body of race science that by degrees ever more assuredly cemented the gap between savage and civilised – was just as political. It simply pretended not to be.

Another quote famously attributed to Mead, again in the absence of any evidence she actually said it, is the line: 'Never doubt that a small group of thoughtful, committed citizens can change the world: indeed, it's the only thing that ever has.' Whoever said this, Mead or not, I don't think they were wrong, but I wish they had made it clear that, all things considered, the change should be for the better, and for our collective good. Many of the ideas of the people featured in this chapter, and those preceding it, from Maslow to the people of Haiti, the metallurgists and artists of historic Benin, First Australians, the Haudenosaunee and Inka, were strong and powerful ones that were 'lost' along the road to civilisation. They were lost in the furthering of an ideal of growth and progress, regardless of the cost. What would have happened to Einstein's ideas if, as the Blackfoot do, we had an understanding that it will affect the next seven generations? Would it have prevented the development of the nuclear bomb? It seems unlikely because in the West the march of progress, the advancement of our civilisation, is so deeply ingrained in the system.

When you are talking about people instead of quantum particles, it's easier to lose sight of what's going on. We don't have many set ideas about quantum particles – a couple of hundred years ago we didn't even know they existed, let alone what to think of them. As we've seen in this book though, we do have very set ideas about how to think about other people and their ideas, particularly those non-Western people that civilisation deemed irrational. How can we look at our world and understand that it is influenced by the previous seven generations? That takes us back nearly a couple of centuries, to the work of Francis Galton, J. G. Frazer, John Lubbock, Hugh Blair, Thomas Babington Macaulay, and all the others. We may not think about them every day, we may not even know their names, but their ideas are still with us in ways that could do with exploding.

As Heavy Head points out, Maslow left Siksiká both a changed man and a changed researcher. He was no longer occupied with ideas of social dominance as so many other scholars and even an only slightly younger version of himself would have it. Instead, he had an idea about what it meant to have the social maturity to be able to live together harmoniously. To me, it seems as though a key difference between these two world-views is how they envision the possibility of change. When Maslow asked them about what they thought about their racist white neighbours, the Blackfoot tribal elders replied that they were not fully developed. They were not niita'pitapi, what Heavy Head describes as 'someone who is completely developed, or who has arrived'. It's possible to read the Blackfoot description of their white neighbours as 'undeveloped' as simply mirroring ideas in Western anthropology that some people are civilised and others exist at various stages of being uncivilised. But the Blackfoot philosophy does not keep people stuck in a single stage of development. Personality is not essential to biology. Change is possible. With Maslow, there could have been a whole new way of looking at people, of looking at individuals within our society, not as loose flotsam on the waves. But something got lost along the way. Even Maslow himself seemed to lose track of his own big idea. Later in his life, he appears to have reverted to his old social-dominance world-view, spouting eugenic ideas in ways that recall Francis Galton (albeit in his own private notebooks).

Nowadays it is common to see the word 'individualism' preceded by the word 'rampant'. The implication is that our self-centredness presents some kind of threat to our way of living and to our wider society at large. Better get your head down and make sure you are the working, productive unit of capitalism you are destined to be – it'll make you happy and will keep you safe and civilised. We didn't get to this point by accident. Somehow, we need to see beyond the supposed progress and advancement of the West and open our eyes to other ways of thinking and being in the world. We need to start imagining what it could mean to be part of something bigger and better than simply looking to ourselves and the narrow limits we place on ourselves based on what we think we are supposed to be. By all means be the best you can be – but be that in the context of your community and the people around you. Perhaps then we might start to move away from ideas that divide us – like civilisa-tion – and focus on what unites us instead.

EPILOGUE

Making the journey to Oxford is always bittersweet for me because, deep inside of a parallel universe, it was supposed to be home. My plan, based on close studies of the works of Dorothy L. Sayers and episodes of *Inspector Morse*, had been to study archaeology and anthropology at Balliol College, get my PhD and then settle into the comfort and the confines of the academic life. I would dress mainly in corduroy, jackets with elbow patches and schlubby cardigans, my glasses threaded with a cord so that, when not in use, they could be worn as a necklace. I would spend my time, between excavations in exotic corners of the globe, teaching and writing papers and books to both academic and public acclaim, the staid regularity of my days peppered by the latest college intrigue or murder on campus. All of this was an impossibility of course. For one thing, Balliol doesn't offer the archaeology and anthropology course, and for another, I don't wear glasses. Most damningly, though, I failed to get into Oxford. Instead, I chose the sordid glamour of a London university and later the even more sordid glamour of a career in the heritage industry and made a name for myself as a troublemaker in university museums, talking about race science, eugenics, decolonisation and all the other topics that make some civilised people clench their jaws or their sphincters (or, on a good day, both). It's to this end that I'm braving the Oxford nostalgia, real and imagined, to go and visit my friend Marenka Thompson-Odlum, Research Curator of Critical Perspectives at the Pitt Rivers Museum.

I first met Marenka when we both kept turning up on the bill of the same museum conferences. As two non-white curators working in predominantly white institutions, we had taken it upon ourselves to tell the colonial stories of our collections. While the museum sector, for the most part, is starting on the long hard journey of addressing the colonial roots and legacies of its work, talking about the idea remains controversial. You may have heard, for instance, that there is a culture war on and that well-established, traditional icons of Western civilisation like the British Museum and the National Trust are under attack from woke liberal snowflakes. Within the civilised haunts of this world, Marenka and I – along with many of our like-minded colleagues – are the barbarians who have already breached the gates. I particularly wanted to talk to Marenka about this because she is both a highly experienced museum professional and also, through her work, an expert at pointing out the mostly invisible ways in which museums in particular, and the Western academy more generally, continue to construct the divide between civilised and uncivilised.

If you've never been to the Pitt Rivers before, the best way for me to describe it to you is to say, 'Imagine a museum.' If you have been there, you're unlikely to have forgotten a large, fairly dark and cavernous hall absolutely full to the brim with an overwhelming quantity of stuff from every corner of the globe. The Pitt Rivers is an example of what's called a universal or encyclopaedic museum collection, compiled with the goal to collect one of every kind of thing and arrange it in an order that could explain how all those things came to be as they are, and what they can tell us about the people who made them.

The Pitt Rivers Collection is so effective at doing this that the overall effect of the display is that of an enormous tidal wave of objects, frozen in space and time. You feel as though, if you were to turn your back on it, at any moment the spell could break and you would be washed away on a flow of antiquity, drowned in the wealth of knowledge of centuries. All of these objects are documentary proof of the social realities they embody. They are data on a monumental scale – you need only sift through them and arrange them in the right order to find the truth. That order, of course, is not neutral. It depends on who's doing the ordering.

While the more overtly colonial and problematic 'objects' – the hugely popular shrunken heads, for example – have been taken off display, Marenka took time out of her busy day to show me how many of the old museum labels continued to do the job of sorting the civilised wheat from the *un*civilised chaff.

Marenka is a warm and generous person. She is calm to her core, and she laughs a lot, often to keep from crying – an understandable hazard in a job when the biases in your catalogues are so overt. The museum's accession registers, for example, list art objects under the banner of 'human form in savage art', 'human form in barbaric art' and 'human form in civilised art'. Here again is that familiar tripartite division, and the suggested progress from one degree to the next, on the journey from savagery to civilisation. Until relatively recently, visitors to the Pitt Rivers had the divide openly pointed out to them in the signage. There was 'Civilised' art in one case, and then 'Savage' art in the case next door. While these category labels had disappeared from the display by the time Marenka turned up (political correctness, to some degree having run its course), she noticed that the words within the labels of the displays continued to tell much the same story.

There are objects from Europe in the Pitt Rivers Museum, but a very particular kind of Europe, stuck in a very particular time. These are the 'primitive' peasant objects, particularly religious charms – symbols of the backward thinking that the Enlightenment would sweep away by flooding them with the bright, rational light of day. The ghosts of these ideas continue to haunt the museum labels. Having carried out a detailed study of the terms used in the labels, and having compared them to the museum catalogue, Marenka found that words like 'modern' and 'civilised' were overwhelmingly used to describe objects from Europe. Words like 'lazy', 'inferior' and 'barbaric', on the other hand, were the special preserve of Africa, Oceania and the Americas. 'The words are changing,' Marenka told me, 'but the meaning is still the same.'

Acknowledgements

This book would not be possible without the work, love and support of really quite a lot of people.

Firstly, on a practical note, enormous and eternal thanks to my colleagues at UCL Science and Technology Studies, particularly Chiara Ambrosio, without whom nothing would have got read and so nothing could have got written.

The book world takes some navigating, so I am so very grateful to my agents Niki Chang and David Evans for making this dream come true; to Aruna Vasudevan and Tom Atkins for their eagle eyes on the text; to Simon Guerrier for his sage advice; and of course, to my editor, the unsinkable Harriet Poland, whose idea it was in the first place.

Thanks and props are due to my critical (that is to say, vitally important, incredibly knowledgeable, generous and encouraging) friends: Jack Ashby, Cerys Bradley, Paul Burnside, Tim Causer, Debbie Challis, Becky Clark, Emily Dawson, Nening Dennis, Victor Ehikamenor, Amanda Moorghen, Alice Procter, David Rooney, Nicola Saunders, Efram Sera-Shriar, Bill Sillar, Erman Sözüdoğru, Rebecca Struthers, Marenka Thompson-Odlum, Alice White and Xine Yao, who set me right when I went wrong. Anything that remains wrong is on me, not them.

Big thanks and so much love to my head cheerleaders: Dr (Mrs) Sonali Das, Paul Burnside, Manchi Chung, Nening

Dennis, Kate Atkins, Tiva Montalbano and the other Women, Anna Cornelius, Lily Garnett, Hana Ayoob and the Neuwrite gang. I'm especially grateful to Roma Agrawal and Angela Saini whose faith ran from cover to cover.

Finally, credit where credit is due: to my science, history and English teachers, Bob Kovach, Janet Nagorski, Maria Tamer, Michael Thompson, Marcia Peté, Joan McGuinness, Erik Torjesen, and Danny Gordon. Special thanks to Charlie Watson, who also taught anthropology and psychology, and Mike Kielkopf – 'precise and concise' remain my watchwords.

Bibliography

Abd El Gawad, H. (2020, November 2). '(Re)claiming the Rosetta: The Rosetta Stone and the (re)writing of Egypt's Modern History'. 100 Histories of 100 Worlds in One Object. https://100histories100worlds.org/reclaiming-the-rosetta/

'Akala | Full Address and Q&A | Oxford Union' [video]. YouTube. (2015, November 26). https://www.youtube.com/watch?v=WUtAxUQjwB4

Álvarez, V. P. (2015). 'The role of the mechanical clock in medieval science'. Endeavour, 39(1), 63–68. https://doi.org/10.1016/j.endeavour.2015.02.004

Amos, O. (2016, July 17). 'Did a London hotel room become part of Yugoslavia?' BBC News. https://www.bbc.com/news/magazine-36569675

Anderson, B. (2016). Imagined Communities: Reflections on the Origin and Spread of Nationalism (revised edition). Verso.

Appiah, K. A. (2018). The Lies That Bind: Rethinking Identity (main edition). Profile Books.

Arnold, K. (2005). Cabinets for the Curious: Looking Back at Early English Museums (first edition). Routledge.

Ashby, J. (2022). Platypus Matters: The Extraordinary Story of Australian Mammals. William Collins.

Bacon, D. S. & Hawthorne, N. (1970). The philosophy of the plays of Shakspere unfolded. AMS Press.

Bacon, F. (2015). Francis Bacon: The Complete Works. Centaur Classics.

Baker, T. (2023, July 13). 'Government given go-ahead to appeal Rwanda deportation block at Supreme Court'. Sky News. https://news.sky.com/story/government-given-go-ahead-

to-appeal-rwanda-deportation-block-at-supreme-court-
12920441

Balch, A. (2022, April 29). 'Nationality and Borders Act becomes law:
Five key changes explained'. The Conversation. http://theconver-
sation.com/nationality-and-borders-act-becomes-law-five-
key-changes-explained-182099

BBC Press Office, 'List of top 100 Britons'. (2022, August 18). https://
www.bbc.co.uk/pressoffice/pressreleases/stories/2002/08_
august/21/100_list.shtml

BBC Radio 4, 'Magna Carta – Episode guide'. (n.d.). BBC. https://
www.bbc.co.uk/programmes/b04y6wdt/episodes/guide

Behuniak, S. M. (2011). 'The living dead? The construction of people
with Alzheimer's disease as zombies'. *Ageing and Society*, 31(1), 70–92.
https://doi.org/10.1017/S0144686X10000693

Bentham, J. (1832). *Auto-icon; Or, Farther Uses of the Dead to the
Living . . .: A Fragment. From the Mss. of Jeremy Bentham.*
(Unpublished).

Bhimani, N. (2022, September). 'Intelligence testing, race and eugenics'. *Wellcome Collection.* https://wellcomecollection.org/articles/
YxDGExEAACMAdaX9

Biewen, J., & Kumanyika, C. (March 2017). 'How Race Was Made'
(No. 2). Retrieved 2 January 2023, from http://www.sceneonradio.
org/episode-32-how-race-was-made-seeing-white-part-2/

Biewen, J., & Kumanyika, C. (May 2017). 'Skulls and Skin' (No. 8).
Retrieved 2 January 2023, from http://www.sceneonradio.org/
episode-38-skulls-and-skins-seeing-white-part-8/

Blackstock, C. (2011). 'The Emergence of the Breath of Life Theory'.
Journal of Social Work Values and Ethics, 8(1).

Blair, H. (1783). *Lectures on Rhetoric and Belles Letters* (Vols 1 and 2).
Creech, Strahan & Cadell.

Bloom, P. (2021, July 9). 'Being in Time'. *New Yorker*.

Bond, S. E. (2018, November 13). 'Pseudoarchaeology and the Racism
Behind Ancient Aliens'. Hyperallergic. http://hyperallergic.
com/470795/pseudoarchaeology-and-the-racism-behind-
ancient-aliens/

Boylston, A. (2012). 'The origins of inoculation'. *Journal of the Royal*

Society of Medicine, *105*(7), 309–313. https://doi.org/10.1258/jrsm.2012.12k044

Bragg, M. (presenter). (2008, May 1). *In Our Time: In The Enclosures of the 18th Century* [radio broadcast]. BBC Radio 4. https://www.bbc.co.uk/programmes/b00b1m9b

Bridgman, T., Cummings, S., & Ballard, J. (2019). 'Who Built Maslow's Pyramid? A History of the Creation of Management Studies' Most Famous Symbol and Its Implications for Management Education'. *Academy of Management Learning & Education*, *18*(1), 81–98. https://doi.org/10.5465/amle.2017.0351

Brody, R. (2019, June 28). 'The Enduring Urgency of Spike Lee's "Do the Right Thing" at Thirty'. *New Yorker*. https://www.newyorker.com/culture/the-front-row/the-enduring-urgency-of-spike-lees-do-the-right-thing-at-thirty

Brown, B. R. (2010). *Until Darwin, Science, Human Variety and the Origins of Race* (1st edition). Routledge.

Bryant, M. (2021, July 31). 'Latin to be introduced at 40 state secondaries in England'. *Observer*. https://www.theguardian.com/education/2021/jul/31/latin-introduced-40-state-secondaries-england

Bullough, O. (2018). *Moneyland: Why thieves and crooks now rule the world and how to take it back* (main edition). Profile Books.

Bullough, O. (2022). *Butler to the World: The book the oligarchs don't want you to read – how Britain became the servant of tycoons, tax dodgers, kleptocrats and criminals*. Profile Books.

Burk, K. (2009). *Old World, New World: The Story of Britain and America*. Abacus.

Burkeman, O. (2021). *Four Thousand Weeks*. Vintage Digital.

Burkeman, O. (presenter). (2017). *Oliver Burkeman Is Busy* [radio broadcast]. BBC Radio 4. https://www.bbc.co.uk/programmes/b07w1dpx/episodes/player

Burstyn, H. L. (1975). 'If Darwin Wasn't the *Beagle's* Naturalist, Why Was He on Board?' *The British Journal for the History of Science*, *8*(1), 62–69.

Cameron, D. (2014). 'British values: Article by David Cameron'. GOV.UK. https://www.gov.uk/government/news/british-values-article-by-david-cameron

Cannadine, D. (presenter). (2018, March 20). *Civilisation: A Sceptic's*

Guide [radio broadcast]. BBC Radio 4. https://www.bbc.co.uk/programmes/b09sn1hj

Carvel, J. (2004, January 8). 'Tebbit's cricket loyalty test hit for six'. *Guardian*. https://www.theguardian.com/uk/2004/jan/08/britishidentity.race

Chakrabarty, D. (2000). *Provincializing Europe: Postcolonial Thought and Historical Difference (New Edition)*. Princeton University Press. https://www.jstor.org/stable/j.ctt7rsx9

Challis, D. (2013). *The Archaeology of Race: The Eugenic Ideas of Francis Galton and Flinders Petrie* (1st edition). Bloomsbury Academic.

Charmantier, I. (2020, September 3). 'Linnaeus and Race'. The Linnean Society. Retrieved 17 June 2023, from https://www.linnean.org/learning/who-was-linnaeus/linnaeus-and-race

Chavez, W. (2017). 'Dec. 29 marks Treaty of New Echota's 182nd anniversary'. Cherokee Phoenix. https://www.cherokeephoenix.org/news/dec-29-marks-treaty-of-new-echotas-182nd-anniversary/article_802b2ef8-7e0f-5749-b932-ba2c12ceeea4.html

Chetty, D., Muse, G., Issa, H., & Tyne, L. (2022). *Welsh (Plural): Essays on the Future of Wales*. Watkins Media Limited.

Chirikure, S. 'Unearthing the truth'. (2021, December 26). *The Economist*. https://www.economist.com/interactive/christmas-specials/2021/12/18/great-zimbabwe-archaeology

Churchill, W. (2008). *Churchill by Himself: The Definitive Collection of Quotations* (R. Langworth, ed.; 1st edition). PublicAffairs.

Clarke, S. (director). (2018, February 18). *The First Brit: Secrets of the 10,000 Year Old Man* [documentary]. Plimsoll Productions.

Coard, B. (1971). *How the West Indian child is made educationally subnormal in the British school system: The scandal of the black child in schools in Britain*. New Beacon for the Caribbean Education and Community Workers' Association.

Coleman, C. G. (2021). *Lies, Damned Lies: A personal exploration of the impact of colonisation*. Ultimo Press.

Collen, I. (2020). 'Language Trends 2020 – Language teaching in primary and secondary schools in England'. British Council. https://www.britishcouncil.org/sites/default/files/language_trends_2020_0.pdf

Community Environmental Legal Defense Fund. (n.d.). 'The Enclosure Movement – CELDF Community Rights'. CELDF. Retrieved 3 January 2023, from https://celdf.org/the-enclosure-movement/

Condamine, C.-M. de L. (1773). *Histoire de l'inoculation de la petite verole, ou Recueil de mémoires, lettres, extraits et autres écrits sur la petite vérole artificielle.* Société Typographique.

Coombes, A. E. (1997). *Reinventing Africa: Museums, material culture, and popular imagination in late Victorian and Edwardian England.* Yale University Press.

Corby, R. (2020, January 31). 'Jill Lepore on Democracy in Peril, Then and Now | The New Yorker Radio Hour' [podcast]. WNYC Studios. https://www.wnycstudios.org/podcasts/tnyradiohour/segments/jill-lepore-democracy-peril-then-and-now-rerun

Crain, C. (2007, January 29). 'Bad Precedent'. *New Yorker.* https://www.newyorker.com/magazine/2007/01/29/bad-precedent

Crain, C. (2016, October 31). 'The Case Against Democracy'. *New Yorker.* https://www.newyorker.com/magazine/2016/11/07/the-case-against-democracy

Crombie, N. (director). (2018, August 23). 'Death' [documentary]. In *Grayson Perry: Rites of Passage.*

Das, S. (2018, March 19). 'Fact check: Were Indigenous Australians once classified under a flora and fauna act?' ABC News. https://www.abc.net.au/news/2018-03-20/fact-check-flora-and-fauna-1967-referendum/9550650

Das, S. (presenter). (2018, November 19). *The Boring Talks: Jeremy Bentham's 'Auto-Icon'* [radio broadcast]. BBC Radio 4. https://www.bbc.co.uk/programmes/m0o1j5j6

Daut, M. L. (2015). *Tropics of Haiti: Race and the Literary History of the Haitian Revolution in the Atlantic World, 1789-1865* (first edition). Oxford University Press.

'David Cameron struggles in mock citizenship test on David Letterman's Late Show – Video'. (2012, September 27). *Guardian.* http://www.theguardian.com/politics/video/2012/sep/27/david-cameron-letterman-late-show-video

Davidovits, J., Huaman, L., & Davidovits, R. (2019). 'Ancient organo-mineral geopolymer in South-American Monuments: Organic matter in andesite stone. SEM and petrographic evidence'. *Ceramics International*, *45*(6), 7385–7389. https://doi.org/10.1016/j. ceramint.2019.01.024

Davies, B. (2020, April 22). 'Freud and his Cigars'. Freud Museum London. https://www.freud.org.uk/2020/04/22/freud-and-his-cigars/

Davis, W. (1997). *The Serpent and the Rainbow* (reissue edition). Pocket Books.

Delbourgo, J. (2017). *Collecting the World: The Life and Curiosity of Hans Sloane*. Penguin.

Demby, G., & Marisol Meraji, S. (2020, June 8). 'A Treacherous Choice And A Treaty Right: Code Switch'. Retrieved 3 January 2023, from https://www.npr.org/2020/03/31/824647676/a-treacherous-choice-and-a-treaty-right

Descartes, R. (1637). *Discours de la méthode pour bien conduire sa raison et chercher la vérité dans les sciences , plus La dioptrique, Les météores et La géométrie qui sont des essais de cette méthode*. https://gallica.bnf.fr/ark:/12148/btv1b86069594

Doyle, A. C. (1920). *Sherlock Holmes Volume 1: The Complete Novels and Stories* (reissue edition). Bantam.

Dr Francis Young [@DrFrancisYoung]. (2021, July 31). 'Many archivists and librarians use Latin every day, because so much was written and published in Latin before 1700. That includes literature; much of the most important Scottish literature of the early modern period was written in Latin' [Tweet]. Twitter. https://twitter.com/DrFrancisYoung/status/1421434904177430530

Drucker, P. F. (1954). *The practice of management* (first edition). Harper & Row.

Druett, J. (2011). *Tupaia: Captain Cook's Polynesian navigator*. Praeger.

Dubner, S. (December 2021). 'The Hidden Side of the Art Market' [podcast]. Retrieved 3 January 2023, from https://freakonomics. com/podcast-tag/the-hidden-side-of-the-art-market/

Earth, Air, Fire, Water: The Cherokee. (1995, July 7). https://www.bbc. co.uk/sounds/play/p033k1yw

Eddy, M. D. (2011). 'The line of reason: Hugh Blair, spatiality and the progressive structure of language'. *Notes and Records of the Royal Society*, 65(1), 9–24. https://doi.org/10.1098/rsnr.2010.0098

Egger, S. A. (2002). *The killers among us: An examination of serial murder and its investigation* (second edition). Prentice Hall.

Emerson, R. W. (n.d.) 'Concord Hymn'. Retrieved 3 January 2023, from https://www.poetryfoundation.org/poems/45870/concord-hymn

Fara, P. (2017). *Pandora's Breeches: Women, Science and Power in the Enlightenment*. Pimlico.

Farout, D. (2016). 'De la Renaissance à la Restauration: Quelques étapes du déchiffrement des hiéroglyphes'. *Les Cahiers de l'École du Louvre*, 9, Article 9. https://doi.org/10.4000/cel.433

Farrar, F. W. (1867). *Aptitudes of Races*. Transactions of the Ethnological Society of London, 5, 115–126. https://doi.org/10.2307/3014218

Fennell, M. (presenter). (2020, November 28). *Stuff the British Stole: Blood Art* [radio broadcast]. https://www.abc.net.au/radionational/programs/stuff-the-british-stole/blood-art/12867832

Fery, G. (n.d.). 'Popular Archeology – Burning the Maya Books: The 1562 Tragedy at Mani'. Popular Archeology. Retrieved 3 January 2023, from https://popular-archaeology.com/article/burning-the-maya-books-the-1562-tragedy-at-mani/

'Five Civilized Tribes'. (n.d.). Retrieved 3 January 2023, from http://www.fivecivilizedtribes.org/Cherokee.html

Fletcher, M. L. M. (1998). 'Listen'. *Michigan Journal of Race and Law*, 3, 523–540.

Forgan, S. (2013). *The Story of Captain Cook: a souvenir guide*. Captain Cook Memorial Museum, Whitby.

Franklin, B. (1784). 'An Economical Project'. *Journal de Paris*.

Frazer, J. G. (1978). *The Golden Bough: A study in magic and religion* (abridged edition). Macmillan.

Freire, P. (2000). *Pedagogy of the oppressed* (thirtieth anniversary edition). Bloomsbury Continuum.

Freud, S. 'Letter from Freud to Fliess, November 2, 1896'. Retrieved 4 January 2023, from https://pep-web.org/browse/document/zbk.042.0202a

Freud, S. (1970). *Letters of Sigmund Freud 1873–1939* (E. L. Freud, ed.). The Hogarth Press.

Freud, S. (2004). *Penguin Great Ideas: Civilisation and its Discontents*. Penguin.

Fukuyama, F. (1992). *The end of history and the last man*. Maxwell Macmillan Canada.

Galton, F. (1874). *English Men of Science: Their Nature and Nurture*. Macmillian & Co.

Galton, F. (1883). *Inquiries Into Human Faculty and Its Development*. Macmillian & Co.

Gammage, B. (2012). *Biggest Estate on Earth: How Aborigines made Australia* (main edition). Allen & Unwin.

Garnett, G. (2018). 'Sir Edward Coke's resurrection of Magna Carta'. In L. Goldman (ed.), *Magna Carta* (pp. 51–60). University of London Press. https://www.jstor.org/stable/j.ctv5136sc.11

Gawande, A. (presenter). (2014, December 13). *The Reith Lectures: The Problem of Hubris* [radio broadcast]. https://www.bbc.co.uk/programmes/b04tjdlj

George Padmore Institute. (2000, 2011). 'Black Education Movement'. https://www.georgepadmoreinstitute.org/collections/the-black-education-movement-1965-1988

Goldstein, A., & Halperin, J. (2017, December 7). '5 Reasons Why It's So Weird That a Little-Known Saudi Prince Bought the "Salvator Mundi"'. Artnet News. https://news.artnet.com/market/salvator-mundi-prince-bader-bin-abdullah-bin-mohammed-bin-farhan-al-saud-1172081

Gould, S. J. (1992). *Ever Since Darwin: Reflections in Natural History*. W. W. Norton & Company.

Gould, S. J. (2006). *The Mismeasure of Man* (revised and expanded edition). W. W. Norton & Company.

Greer, B. (2019). 'Fearsome One-Eyed Queens' [podcast]. Retrieved 2 January 2023, from https://www.audible.co.uk/pd/Ep-2-Fearsome-One-Eyed-Queens-Podcast/B08DHDTK88

Guha, R. (2018). *Gandhi 1914–1948: The Years That Changed the World* (first edition). Allen Lane.

Hall, C. (2014). 'Bereavement theory: Recent developments in our understanding of grief and bereavement'. *Bereavement Care, 33*(1), 7–12. https://doi.org/10.1080/02682621.2014.902610

Hall, E., & Stead, H. (2020). *A People's History of Classics: Class and Greco-Roman antiquity in Britain*. Routledge/Taylor & Francis Group.

Halmhofer, S. (2021, October 5). 'Did Aliens Build the Pyramids? And Other Racist Theories'. SAPIENS. https://www.sapiens.org/archaeology/pseudoarchaeology-racism/

Handy, J. (2019). '"The enchantment of property": Arthur Young, enclosure, and the cottage economy in England, 1770–1840'. *Journal of Agrarian Change, 19*(4), 711–728. https://doi.org/10.1111/joac.12334

Haney, J. L. (1944). 'Of the People, by the People, for the People'. *Proceedings of the American Philosophical Society, 88*(5), 359–367.

Harford, T., & Wright, A. (2020). 'How To End A Pandemic (No. 14)'. Retrieved 2 January 2023, from https://timharford.com/2020/07/cautionary-tales-dark-winter-bright-spring/

Harloe, K. (presenter). (2021, June 28). *Detoxifying the Classics* [radio broadcast]. BBC Radio 4. https://www.bbc.co.uk/programmes/m000x72t

Harrington, B. (2016). *Capital without Borders: Wealth Managers and the One Percent*. Harvard University Press.

Harvey, J. (presenter). (2019). *Could an ancient Athenian fix Britain?* [radio broadcast]. BBC Radio 4. https://www.bbc.co.uk/sounds/play/m000b5ks

Hay, S. N. (1962). 'Rabindranath Tagore in America'. *American Quarterly, 14*(3), 439–463. https://doi.org/10.2307/2710456

Haynes, N. (2021). *Pandora's jar: Women in the Greek myths*. Picador.

Heavy Head, R. (2018, March 28). 'Naamitapiikoan Blackfoot Influences on Abraham Maslow'. https://www.youtube.com/watch?v=WTO34FLv5a8

Hegel, G. W. F. (1830). *Enzyklopädie der philosophischen Wissenschaften im Grundrisse*. Felix Meiner.

Henderson, J. (n.d.). 'Caecilius Statius: Fragments not Assigned to any Play'. Loeb Classical Library. Retrieved 3 January 2023, from https://www.loebclassics.com/view/caecilius-plays/1935/pb_LCL294.553.xml

Henley & Partners. (2022). 'Passport Index'. https://www.henley-global.com/passport-index

Hicks, D. (2020). *The Brutish Museums: The Benin Bronzes, Colonial Violence and Cultural Restitution*. Pluto Press.

Hoffman, E. (1999). *The Right to Be Human: A Biography of Abraham Maslow* (second edition). McGraw-Hill Education.

Holland, T. (2005). *Rubicon: The Last Years of the Roman Republic* (illustrated edition). Anchor Books.

Holy Bible: King James Version. (2011). Collins.

Hughes, B. (presenter). (2017, April 29). *The Ideas That Make Us* [radio broadcast]. BBC Radio 4. https://www.bbc.co.uk/programmes/b03b2zb9

Hurston, Z. N. (2022). *Tell My Horse: Voodoo and Life in Haiti and Jamaica*. Grapevine India.

Hyland, S. (2017). 'Writing with Twisted Cords: The Inscriptive Capacity of Andean Khipus'. *Current Anthropology*, *58*(3), 412–419. https://doi.org/10.1086/691682

Jackson, A. (1835). 'A letter from President Andrew Jackson to the Cherokee Nation about the benefits of voluntary removal'. https://dp.la/primary-source-sets/cherokee-removal-and-the-trail-of-tears/sources/1506

Janega, A. D. E. (2017, May 26). 'There's no such thing as the "Dark Ages", but OK'. Going Medieval. https://going-medieval.com/2017/05/26/theres-no-such-thing-as-the-dark-ages-but-ok/

Jasanoff, M. (2009). *Edge of Empire: Conquest and Collecting in the East 1750–1850*. Harper Perennial.

Johansen, B. E. (1982). *Forgotten Founders: How the American Indian helped shape democracy*. Harvard Common Press.

Jones, J. (2018, October 14). 'The Da Vinci mystery: Why is his $450m masterpiece really being kept under wraps?' *Guardian.* https://www.theguardian.com/artanddesign/2018/oct/14/leonardo-da-vinci-mystery-why-is-his-450m-masterpiece-really-being-kept-under-wraps-salvator-mundi

Kaufman, S. B. (n.d.). 'Who Created Maslow's Iconic Pyramid?' Scientific American Blog Network. Retrieved 5 January 2023, from https://blogs.scientificamerican.com/beautiful-minds/who-created-maslows-iconic-pyramid/

Kendi, I. X. (2017). *Stamped from the Beginning: The Definitive History of Racist Ideas in America* (first edition). Vintage Digital.

Kennedy, J. F. (1961, January 9). 'The City Upon a Hill'. https://www.jfklibrary.org/learn/about-jfk/historic-speeches/the-city-upon-a-hill-speech

Kenyon-Flatt, B. (2021, March 19). *How Scientific Taxonomy Constructed the Myth of Race*. SAPIENS. https://www.sapiens.org/biology/race-scientific-taxonomy/

Kickingbird, K., & Kickingbird, L. (n.d.). 'Foundations of American Democracy'. Retrieved 3 January 2023, from http://www.kickingbirdassociates.com/articles/foundations-of-american-democracy/

Kilcher, A. (2010). *Constructing Tradition: Means and Myths of Transmission in Western Esotericism*. BRILL. https://doi.org/10.1163/ej.9789004191143.i-474

Kirby, T. (director). (2019, June 24). *The Unwanted – The Secret Windrush Files* [documentary]. Uplands Television.

Koolmatrie, J. (2018, January 26). 'The myth of Aboriginal stories being myths'. TEDxAdelaide, Adelaide. https://www.youtube.com/watch?v=aUIgkbExn6I

Kübler-Ross, E., & Byock, M. D. I. (2011). *On Death and Dying: What the Dying Have to Teach Doctors, Nurses, Clergy & Their Own Families* (reissue edition). Scribner.

Kumar, K. (2017). *Visions of Empire – How Five Imperial Regimes Shaped the World*. Princeton University Press.

Lame Deer, & Erdoes, R. (2009). *Lame Deer, seeker of visions*. Simon & Schuster.

Larson, V. T. (1999). 'Classics and the Acquisition and Validation of Power in Britain's "Imperial Century" (1815–1914). *International Journal of the Classical Tradition*, 6(2), 185–225.

'The Last Act Of Jeremy Bentham'. (1832, June 10). *The Examiner*. https://www.britishnewspaperarchive.co.uk/viewer/bl/0000054/18320610/009/0010

Lauren, J. (2018, December 20). 'The Serial Killer and the "Less Dead"'. The Cut. https://www.thecut.com/2018/12/how-serial-killer-samuel-little-was-caught.html

Lawley, S. (presenter). (2002, December 13). *Desert Island Discs: Linton Kwesi Johnson* [radio broadcast]. BBC Radio 4. https://www.bbc.co.uk/programmes/p00947g4

Legislation.gov.uk (1947). 'Polish Resettlement Act, (1947)'. https://www.legislation.gov.uk/ukpga/Geo6/10-11/19

Lepore, J. (2005, October 5). 'Not So Fast'. *The New Yorker*.

Lepore, J. (2018). *These Truths: A History of the United States* (illustrated edition). W. W. Norton & Company.

Light, A. (1991). *Forever England: Femininity, literature, and conservatism between the wars.* Routledge.

Lindqvist, S. (2018). *Exterminate all the brutes* (J. Tate, trans.). Granta.

Little, B. (n.d.). 'Why Bibles Given to Slaves Omitted Most of the Old Testament'. History Channel. https://www.history.com/news/slave-bible-redacted-old-testament

Littlewood, R., & Douyon, C. (1997). 'Clinical findings in three cases of zombification'. *The Lancet, 350*(9084), 1094–1096. https://doi.org/10.1016/S0140-6736(97)04449-8

Loewen, J. W. (1996). *Lies my teacher told me: Everything your American history textbook got wrong.* Simon & Schuster.

Lowry, R. (1985). *The Journals of Abraham Maslow.* Viking.

Luckhurst, R. (2015). *Zombies: A Cultural History.* Reaktion Books.

Macaulay, T. B. (1835). 'Minute on Education' (p. Calcutta). Bureau of Education. http://www.columbia.edu/itc/mealac/pritchett/00generallinks/macaulay/txt_minute_education_1835.html

Mann, C. C. (2006). *1491: The Americas before Columbus.* Granta Books.

Mantel, H. (presenter). (2017, June 13). *The Reith Lectures: Hilary Mantel* [radio broadcast]. https://www.bbc.co.uk/programmes/b08tcbrp

Marmoy, C. F. A. (1958). 'The "Auto-Icon" of Jeremy Bentham At University College, London'. *Medical History, 2*(2), 77–86. https://doi.org/10.1017/S0025727300023486

Marshall, J. (1823). 'Johnson & Graham's Lessee v. McIntosh, 21 U.S. 543 (1823)'. Justia Law. https://supreme.justia.com/cases/federal/us/21/543/

Marshall, J. (1832). 'Worcester v. Georgia, 31 U.S. 515 (1832)'. Justia Law. https://supreme.justia.com/cases/federal/us/31/515/

Maslow, A. H. (1943). 'A theory of human motivation'. *Psychological Review*, *50*, 370–396. https://doi.org/10.1037/h0054346

Maslow, A. H. (1954). *Motivation and Personality*. New York, Harper.

Maslow, A. H., & Honigmann, J. J. (1970). 'Synergy: Some Notes of Ruth Benedict'. *American Anthropologist*, *72*(2), 320–333.

Masson, M. (1986). *The Complete Letters to Wilhelm Fliess, 1887–1904* (new edition). Harvard University Press.

Maxwell, L. M., Musson, S., Stewart, S., Talarico, J., Taylor, E. (2012). *Haarfarbentafel*. University College London.

Mbembe, A. (2019). *Necropolitics*. Duke University Press Books.

McGregor, H., & Kosman, M. (July 2021). 'Book 4, Ep. 2 | The Nation State'. Retrieved 4 January 2023, from https://www.ohwitchplease. ca/episodes/blog-post-title-four-rjma3-zmndk-nk2wn-8tsrj-4kl73-tm4e4-j5y6e-tm8x8-6bhf4-tx3hd-daltb-bhzrr-elhsx-jzs87-jx2kz-sxrga-en4gl-lh8er-h2axc

Medrano, M., & Urton, G. (2018). 'Toward the Decipherment of a Set of Mid-Colonial Khipus from the Santa Valley, Coastal Peru'. *Ethnohistory*, *65*(1), 1–23. https://doi.org/10.1215/00141801-4260638

Meghji, A. (2017, October 8). 'Remembering Stuart Hall: Race and nation in Brexit Britain'. Black History Month 2022. https://www. blackhistorymonth.org.uk/article/section/news-views/ remembering-stuart-hall-race-nation-brexit-britain/

Michel, K. L. (2014, April 19). 'Maslow's hierarchy connected to Blackfoot beliefs'. *A Digital Native American*. https://lincolnmichel. wordpress.com/2014/04/19/maslows-hierarchy-connected-to-blackfoot-beliefs/

Montin, E. (1908). *Introduction to J. Rousseau's Émile: Or, Treatise on education by Jean-Jacques Rousseau* (W. H. Payne, trans.). Appleton & Company.

Moore, L. (2022). *In Search of Us: Adventures in Anthropology* (main edition). Atlantic Books.

Mosby, I., & Millions, E. (2021). 'Canada's Residential Schools Were a Horror'. *Scientific American*. https://www.scientificamerican.com/ article/canadas-residential-schools-were-a-horror/

Moser, S. (2006). *Wondrous Curiosities – Ancient Egypt at the British Museum* (first edition). University of Chicago Press.

Moss, C. (2022, March 13). 'King Tut's Alien Dagger Conspiracies Have Gotten Insane'. The Daily Beast. https://www.thedailybeast.com/king-tuts-alien-dagger-conspiracies-have-gotten-insane

Mukherjee, S. (n.d.). 'Assam Tea Gardens Have Their Own Time! Here's The Story Of "Bagan Time"'. Vahdam Global. Retrieved 3 January 2023, from https://www.vahdam.global/blogs/news/assam-tea-gardens-have-their-own-time-here-s-the-story-of-bagan-time

Mussai, R. (2014). 'Black Chronicles II'. https://autograph.org.uk/exhibitions/black-chronicles-ii

Neame, R. (director). (1969, February 24). The Prime of Miss Jean Brodie [film]. Twentieth Century Fox.

Neate, R. (2019, June 10). 'Leonardo masterpiece "being kept on Saudi prince's yacht"'. Guardian. https://www.theguardian.com/business/2019/jun/10/da-vinci-salvator-mundi-saudi-prince-yacht

Ngũgĩ wa Thiong'o. (1986). Decolonising the mind: The politics of language in African literature. Heinemann.

Oberhaus, D. (2018, November 30). 'This New Atomic Clock Is So Precise Our Ability to Measure Gravity Constrains Its Accuracy'. Vice. https://www.vice.com/en/article/ev3a4e/nist-new-atomic-clock-map-of-earth-gravity

O'Keefe, E. A. (1984). 'Towards an Understanding of the Significance of "The Dreamtime" to Aboriginal People'. The Australian Journal of Indigenous Education, 12(4), 50–56. https://doi.org/10.1017/S0310582200013407

O'Rourke, J. (director). (2018). Akala's Odyssey [documentary]. BBC 4.

O'Toole, G. (2013, April 23). '"What Do You Think of Western Civilization?" "I Think It Would Be a Good Idea"'. Quote Investigator. https://quoteinvestigator.com/2013/04/23/good-idea/

Paine, T. (1995). Thomas Paine: Collected Writings (LOA #76): Common Sense / The American Crisis / Rights of Man / The Age of Reason / pamphlets, articles, and letters. Library of America.

Painter, N. I. (2011). The History of White People (illustrated edition). W. W. Norton & Company.

Pearson, K. & Moule, M. (1925) 'The Problem of Alien Immigration into Great Britain Illustrated by an Examination of Russian and Polish Jewish Children'. Annals of Eugenics 1: 5-127.

Petrie, W. M. F. (1931). *Seventy Years in Archaeology*. Sampson, Low, Marston & Co. Ltd.

Pikirayi, I. (2013). 'Great Zimbabwe in Historical Archaeology: Reconceptualizing Decline, Abandonment, and Reoccupation of an Ancient Polity, A.D. 1450–1900'. *Historical Archaeology*, 47(1), 26–37. https://doi.org/10.1007/BF03376887

Pizarro, P. (1969). *Relation of the Discovery and Conquest of the Kingdoms of Peru* (P. M. Means, trans.). Kraus Reprint.

Plato, & Lane, M. (2007). *The Republic* (H. D. P. Lee & D. Lee, trans.). Penguin Classics.

Porlan, M. (2016, December 19). 'The Secret Life of Time'. *New Yorker*.

Portillo, M. (presenter). (2007, April 29). *Magna Carta: Things We Forgot to Remember* [radio broadcast]. BBC Radio 4. https://www.bbc.co.uk/programmes/b00771y0

Press, A. (2021, October 4). 'Henrietta Lacks' estate sues drug company that sold her cells'. *Guardian*. https://www.theguardian.com/business/2021/oct/04/henrietta-lacks-estate-sues-pharmaceutical-cells

Procter, A. (2020). *The Whole Picture: the colonial story of the art in our museums and why we need to talk about it* (illustrated edition). Cassell.

Punt, S. (2017, September 23). 'Taking the Pissoir?' https://soundcloud.com/punt-pi/taking-the-pissoir

Ramirez, A. (2020). *The Alchemy of Us: How Humans and Matter Transformed One Another*. MIT Press.

Ravilochan, T. (2021, June 15). 'What I Got Wrong: Revisions to My Post about the Blackfoot and Maslow'. Medium. https://gatherfor.medium.com/i-got-it-wrong-7d9b314fadff

Ravilochan, T. (2022, July 13). 'Could the Blackfoot Wisdom that Inspired Maslow Guide Us Now?' Medium. https://gatherfor.medium.com/maslow-got-it-wrong-ae45d6217a8c

Rawls, J. (1999). *A theory of justice* (revised edition). Belknap Press of Harvard University Press.

Redman, S. J. (2016). *Bone Rooms: From Scientific Racism to Human Prehistory in Museums* (illustrated edition). Harvard University Press.

Rhodes Must Fall Oxford [@RMF_Oxford]. (2015, October 23). 'Pitt-Rivers museum is one of the most violent spaces in

Oxford' [Tweet]. Twitter. https://twitter.com/RMF_Oxford/status/657603704695189504

Richardson, R. (2001). *Death, Dissection and the Destitute* (new edition). University Of Chicago Press.

Roberts, D. (2012). *Fatal Invention: How Science, Politics, and Big Business Re-create Race in the Twenty-first Century*. The New Press.

Rogers, K. (2022, March 2). 'Commerce Secretary Gina Raimondo is the designated survivor during the State of the Union'. *New York Times*. https://www.nytimes.com/2022/03/01/us/politics/gina-raimondo-sotu-designated-survivor.html

Rooney, D. (2021). *About Time: A History of Civilization in Twelve Clocks*. Penguin.

Rousseau, J.-J. (1991). *Emile; or On Education*. Penguin Classics.

Royal Society. (n.d.). 'History of the Royal Society'. Retrieved 2 January 2023, from https://royalsociety.org/about-us/history/

Said, E. W. (1978). *Orientalism*. Pantheon Books.

Saini, A. (2019). *Superior: The Return of Race Science*. Fourth Estate.

Sands, P. (2016). *East West Street: On the origins of genocide and crimes against humanity*. Weidenfeld & Nicolson.

Sarr, F., & Savoy, B. (2018). 'Report on the restitution of African cultural heritage' (D. S. Burk, trans.). https://drive.google.com/file/d/1jetudXp3vued-yA8gvRwGjH6QLOfss4-/view?usp=sharing&usp=embed_facebook

Schama, S. (presenter). (2022, August 22). *Simon Schama: The Great Gallery Tours – The Courthauld* [radio broadcast]. BBC Radio 4. https://www.bbc.co.uk/programmes/m000kw4s

Schillace, B. (2015). *Death's Summer Coat: What the History of Death and Dying Can Tell Us About Life and Living*. Elliott & Thompson.

Schjeldahl, P. (2017, November 27). 'Masters and Pieces: Leonardo, Michelangelo, and Munch'. *New Yorker*. https://www.newyorker.com/magazine/2017/11/27/masters-and-pieces-leonardo-michelangelo-and-munch

Shakespeare Birthplace Trust. (n.d.). 'The Shakespeare Authorship Question'. Retrieved 2 January 2023, from https://www.shakespeare.org.uk/explore-shakespeare/shakespedia/william-shakespeare/shakespeare-authorship-question/

Shakespeare, T. (2020, September 29). *Lives Unworthy of Life? Disability Pride Versus Eugenics | Birkbeck Institute for the Study of Antisemitism*. Birkbeck Institute for the Study of Antisemitism |. https://bisa.bbk.ac.uk/event/lives-unworthy-of-life-disability-pride-versus-eugenics/

Shannon, L. (director). (2021, June 1). *Subnormal: A British Scandal* [documentary]. BBC. https://www.bbc.co.uk/programmes/m000w81h

Shapiro, J. (2011). *Contested Will: Who Wrote Shakespeare?* Faber & Faber.

Shukla, N. (ed.). (2016). *The Good Immigrant*. Unbound.

Silverman, K. (1984). *Life and Times of Cotton Mather*. Joanna Cotler Books.

Solly, M. (2022, March 16). 'What Happened the Last Time the U.S. Tried to Make Daylight Saving Time Permanent?' *Smithsonian Magazine*. https://www.smithsonianmag.com/smart-news/what-happened-the-last-time-the-us-tried-to-make-daylight-saving-time-permanent-180979742/

Sosteric, M. (2021, January 13). 'Abraham Maslow was a Eugenicist'. Medium.https://dr-s.medium.com/abraham-maslow-was-a-eugenicist-b3ba9a85f5ab

Spiegelman, A. (2003). *The Complete MAUS, English Edition*. Penguin.

Stewart, M. (2010). *The Management Myth – Debunking Modern Business Philosophy* (reprint edition). W. W. Norton & Company.

Stocking, G. W. (ed.). (1984). *Observers Observed: Essays on Ethnographic Fieldwork: 1*. University of Wisconsin Press.

Taylor, D. & Quinn, B. (2023, June 29). 'Braverman plan to send asylum seekers to Rwanda unlawful, appeal court rules'. *Guardian*. https://www.theguardian.com/uk-news/2023/jun/29/plan-to-send-asylum-seekers-to-rwanda-is-unlawful-uk-appeal-court-rules

Taylor, F. W. (1911). *The Principles of Scientific Management*. Harper & Brothers.

Teignmouth, Lord, & Jones, W. (eds). (2013). 'The Third Anniversary Discourse, on the Hindus, delivered 2d of February, 1786'. In *The Works of Sir William Jones: With the Life of the Author by Lord Teignmouth* (Vol. 3, pp. 24–46). Cambridge University Press. https://doi.org/10.1017/CBO9781139506922.005

'Theresa May's conference speech' [video]. (2016, October 5). *The Spectator*.https://www.spectator.co.uk/article/full-text-theresa-may-s-conference-speech/

Thomas, M. (2020, June 8). 'The Thing About Us: The Charter of the Forest' [podcast]. Retrieved 3 February 2023, from https://podcasts.apple.com/gb/podcast/the-things-about-us-the-charter-of-the-forest/id1506198366?i=1000477110834

Tietz, T. (2021, June 29). 'Leo Frobenius and the Theory of Cultural Morphology'. SciHi Blog. http://scihi.org/leo-frobenius/

van Wyhe, J. (ed.) (2002). 'The Complete Work of Charles Darwin Online'. http://darwin-online.org.uk/

Van der Donck, A. (1993). *A Description of the New Netherlands* (C. Gehring, trans.). State Museum of New York.

Vasari, G. (1550). *Le vite de più eccellenti architetti, pittori et scultori italiani, da Cimabue insino a'tempi nostri: Descritte in lingua toscana, da Giorgio Vasari … Con una sua utile … introduzzione a le arti loro*. L. Torrentino. http://catalogue.bnf.fr/ark:/12148/cb31545572n

Vedantam, S. (2016, October 25). 'Filthy Rich' [podcast]. Retrieved 3 January 2023, from https://www.npr.org/2016/10/25/499213698/whats-it-like-to-be-rich-ask-the-people-who-manage-billionaires-money

Vega, G. de la. (1609). *Primera parte de los commentarios reales: Que tratan del origen de los Yncas, reyes que fueron del Peru, de su idolatria, leyes, y gouierno en paz y en guerra: de sus vidas y conquistas, y de todo lo que fue aquel imperio y su republica, antes que los españoles passaran a el*. Lisboa : En la officina de Pedro Crasbeeck. http://archive.org/details/primerapartedelooovega

Verde, T. (2018, October). 'Egyptology's Pioneering Giant'. AramcoWorld.https://www.aramcoworld.com/Articles/September-2018/Egyptology-s-Pioneering-Giant

Vich, M. (2008). 'Maslow's Leadership Legacy'. *Journal of Humanistic Psychology*, 48(4), 444-445. https://doi.org/10.1177/0022167808320540

Vincent, N. (2012). *Magna Carta: A very short introduction* (first edition). Oxford University Press.

Virgil. (1697). *The Aeneid* (Dryden trans.) Retrieved 2 January 2023, from https://oll.libertyfund.org/title/dryden-the-aeneid-dryden-trans

Vitale, T. (director). (2016, December 4). 'Rome' [television programme]. In *Anthony Bourdain: Parts Unknown*.

Vowell, S. (2020, September 4). 'Trail of Tears (No. 716)' [podcast]. Retrieved 3 January 2023, from https://www.thisamericanlife.org/716/trail-of-tears

Wagner, K. A. (2017). *The Skull of Alum Bheg: The Life and Death of a Rebel of 1857*. C. Hurst & Co. Publishers Ltd.

Webster, W. (2022). *Imagining Home: Gender, Race and National Identity, 1945–1964* (first edition). Routledge.

Weiss, R. A. & Esparza, J. (2015, April 19). 'The prevention and eradication of smallpox: A commentary on Sloane (1755) "An account of inoculation"'. *Philosophical Transactions B, 370*, 1666. https://doi.org/10.1098/rstb.2014.0378

Wilentz, A. (2013). *Farewell, Fred Voodoo: A Letter from Haiti*. Simon & Schuster.

Williams, E. E. (1994). *Capitalism & Slavery* (first edition). University of North Carolina Press.

Wilson, J. (presenter). (2019, May 1). *Front Row: Leonardo da Vinci 500th Anniversary, Salvator Mundi* [radio broadcast]. BBC Radio 4. https://www.bbc.co.uk/sounds/play/m0004mgw

Woolf, D. R., Feldherr, A., Foot, S., Hardy, G., Robinson, C. F., & Hesketh, I. (2011). *The Oxford History of Historical Writing: Volume 2: 400–1400*. Oxford University Press.

Working with Indigenous Australians. (n.d.). 'Homepage'. Retrieved 3 January 2023, from http://www.workingwithindigenousaustralians.info/index.html

Working with Indigenous Australians. (n.d.). 'The Dreaming'. Retrieved 3 January 2023, from http://www.workingwithindigenousaustralians.info/content/Culture_2_The_Dreaming.html

Wu, T. (2015, August 21). 'You Really Don't Need to Work So Much'. *New Yorker*.

Wyhe, J., & Kjærgaard, P. (2015). 'Going the Whole Orang: Darwin, Wallace and the Natural History of Orangutans'. *Studies in History and Philosophy of Biological and Biomedical Sciences, 21*. https://doi.org/10.1016/j.shpsc.2015.02.006

Yang, J. L. (2020). *One Mighty and Irresistible Tide: The Epic Struggle Over American Immigration, 1924–1965*. W. W. Norton & Company.

'Zora Neale Hurston on Zombies' [video]. (1943, January 25). YouTube. https://www.youtube.com/watch?v=YmKPjh5RX6c

Notes

Epigraph

p. vii   'A great portion . . .' Hay (1962).

Introduction

p. xi   'The quip was first attributed . . .' O'Toole (2013).
p. xi   'To start with, Mohandas Karamchand Gandhi . . .' Guha, R. (2018).
p. xiii   'For the ancient Greeks . . .' Cannadine (2018).

Chapter 1: Nullius in verba

p. 1   'In old-fashioned . . .' Maxwell et al. (2012).
p. 2   'These laws would go on . . .' Sands (2016).
p. 2   'We could say with some certainty . . .' Maxwell et al. (2012).
p. 4   'One of the most celebrated . . .' Fara (2017).
p. 5   'When, after years of lobbying . . .' Royal Society (n.d.).
p. 5   'For Enlightenment thinkers . . .' Descartes (1637).
p. 6   'When it came to computing...' Spiegelman (2003).
p. 8   'He spent much of his life . . .' Galton (1883).
p. 10   'Before this time . . .' Greer (2019).
p. 10   'In 1735, for example . . .' Charmantier (2020), Kenyon-Flatt (2021).
p. 11   'These, according to Blumenbach . . .' Lindqvist (2018).
p. 11   'For much of the eighteenth century . . .' Brown (2010).
p. 14   'This infamously culminated . . .' Shakespeare (2020).

p. 15 'The Museum Studies student research . . .' Maxwell et al. (2012), Pearson and Moule (1925).

p. 17 'Translations of Virgil's text. . .' Frazer (1978).

p. 18 'James Cowles Prichard . . .' Lindqvist (2018).

p. 21 'The very early boom of the plantation colonies . . .' Biewen and Kumanyika (March 2017) and (May 2017).

p. 21 'The scientific categorization of . . .' Kendi (2017), Painter (2011).

p. 21 'It is a painful irony . . .' Roberts (2012).

Chapter 2: Knowledge is power

p. 25 'I wish this were . . .' Wagner (2017).

p. 26 'My particular favourite . . .' Neame (1969).

p. 26 '"To me," she says . . .' Ibid.

p. 26 'Here Jean Brodie is concisely summarising . . .' Rousseau (1991).

p. 27 'Rousseau was not . . .' Montin (1908).

p. 28 'The public historian . . .' Bryant (2021).

p. 28 'Historians like Francis Young . . .' Dr Francis Young [@ DrFrancisYoung] (2021).

p. 28 'We know Latin . . .' Bryant (2021).

p. 29 'A 2020 British Council survey . . .' Collen (2020).

p. 29 'Both "the classics" and "class" . . .' Hall & Stead (2020).

p. 31 '"the language of . . ."' Ibid.

p. 32 '*Tu regere imperio* . . .' Virgil (1697).

p. 33 'It's this co-opting . . .' Harloe (2021).

p. 33 'As Benjamin Jowett, . . .' Larson (1999).

p. 34 'Today, Macaulay is . . .' Macaulay (1835).

p. 34 'An intermediary class . . .' Ibid.

p. 39 'In their book *A People's History of the Classics* . . .' Hall & Stead (2020).

p. 40 'Within Britain itself . . .' Chetty et al. (2022).

p. 40 'In British settler colonies . . .' Mosby & Millions (2021).

p. 41 'Culture is as much . . .' Said (1978).

p. 41 'As such, it is not simply . . .' Ngũgĩ wa Thiong'o (1986).

p. 41 'One of these was a leaked report . . .' George Padmore Institute (2000).

p. 42 'In the 1920s, psychologists . . .' Bhimani (2022).

p. 42 'Standardised intelligence tests . . .' Shannon (2021).

p. 42 'A few years after the Haringey school reports, . . .' Coard (1971).

p. 42 'Speaking to Sue Lawley . . .' Lawley (2002).

p. 43 'Professor Gus John . . .' Shannon (2021).

p. 44 'Alongside this, the Black Saturday Schools . . .' Akala [@akalamusic] (2018).

p. 44 'This is Kingslee, . . .' Ibid.

p. 44 'He has spoken more recently. . .' 'Akala | Full Address and Q&A' (2015).

p. 46 'The educational theorist Paulo Freire . . .' Freire (2000).

Chapter 3: The pen is mightier than the sword

p. 49 'One of the first people . . .' Shakespeare Birthplace Trust (n.d.).

p. 50 'These anti-Stratfordian arguments . . .' Bryson & Shakespeare (2009).

p. 52 'What records there are, . . .' Shapiro (2011).

p. 52 'Francis Galton was influential . . .' Galton (1874).

p. 53 "stupid, illiterate, third-rate play actor' . . .' Bacon & Hawthorne (1970).

p. 54 "Homer' was more likely . . .' McCoy (2021).

p. 54 'If anything, the Greek epics . . .' O'Rourke (2018).

p. 54 'Even in what we know from works . . .' Haynes (2021).

p. 56 'In his *Third Anniversary Discourse on the Hindus* . . .' Teignmouth & Jones (2013).

p. 56 'It's now generally thought . . .' Farout (2016).

p. 58 'Blair divided the progress of history . . .' Eddy (2011).

p. 59 "though among barbarous nations, . . .' Blair (1783), Eddy (2011).

p. 59 "The more any nation is . . .' Ibid.

p. 59 'It's telling that when Captain Cook . . .' Forgan (2013).

p. 61   'Over the following centuries, Western historians . . .' Mann (2006).

p. 63   '"the point of a pin" . . .' Pizarro (1969) in Mann (2006).

p. 64   'Nearly one hundred years later, . . .' Medrano & Urton (2018).

p. 65   'Even better, Sabine Hyland, . . .' Hyland (2017).

p. 66   'recorded on knots . . .' Vega (1609).

p. 66   'Two and a half decades earlier, . . .' Ibid.

p. 66   'It was the same trick . . .' Fery (n.d.).

p. 68   'When he visited there in 1871, . . .' Chirikure (2021).

p. 69   'Some other things are worth clarifying . . .' Halmhofer (2021), Bond (2018), and Moss (2022).

p. 69   'a capital mistake . . .' Doyle (1920).

p. 69   'As medieval historians . . .' Janega (2017).

p. 69   'Over several centuries, starting in 1402, . . .' Woolf et al. (2011).

p. 69   'In the Caribbean, . . .' Little (n.d.).

Chapter 4: Justice is blind

p. 72   'When, some time in the second century . . .' Henderson (n.d.).

p. 73   'The writer and literary critic . . .' Light (1991).

p. 74   'In Ancient Greek, . . .' Hughes (2017).

p. 74   'As the title of his incredibly powerful. . .' Brody (2019).

p. 75   'In 2012, David Cameron . . .' 'David Cameron Struggles' (2012).

p. 76   'In June 2014, a year ahead . . .' Cameron (2014).

p. 77   'That being said, . . .' Vincent (2012).

p. 81   'It was thanks to Coke . . .' Garnett (2018).

p. 81   'The Charter of the Forest . . .' Portillo (2007).

p. 82   'Fundamentally, these were . . .' Thomas (2020).

p. 83   'One of the great advocates . . .' Handy (2019).

p. 83   'For Young and its other fans, . . .' Bragg (2008).

p. 84   'Over three hundred years . . .' Community Environmental Legal Defense Fund (n.d.).

p. 85   'The land that history books refer to . . .' *Earth, Air, Fire, Water* (1995).

p. 86   'When the Europeans did turn up . . .' Five Civilized Tribes (n.d.).

p. 87   'The Cherokee Nation was avid . . .' Vowell (2020).

p. 88   'The following year, in 1828, . . .' Chavez (2017).

p. 89   'One of the earliest incarnations of the discovery doctrine, . . .' Chappell (2023)

p. 90   'The Supreme Court had another answer . . .' Marshall (1832).

p. 90   '". . . the tribes of Indians inhabiting . . .' Ibid.

p. 92   'In another landmark ruling . . .' Marshall (1832).

p. 92   'In a 2020 interview . . .' Demby & Marisol Meraji (2020).

p. 92   'If you never came across him . . .' Vowell (2020).

p. 92   'As far as Andrew Jackson was concerned, . . .' Crain (2007).

p. 93   'He had run his presidential campaign . . .' Loewen (1996).

p. 93   'In March 1835, Jackson wrote an open letter . . .' Jackson (1835).

p. 94   'While Chief John Ross was adamant . . .' Chavez (2017).

p. 95   'In her one-woman play . . .' Quoted in Demby & Marisol Meraji (2020).

p. 96   'Writing about his experience . . .' Fletcher (1998).

p. 96   'In his 1971 book, *A Theory of Justice*, . . .' Rawls (1999).

Chapter 5: Power to the people

p. 101   'Lincoln's brief and astonishingly moving speech . . .' Haney (1944).

p. 103   'In 1961, John F. Kennedy set up . . .' Kennedy (1961).

p. 104   'The prolific spread of democracy . . .' Fukuyama (1992).

p. 106   'Whether in the United States, . . .' Corby (2020).

p. 107   'It's important to point out . . .' Harvey (2019).

p. 108   'The Athenians did have elected . . .' Ibid.

p. 109   'Socrates, as portrayed in Plato's *Republic* . . .' Plato & Lane (2007).

p. 110   'It was the foundation of the United States of America . . .' Lepore (2018), Burk (2009).

p. 111   'Through its own self mythology, . . .' Holland (2005).

p. 113   'The Haudenosaunee (called the Iroquois League . . .' Johansen (1982).

p. 113   'According to a Dutch lawyer . . .' Van der Donck (1993).

p. 114   'As early as 1751, that old charmer Benjamin Franklin . . .' Kickingbird & Kickingbird (n.d.).

p. 114   'As Thomas Paine, . . .' Paine (1995).

p. 119   'Was Winston Churchill really just . . .' Churchill (2008).

p. 119   'All of this, of course, is even before . . .' Harvey (2019).

p. 121   'Ever since the Cold War, . . .' Rogers (2022).

Chapter 6: Time is money

p. 124   "There are three tenses or times,' Augustine wrote, . . .' Porlan (2016).

p. 127   'Coming into the modern era, . . .' Álvarez (2015).

p. 127   'As the historian David Rooney has pointed out, . . .' Rooney (2021).

p. 130   'When, in 1784, the eminently quotable Benjamin Franklin . . .' Franklin (1784).

p. 130   'A century on, though, . . .' Mukherjee (n.d.).

p. 131   'Daylight Saving Time is now a common part . . .' Solly (2022).

p. 131   'Industrialisation was a key historical development . . .' Williams (1994).

p. 132   'The manufacturing industries . . .' Ramirez (2020).

p. 132   'Much of this was enabled by . . .' Stewart (2010).

p. 133   'The management doyen Peter Drucker . . .' Drucker (1954).

p. 134   'Working people cottoned on to this . . .' Lepore (2005).

p. 135   'Darwin came on board as a companion . . .' Burstyn (1975).

p. 135   'On 16 January 1836, Darwin wrote . . .' van Wyhe (2002).

p. 135   '"they appear to me . . ."' Ibid.

p. 136   'This is a far from straightforward story: . . .' Brown (2010).

p. 136   'The Fuegians he mentioned in his journal . . .' Wyhe & Kjærgaard (2015).

p. 138   'Writing of the Fuegians, . . .' van Wyhe (2002).

p. 138   'The English name given to this worldview is the Dreaming, . . .' O'Keefe (1984).

p. 139   'The Dreaming encompasses some 7.7 million square kilometres . . .' Gammage (2012).

p. 141   'Describing the country inland from Port Stephens, . . .'
Dawson (1826) quoted in Gammage (2012).

p. 142   'Over the following century, . . .' Coleman (2021), Saini (2019).

p. 143   'It took Western scientists eighty-five years . . .' Ashby (2022).

p. 143   'Collaborative research . . .' Koolmatrie (2018).

p. 143   'There is a longstanding myth . . .' Das (March 2018).

p. 144   'The Indian historian Dipesh Chakrabarty . . .' Chakrabarty (2000).

p. 144   'Busy is both a state of being . . .' Burkeman (2017).

p. 145   'In 1964, *Life* magazine had published . . .' Wu (2015).

p. 146   'In his book *Four Thousand Weeks*, Oliver Burkeman . . .' Burkeman (2021).

Chapter 7: Your country needs you

p. 152   'even post-Brexit, . . .' Henley & Partners (2022).

p. 153   'Writing in 1830, the German philosopher Georg Wilhelm Friedrich Hegel . . .' Hegel (1830) in Appiah (2018).

p. 153   'It's almost impossible to look into . . .' Anderson (2016).

p. 156   'As a self-avowed . . .' McGregor & Kosman (2021).

p. 156   'And, as the cultural theorist . . .' Hall quoted in Mussai (2014).

p. 157   'The history of UK immigration laws . . .' Kirby (2019).

p. 158   'In the immediate aftermath of the Second World War, . . .' Legislation.gov.uk (1947).

p. 158   'There was a clear understanding, . . .' Webster (2022).

p. 159   'Across the Atlantic the United States . . .' Yang (2020).

p. 159   'Britain couldn't openly be seen . . .' Kirby (2019).

p. 161   'The model of Cheddar Man . . .' Clarke (2018).

p. 162   'In 2022, as I was writing . . .' Balch (2022).

p. 162   'The powers of this . . .' Taylor & Quinn (2023), Baker (2023).

p. 164   'It's part of the job description . . .' Amos (2016).

p. 166   'When the Prince and his family . . .' Ibid.

p. 167   'Researchers who look into . . .' Vedantam (2016).

p. 167   'In her book, *Capital Without Borders*, . . .' Harrington (2016).

p. 168   'Along with their money, . . .' Bullough (2018).

p. 168   'Bullough argues that, . . .' Bullough (2022).

p. 170   'At the Conservative Party Conference in 2016, . . .' 'Theresa May's conference speech' (2016).

p. 170   '"Empires come and go," wrote Stuart Hall, . . .' Meghji (2017).

p. 171   'In April 1990, Norman (later Lord) Tebbit . . .' Carvel (2004).

p. 172   'This is the experience of many immigrants . . .' Shukla (2016).

Chapter 8: Art for art's sake

p. 173   'It's the sixteenth-century Italian painter, . . .' Vasari (1550).

p. 174   'Today, whether they are a realist, . . .' Dubner (2021).

p. 175   'Conceptual art is said to have been born . . .' Punt (2017).

p. 176   'Courtauld pulled on the mantle . . .' Schama (2022).

p. 178   'Peter Schjeldahl at the New Yorker . . .' Schjeldahl (2017).

p. 179   '*Salvator Mundi* had not always been . . .' Jones (2018).

p. 180   'The tactic seemed to work . . .' Neate (2019).

p. 183   'For Lewis, and others, it appears the situation is simple . . .' Goldstein & Halperin (2017), Wilson (2019).

p. 186   'It was during the sixteenth century . . .' Moser (2006).

p. 187   'The Wormianum was one . . .' Arnold (2005).

p. 187   'The British Museum, originally founded . . .' Delbourgo (2017).

p. 188   'The skulls were sent back . . .' Redman (2016).

p. 188   'For example, when we hear . . .' Jasanoff (2009).

p. 188   'When this attempt failed, the . . .' Verde (2018).

p. 189   'The fact that Egyptian objects . . .' Procter (2020).

p. 189   'In his autobiography published in 1931, . . .' Petrie (1931).

p. 189   'In her book *The Archaeology of Race*, . . .' Challis (2013).

p. 190   'The Egyptian archaeologist Heba Abd El Gawad . . .' Abd El Gawad (2020).

p. 190   'If you are interested in looking at African art . . .' Coombes (1997).

p. 191   'In his book, *Small Wars*, . . .' quoted in Hicks (2020).

p. 193   'We know there was looting . . .' Ibid.

p. 194   '"It's like seeing your grandmother . . .' quoted in Fennell (2020).

p. 194 'As part of its campaigns, in 2015, . . .' Rhodes Must Fall Oxford [@RMF_Oxford] (2015).

p. 195 'In the early decades . . .' Tietz (2021).

p. 195 'The case of African objects in Western museums . . .' Sarr & Savoy (2018).

p. 196 'Speaking in an interview . . .' quoted in Fennell (2020).

p. 197 'The Cameroonian historian and philosopher . . .' Mbembe (2019).

Chapter 9: Death is the great equaliser

p. 199 'The ninth of June 1832 . . .' 'The Last Act Of Jeremy Bentham' (1832).

p. 199 'Smith's next move was . . .' Marmoy (1958).

p. 202 'The thing is shrouded in myths . . .' Das (November 2018).

p. 204 'Towards the end of his life, . . .' 'The Last Act' (1832).

p. 204 'The historian Ruth Richardson argued . . .' Richardson (2001).

p. 206 'The idea of the "less dead" was . . .' Lauren (2018), Egger (2002).

p. 207 'The Victorians, in particular, . . .' Schillace (2015).

p. 208 'We're going to look at Freud . . .' Hall (2014).

p. 208 'It's worth pointing out that . . .' Freud (1896), Masson (1986).

p. 208 'The well-known five stages . . .' Kübler-Ross & Byock (2011).

p. 209 'In St Paul's first letter to the Corinthians, . . .' Holy Bible, (2011), 1 Corinthians 15:26.

p. 210 'The Toraja people, who live . . .' Crombie (2018).

p. 210 'That was the year of a small, . . .' Littlewood & Douyon (1997).

p. 211 'A German Jewish immigrant . . .' Moore (2022).

p. 211 'Hurston's study of Vodou . . .' Hurston (2022).

p. 212 '"I do know that people" . . .' 'Zora Neale Hurston on Zombies' (1943).

p. 213 'Cultural historian Roger Luckhurst . . .' Luckhurst (2015).

p. 213 'Journalist Amy Wilentz . . .' Wilentz (2013).

p. 213 'Perhaps it's unsurprising . . .' Daut (2015).

p. 213 'In the 1980s, a Harvard anthropologist . . .' Davis (1997).

p. 216 'According to Littlewood and Douyon, . . .' Littlewood & Douyon (1997).

p. 217 'In the West, the word "zombie" conjures . . .' Luckhurst (2015).

p. 217 'When it comes to social care, . . .' Behuniak (2011).

p. 218 'The doctor and writer Atul Gawande . . .' Gawande (2014).

p. 220 'The writer Hilary Mantel . . .' Mantel (2017).

Chapter 10: We're all in this together

p. 224 "One cannot smoke and play cards . . .' Freud (1970).

p. 226 "'The development of civilization, . . .'" Freud (2004).

p. 227 'He wedged his mouth open . . .' Davies (2020).

p. 233 'We saw from his work . . .' Stocking (1984).

p. 234 'For Benedict, the big question . . .' Maslow & Honigmann (1970).

p. 235 'I learned the story of Maslow's time . . .' Heavy Head (2018).

p. 238 'Instead, it was the invention of a psychologist . . .' Bridgman et al., (2019).

p. 241 "'That top segment, that self-actualisation,". . .' Heavy Head (2018).

p. 241 'Rather than progress from one stage . . .' Ravilochan (2022), Blackstock (2011).

p. 242 "'The more I got to . . ."' Hoffman (1999).

p. 242 "'Before our white brothers came" . . .' Lame Deer & Erdoes (2009).

p. 243 "'One day, just after Pearl Harbour," . . .' Hoffman (1999).

p. 244 'Mead was one of the cohort of researchers . . .' Moore (2022).

p. 246 'As Heavy Head points out, . . .' Heavy Head (2018).

p. 246 'Even Maslow himself seemed . . .' Lowry (1985), Sosteric (2021).